Lineberger Memorial
Library

DEATH ANXIETY

This book, DEATH ANXIETY:
The Loss of the Self
by James B. McCarthy
was originally entitled:
FEARFUL LIVING:
The Fear of Death

James B. McCarthy

DEATH ANXIETY

The Loss of the Self

GARDNER PRESS, INC., NEW YORK
Distributed by the HALSTED PRESS
DIVISION OF JOHN WILEY & SONS, INC.
New York · Toronto · London · Sydney

GARDNER PRESS, INC.
19 Union Square West
New York, N.Y. 10003

Distributed solely by the Halsted Press Division
of John Wiley & Sons, Inc., New York

Library of Congress Cataloging in Publication Data

McCarthy, James B
    Fearful living.

    1. Fear of death. 2. Psychology, Pathological.
I. Title.
RC552.F42M33   616.8′5   78-13436
ISBN 0-470-26508-6

Printed in the United States of America

*This Book is Dedicated
To My Teachers and Patients*

Contents

Preface

The development of this volume has been greatly aided by the encouragement of my family, friends and colleagues. I would like to express my appreciation to the Psychology Department of Queens Children's Hospital for their active support of this work. I feel particularly grateful to the following colleagues for their thoughtful comments on various chapters of the manuscript: Drs. Manuel Domingo and Gladys Guarton of Queens Children's Hospital, Robert Katz of the Institute for Contemporary Psychotherapy, John Ozehosky of C.W. Post College, Long Island University, and Irving Weinstein of the Lincoln Institute for Psychotherapy, and to Mrs. Ann Raggi of Hillcrest Hospital for her patience and diligence in preparing the manuscript.

Introduction

Death anxiety refers to the fear of one's own death in a physically healthy individual. Marked death fears betray a neurotic anxiety that delivers a significant statement about personality functioning. The nature of the relationship between neurotic living and the fear of death has been a source for speculation in both personality theory and psychotheraputic clinical work. For Carl Jung the fear of death emerged as the main source of neurotic misery only in the second half of human life within the context of a failure to fully accept the limits of one's future prospects, accomplishments, and physical capabilities. Death anxiety in this view lies rooted in an agnostic, materialistic self-alienation. It takes the form of scientific misgivings about the reality of God's existence or a disbelief in the possibility of life after death. Jung pointedly called twentieth-century man to task for this pseudo-scientific, anti-spiritual stance and clearly identified mental health and the resolution of death fears with a prototypical religious outlook in his *Modern Man in Search of a Soul*. Ernest Becker posited an opposing view in *The Denial of Death:* that adjustment problems and disturbing psychic phenomena of divergent types ranging from depression, schizophrenia, and neurosis to sexual perversions can all be essentially reduced to the fear of death. The existential psychoanalysts—to an extent, Alfred Adler and Becker have argued that mental illness constitutes a failure of transcendence of the fear of death, "failed heroics" in achieving such transcendence, born out of ignorance and a lack of courage. Erich Fromm and the neo-Freudian psychoanalytic theoreticians have redefined neurotic problems in living in terms of embeddedness in the dependent, fearful, security-conscious, emotional fabric of childhood. From this vantage point, adult neurotics simultaneously fear life and death in that they are robbed of the full richness of relatedness by a dependent clinging to the secure psychic moorings of childhood. The culturalist emphasis on the loss of freedom in neurosis places an entirely different focus on what is therapeutic about psychotherapy or psychoanalysis. The contemporary psychoanalyst therefore assists the neurotic patient in breaking free from fearfulness via attempts at self-scrutiny and dialogue in the analytic exchange.

The twofold purpose of this volume is to trace the expression of death anxiety in neurosis and to address the need for a heightened understanding of the interrelationship between the fear of death, depression, and separation conflicts in adjustment problems. The designation of a fear of death complex does not connote a disease entity or clearly delineated psychological dysfunction. Death anxiety will be defined as the neurotic fear of the loss of the self. I will propose that neurotic death fears express the depression and separation anxiety inherent in this fear of the loss of the self. The fear of death complex then refers to an interwoven psychodynamic pattern that, in my view, adheres to adjustment problems from early childhood to senescence. It arises in a developmental context and persists in its tripartite array in a backward and forward ebb of unconscious and conscious processes throughout life. This book is intended for both, practicing psychotherapists and students, as a psychoanalytic companion piece that provides a framework for understanding and integrating the voluminous body of knowledge on the psychology of death that has accumulated in the last decade. Of particular importance to the clinician reader is the stress on the role of depression in death anxiety and death-related attitudes present in neurotic conflicts.

The organization of the book consists of an assortment of essays that intersperse the elaboration of the central theme of death anxiety with its implications in psychological research, psychoanalytic practice, religion, and philosophy. The book began in part from an interest in the role of religion and existential issues in neuroses and in the formation of fears about death. It also was developed partly from therapeutic work with depressed patients who revealed anxiety and puzzling, conflicting attitudes about death. A deepening curiosity about these phenomena gave rise to a need to evaluate and synthesize the contributions on death anxiety from these diverse areas. The need then became clearer for a psychoanalytic investigation of death anxiety that might add depth to the discordant and contradictory literature on death and dying.

The book's history reflects an attempt to summarize seminal contributions on the fear of death from all of the above fields. It relies on literary and mythological plots as well as clinical material and research studies to document the importance of death anxiety. Through the development of this inquiry and the relevant research, there emerges an emphasis on death anxiety's intrusion in neurotic patterns of living. In psychotherapy, scrutiny of the patient's fear of the loss of the self yields an appreciation of the complexity of the struggle to find a mode of defensiveness that insures psychological survival. Beginning with its manifestations in common place defenses and its origin in early childhood, death anxiety can achieve psychological representation as the fear of the loss of the self. Death fears develop in childhood, indistinguishable from depression and separation anxiety, only to be later integrated into characterological trends that symbolize one's neurotic problems. The fear of death is to some extent universal. In intense death anxiety; the fear of the loss of the self parallels feelings of helplessness and depression. Depression can be understood in this context as both an expression and a defense against death anxiety.

The chapters on religion and purpose in life have been included for several reasons. Beginning with Freud religion has been described by many investigators as the ideal depository for neurotic death fears. Genuine religious commitment needs to be differentiated from the self-serving facade of a religious retreat from death anxiety. The interplay between death anxiety and lack of purpose in life will be supported by a brief account of cultural influences on identity problems and the psychology of the cult. Three neurotic styles for coping with death anxiety will be defined in terms of the excessive use of avoidance, agression, and withdrawal. The expression of the self in the defense against death anxiety corresponds to the individual's attitudes towards life roles. Threats to the self and the neurotic fear of the loss of the self are revealed in the course of the patient's experience in psychotherapy. The existential psychoanalysts have devoted careful attention to death fears and their concept of existential anxiety provides a phenomenological description of the depression, passivity and purposelessness of intense death anxiety. Both the transference and the patient's symbolic language give evidence of his or her death fears and wishes. Particularly in the transference and at points of resistance to growth, the psychotherapeutic work uncovers the patient's unique blend of death anxiety and personality problems. Psychoanalytic psychotherapy provides the medium for the growth of the self, while allowing for the unraveling of the threats to the patient's self.

SECTION 1

The Meaning of
Death Anxiety

CHAPTER ONE

The Fear of Death

Ingmar Bergman's *The Seventh Seal* fascinates viewers partially because of the imagery of the scenes in which the knight plays chess with the personification of death, and in greater part because of the juxtaposition of scenes of vitality, family life, and warmth with images of suffering, war, and death, all of which parallel the moves on the chess board. That engrossing contest reflects a symbolic struggle between life and death which has permeated Western philosophy, art, and literature for centuries. Part of the fascination with death in recent years, the interest in the treatment of the dying, and the research on the psychology of death is derived from the meaning of death and death fears in the unconscious.

The knight's battle with death may symbolize an unconscious, struggle between life and death anxiety in one's inner psychological world—just as the king, queen, pawns, and other chess pieces are symbolical representations of father, mother, and significant others. Their progress across the chess board falls between the contrasting images of life and death. Although the fear of death is universal, it is an emotionally significant covert factor only in some individuals. Others are overtly fearful and quite conscious of their uncertainty, which like the chess pieces falls in "the valley of the shadow of death." The degree of that awareness and the influence of death anxiety on psychological events will be the main thesis of this work. The unpredictability of the outcome of the chess match in the *Seventh Seal* marks each moment with an indelible stamp that can fill the knight with the exhilaration of the challenge or carry him into fear and exisitential despair. What complicates the matter even further is that in each developmental phase of life the fear of death can be represented differently and arise from a different situational context. The meaning of death fears, and how they unfold and are avoided, needs to be broadly traced before the focus of inquiry shifts to include specific psychological variables in death fears.

The limited amount of scientific research on death anxiety, the fear of death (thanatophobia) until the 1970s stands in sharp contrast to the considerable theoretical and speculative attention devoted to the issue in recent years.[1] Much of the early work on the psychological meaning of the anticipation and fear of death began with Freud's delineation in *The Ego and the Id:*

It would seem that the mechanisms of the fear of death can only be that the ego relinquishes its narcissistic libidinal cathexis in a very large measure—that is, that is gives up some external object in other cases in which it feels anxiety. I believe that the fear of death is something that occurs between the ego and the superego. We know that the fear of death makes its appearance under two conditions . . . namely, as a reaction to an external danger and as an internal process, as for instance in melancholia. . . . These considerations make it possible to regard the fear of death, like the fear of conscience, as a development of the fear of castration.[2]

While not fully defining that internal process by which the fear of death arises, Freud originally subsumed the question under the topic of the death instinct. The death instinct consisted of an internal biologically based drive in man, which is represented in the ego as aggressive impulses, and the dichotomy between Eros and Thantos was described as pulling man in opposing directions. Ernest Jones reported examples of Freud's pessimistic, fatalistic view of Thanatos, his speculations on the meaning of death, and his predictions of the year of his own death while he was still in robust health.[3] Others have suggested that the sociocultural study and religious writings of Freud's final painful years may have partially reflected a solution to anxiety about his own death.

Investigations concerning the fear of death were carried out in the 1930s within a psychoanalytic framework by Bromberg and Schilder and others.[4] Castration anxiety was considered to be a crucial variable with respect to the fear of death, but Bromberg and Schilder cautioned that fear of death need not necessarily be pathological. They claimed that attitudes toward death found in neurotics and psychotics could also be found in normal adults. In addition, earlier studies had suggested that fear of death in children might be due to excessive physical restraint, masturbation guilt, fear of darkness, or separation anxiety, and not necessarily just castration anxiety[5,6] and feelings of guilt about homicidal impulses. Some investigators claim that the fear of death is inborn, just as is a fear of annihilation of the personality,[8] while Jungians attribute its origin to the psychology of archetypes that arise from the collective unconscious.

A more recent study speculated that the fear of death may be based on a child's fear of the loss of primary narcissism as well as a fear of retaliation for his destructive fantasies.[9] The fear of death is manifested most openly among people with high self-esteem, since death represents the end of opportunities to pursue goals important to one's self-esteem.[10] How can these studies be accounted for in the psychoanalytic view? Can anxiety about death, simply originate from castration anxiety and witnessing the primal scene? How might it be differentiated from a fear of death that is due to real environmental threats. Experimental attempts to address these issues were typified by statistically designed studies. Sarnoff and Corwin, for example, predicted successfully that male undergraduates who had a high degree of castration anxiety would show a greater increase on a Fear of Death Scale after being presented with sexually arousing stimuli than subjects who showed a lower degree of castration anxiety.[11] By using a before and, after design, they obtained a significant correlation between the subjects' degree of castration anxiety and the degree of fear of death, thereby supporting their view that fear of death is in some way related to castration anxiety.

Both theeoretical and experimental studies on the fear of death are at best contradictory and confusing. Furthermore, the latter seem superficial and the former studies that adhere to the psychoanalytic explanation of death anxiety reflect a reductionistic model of personality functioning that can be traced back to Freud's espousal of the importance of maintaining harmony or balance in mental life. This reductionistic model remains inadequate as a universal explanation for the dynamic significance of attitudes toward death to both practicing psychotherapists and research psychologists. In fact, negative emotions such as anxiety and depression need not necessarily be present in either the last few hours of life or a patient's fantasies and attitudes about the prospect of his own death. Some elderly people close to death welcome and anticipate it with relative acceptance and with a freedom from anxiety.[12]

The fear of death issue can be understood in existential terms as the problem of finding meaning in one's life. Viktor Frankl described the realization of the inevitability of death as a universal existential crisis.[13] The existential position holds up to pointed criticism the interpretation of concerns about the meaning of ones' life and death in terms of castration fears or Oedipal issues because such interpretations involve a fundamental misunderstanding of the universal experience of existential despair. Rollo May, the American existentialist, has expressed some particular dissatisfaction with the classical psychoanalytic explanations of death anxiety.[14] May added to the existential neo-Freudian position, which emphasizes that confrontation with death gives the most positive meaning to life. The inescapability of death forces man to face the potential of being in himself and others. It gives a concrete reality to individual life that may serve to enrich experience in the present. The absoluteness of death thereby gives an absolute quality to each fleeting moment of life. Erich Fromm claimed that man's awareness of his own death produces anxiety that can only be dealt with by recognizing one's individuality.[15] According to Fromm and the existential analysts, man's awareness of death gives him the responsibility for finding meaning in life.

Research psychologists have studied this same issue through experimentation while psychoanalysts grapple with its implications in clinical practice. The philosopher Jacques Choron delineated three components to the fear of death: the fear of dying, the fear of what happens after death, and the fear of ceasing to be.[16] The psychological scrutiny of these dimensions of death anxiety comes into clearer focus when the distinction is made between situations where death is a very real threat as opposed to those where death or its inevitability is merely thought about in an abstract way. The fear of dying and ceasing to be involves myriad factors extending from a fear of pain, suffering, helplessness, dependency, and loss of control of one's physical and mental abilities at one end of a continuum to fear of abandonment and of being separated from loved ones and loss of one's own love for others at the other end. The unconcious and deeply personal meanings of death anxiety are superordinate to the more conscious expectations of sadness, emotional suffering, mourning the living and mourning for oneself, guilt or acceptance in one's failures and disappointment over missed opportunities for living. The fear of the unknown, including fear of punishment, serves as an additional source of anxiety if one believes in an afterlife.

A point of departure for an overview of defense mechanisms people use to avoid fears of death can be found in a research project of condemned prisoners waiting for their death sentence to be carried out. Drs. Harvey Bluestone and Carl McGahee conducted psychiatric interviews with nineteen prisoners on Sing Sing's death row.[17] On a logical basis, one would expect overwhelming depression or anxiety of someone in such a state, but, on the contrary, a consistent pattern of personality defenses was noted that served to mitigate their overt expression. Denial was the most frequently used defense. It proved successful when the prisoners minimized their situation, refused to think of their fate, or isolated and detached themselves from any intense feelings. The other most common defenses included projection by means of a delusion of being persecuted and obsessive rumination. Projection or the attribution to another of one's own unconscious feelings serve not only to ward off depression and anxiety; it also helped to reduce the intensity of the prisoners' feelings about the helplessness of their fate and the rage that accompanied it. Obsessive rumination involves putting oneself under consistent pressure to think constantly about any topics that will evade depression and anxiety. Working on their appeals, hope for repeal of the death sentence and preoccupation with the legal issues of their case served this function for some prisoners. Preoccupation with religion served others. On the whole, the prisoners did not become overwhelmed with depression or anxiety on death row because of the effectiveness of their defense mechanisms and the apparent intactness of their personality structures.

It is only a small jump to see how similar the inmates' reactions are to those of ordinary people striving to avoid fear and suffering in the contemplation of death. Projection, denial, rumination, isolation, and other mechanisms of defense are quite commonly employed to that end. Displacement, another defense mechanism, involves defusing powerful emotions by deflecting them to people who are secondary objects of the feelings. Displacement of the fear of death ranges from a fear of attack by hostile forces and fear of the unknown and the dark in children, to fear of disaster, accidents, and injuries. The religious zealot proselytizing in the city streets "to repent, for the end of the world is at hand" may be reacting to his or her unrecognized or unacknowledged fear of death. Reaction formation consists of the denial of an unconscious feeling by the adoption of an opposite attitude. Traces of a reaction formation to fear of death may be involved in some joyous mourning rituals and funeral customs, in the sense of bravado of the combat soldier and in his loyalty and belief in the collective strength, power, and valor of his company or division. The medical student's playfulness and nonchalance with the cadaver during dissections constitutes a well-adapted use of denial and reaction formation to the fear of death. The repression of the fear of aging and death may underlie the American fascination with youth and the increasingly popular surgical attempts to slow down or reverse the aging process. In some artists, sublimation and compensation become involved in their creative process chiefly as a means for struggling with thoughts of death or death anxiety. Sublimation is the gratification of unacceptable impulses or feelings by channeling them into socially acceptable activities which permit compensation via involvement in some activity that will hold off feelings of inadequacy and inferiority. Consider, for example, the title Gaughin gave to one of his paintings, Life, or the use of brilliant hues of color made by the impressionists and fauvists in contrast to Picasso's somber use of achromatic color and death symbolism in Guernica. Rationalization—the justification of shortcomings in behavior or of unfavorable outcomes in situations by finding good reasons for them— and undoing—a kind of magical repetition of phrases or actions in order to wipe out guilt—are additional normal defensive operations. Freud's clarification of the unconscious purpose of religious ceremonies, prayers, and rituals brought the nature of these activities into sharp relief; the same defensive relationship may hold for the attempt to assuage the fear of death through religion.[19] All of the defense mechanisms used to alleviate or ward off anxiety can be quite efficient in defending against the fear of death.

Perhaps the most widely used security operation that holds the fear of death at bay is the "manic defense," a concept illuminated by Donald Winnicott and derived from the early work of Melanie Klein.[20] Some use of the manic defense is a normal part of ordinary life. However, the extent to which a person experiences severe depressive anxiety infuences the degree to which he or she will be able to pay close attention to the nuances of inner psychological reality. Manic activity, constant involvement in physical activity, or even fantasy can mark an attempt to deny inner reality and depression. Ideas about death are included in the fantasy content of Klein's phase of the depressive position in infancy. Following this point of view one step further, Winnicott explains that a great variety of activities can provide reassurance against death. This activity conforms to the struggle to avoid inner depression and conflicts arising between internal objects. When pursued to an extreme, the most ordinary healthy, positive daily activities and interests can involve a manic defense against depression and concerns about death. Being "too busy to think"—that is, preoccupied with work, sports, music, the arts, cars, gadgets, and material objects—can have such a connotation. The need to be constantly occupied, the inability to tolerate aloneness with oneself, the rush to fill leisure time with social life, or some activity at the expense of any opportunity for introspection are illustrative of the manic defense against depression and fear of death.

In *Death and the Mid-Life Crisis,* Elliot Jacques documents the possible extent of such denial in case studies.[21] As the midlife point is reached, one cannot help but react to the inevitability of one's death. The slow but certain changes in one's body and appearance and the passage of time force some confrontation with the reality of death. Either acceptance of death or denial and defense against it can then result. In the Kleinian view, the outcome at that time will be greatly influenced by the events of the period of the infantile depressive position.[22] However, Klein assumes the idea of death, is primary and that it exists in the unconscious. Nevertheless, the midlife crisis does provide one stimulus for a possible integration of the relationships between depression, characterotological problems, and how one handles the eventuality of death. It is precisely at those points in life from age thirty-five into middle age, when awareness of death reaches consciousness, that depression can emerge and, in response, the manic defense. In old age the gradual loss of physical strength, vitality, sexual potency, the loss of friends and loved ones, retirement, and sickness necessitate coming to terms with death in some way. In young adulthood the manic defense may be present though not in high operation because the depressive position is not in the foreground. Yet the manic defense can be clearly operating in the background throughout life, except if it is worked through during in-depth psychotherapy or if it is shattered by circumstance, as may occur in the process of mourning the death of a loved one. Manic behavior and defensive denial of fears about death run parallel to the general tendency to feel the urge to flee in the face of psychological danger. For example, the flight from battle of the young soldier in The *Red Badge of Courage* partially represented a retreat from fear and the possible threat of his destruction. The swiftness of his desertion in response to inner terror is analogous to the driven, anxious, restless, empty pleasure of manic activities undertaken to defend against thoughts about and fear of death.

Just as the artist may aim to achieve a kind of immortality in creative self-expression, the everyday activities of life taken as a whole can represent a pseudo-victory in the denial of death. What might be called the cultural defense against fears of death involves the collectively creative response of a society to preserve its immortality. Cultural values and traditions certainly can be ingrained in an individual so that there is both the avoidance of death fears and the need to conform to modes of dealing with death and existential anxiety. The success of the funeral parlor business in the United States and the whole gamut of codified acceptable behavior in mourning or visiting relatives of the dead all still becry a taboo against death and a strong fear of it. Beginning with Otto Rank's assumption that man creates culture in order to maintain his spiritual self, Robert Lifton developed a psychosocial view of historical conditions. According to Lifton,[23] the purpose of cultural life lies in maintaining modes of immortality for a society and providing avenues for its expression. The effect of historical events is to develop a "collective sense of immortality," and fears of death are sharply limited by relating to a particular society's modes of immortality. Pertinent examples included the popularity of the "counterculture" in the United States during the 1960s and 1970s and Mao tse-Tung's cultural revolution in China.[22] Ancient mythology, folklore, and literature abound with references to the same theme. In Greek legends extraordinary strength, valor, and accomplishment often led to the protagonist's finding favor with the gods and at times being transformed into a god who was worshipped by future generations, as was the case with Ulysses and Daedalus. Finally, the symbolic expression of the fear of death and its avoidance may lie beneath the currently popular absorption with spiritualism, devils, exorcism, and witchcraft. The need to identify, label, and become familiar with "spirits" grows out of a wish to objectify and control the unfamiliar, terrifying, unconscious feelings within the psyche.

How do death fears develop and what meaning do they have? What complex network of factors tips the balance of psychological defense from disspassionate resignation to death to confrontation or a renewed purpose in life? Assuming that the idea of death does develop in early childhood, an assumption to be examined in a later chapter, what is the origin of death anxiety? A brief historical tracing of analytic theory will introduce this discussion. Based on Freud's treatment of anxiety, a parsimonious explanation lies in grasping the helplessness and lack of psychological and physical resources possessed by the young child.[24] The basis of all feelings of security in infancy (which may be defined as relative freedom from anxiety) comes from a secure, loving, nurturing relationship with the mother. Developmental psychologists and psychiatrists such as John Bowlby can trace the origin of insecurity and anxiety to the earliest weeks of life. The well-adjusted mother feels little prolonged uneasiness about the newborn's fragility and total helplessness, and even the inexperienced mother with her first child adjusts to the infant through a biological–psychological dialogue. The protected, well-nourished, and loved baby, cared for by the "good enough mother," in Winnicott's terminology, begins life with basic security. The continued emergence throughout the first year of life of a sense of magical powers and control over the environment is a consequence of the complete security and gratification of the infant's needs in the symbiotic union with the mother. Freud theorized that the close connection between the expression of a need (the infants need for the breast or bottle, for physical contact, to be changed, turned, moved, or to be covered) and the gratification of that need occurs in the context of the existence of an imagined or hallucinated mental image of the mother. It is as if the breast only has to be imagined or thought about for it to appear.

Frustration of the infant's needs is an inevitable occurrence which in no serious way detracts from security maintenance in the healthy mother-child relationship. In fact, it is an essential part of the child's ego development that need satisfaction can never be perfect, nor does frustration destroy the infant's sense of omnipotence or magical power over his environment. Charles Wahl[25] suggests, that this infantile omnipotence can provide a basis for children's handling of the fear of death. At an earlier stage, the symbiotic union provides the basis for the baby's anxiety reduction. The child later holds in check anxiety about death and anxiety in general by the retention of some remnants of infantile omnipotence which have evolved into secure trust in the parents and relative freedom from crippling anxiety. Just as Freud initially saw anxiety in infancy as a consequence of the infant's helplessness, he at first saw death anxiety as a fear of the mother's absence and her not returning. Ernest Jones interpreted the wish to die as the wish to sleep with the mother in order to return to her womb and interpreted heaven, our "place of birth," as a symbol of the mother's womb.[26] Others believe that the most beautiful of all dreams is one that involves as its content death and reunion with the primal mother.[27] In psychoanalytic theory, the fear of death arises from the period of infancy, called the oral period, when there is the threat of destruction from the "terrible mother." This concept of the "bad or terrible mother" no way implies any deliberate mistreatment of the infant; it implies unrelatedness on the part of the mother. In interpersonal psychoanalytic theory, projection onto the mother of the infant's own hateful, destructive, devouring feelings for her might be understood as a possible response to "aloneness" and the mother's unavailability.

Several factors contribute to this version of death anxiety arising from early object relations. The first is the baby's utter helplessness and dependency. Second is the gradual development of a sense of the constancy of the mother as well as important others and objects in the child's environment. At one early point in development, any object out of the baby's sight is thought to no longer exist. Fear of loss of the mother and the fear of helplessness become equated with the fear of death. The young child's inability to distinguish clearly between thought, fantasy, and action as well as a lack of understanding of causal relationships further influence death fears. If the wish for mother to appear can result in quick arrival at the crib or playpen, then perhaps hostile wishes can result in her disappearance. The magical world of infancy gives way only gradually to a sophisticated grasp of cause and effect, and the Piagetian research indicates that the specific age at which this is accomplished varies with the mental abilities of each child. Melanie Klein's concept of infantile ambivalence is also pertinent to infantile hostility and death anxiety. Frustration, inhibition, and inevitable lack of total gratification by the parents give rise to ambivalent or contradictory powerful feeling states. Thus, the good, permissive, gratifying mother is loved, whereas the frustrating or punishing mother is hated.

Varying degrees of tolerance for such ambivalent feelings correlates with the young child's need for unambiguous emotional communication from parents. The relative ease or difficulty in integrating contradictory feelings for parents complicates hostility for the parents which contributes further to death fears in children. From the perspective of developmental psychology, the child's developing ego functions have to cope with ambivalent feelings for parents in the midst of the remnants of infantile grandiosity and magical thinking. The child needs protection from overpowering feelings of helplessness, anxiety, vulnerability and fear of loss of security. Part of the fear of separation entails dependence on the parents' power for the child's psychological survival. The fear of death grows within the context of these psychodynamic forces in children, and some children need a great deal of reassurance against death anxiety, which was expressed in the centuries old prayer "Now I lay me down to sleep, I pray the Lord my soul to keep; if I should die before I wake, I pray the Lord my soul to take." Whatever the unconscious significance of children's specific death fears in stories, myths, or fairy tales, the need to conquor their fear of helplessness and the fear of death provides part of the basis for their fascination with the angry witch, cruel stepmother, hungry wolf, monsters, giants, ghosts, and dragons.[27] These characters personify and portray in dramatic events each of the above factors from magic to ambivalence, thereby providing children with the opportunity to work through and achieve mastery of their death anxiety.

One of the earliest psychoanalytic papers on the fear of death still pertains to the question of the meaning of death fears as they evolve in children. Mary Chadwick's "Notes Upon the Fear of Death" begins with the postulation that helplessness in childhood is the origin of fear of death, wherein death may be symbolized as either the loss of love or the loss of the penis, which can become identified with the loss of the self.[29] In her view, death is represented to children, and perhaps to adults also, as either a hostile, violent destruction carried out by a cruel father or a longed-for regression to prenatal life in which death is represented as complete protection and security in the mother's womb. Analogous to this are the Old Testament descriptions of the wrath of the angry God the Father, who gives life to man and woman in the Garden of Eden and then banishes them from paradise, and the warmth and nurturance connoted by the espression "Mother Earth." Edgar Allan Poe's obsession with the theme of the death of a beautiful woman expressed a central dynamic of his melancholic personality, and his poem "Annabel Lee" falls into a clear perspective in light of Chadwick's formulation:

For the moon never beams, without bringing me dreams
    of the beautiful Annabel Lee;
And the stars never rise, but I feel the bright eyes
    of the beautiful Annabel Lee;

And so, all the night tide, I lie down by the side
    of my darling—my darling—my life and my bride;
In the sepulchre there by the sea—
    In her tomb by the pounding sea.[30]

In psychoanalytic terms, the poem would be interpreted on two levels: as a yearning for restored union with the Oedipal mother and as a clear unconscious wish to return to an earlier state of total dependency and psychic merger in the mother's womb. Chadwick presents four varieties of expression of death fears in children: it occurs (a) as a result of parental threats of punishment; (b) in response to death wishes directed toward the parents; (c) as a result of physical retraint put on them; (d) in correlation with the fear of the dark or of becoming blind. Being restrained from moving almost always produces an anxiety reaction in children, who will often exclaim, "Stop, you're killing me," when restrained. Kinesthesis, movement and muscular exertion all are involved in the child's use of the body to explore, manipulate and control the world. Movement is the first ego function of which the infant is capable, and its loss can signify destruction. Our American fascination with speed in sports, cars and all means of transportation may indirectly symbolize the need for power in movement. Perhaps breaking a new world's record in track or sport car racing represents not only personal achievement and triumph over physical limitations and the laws of physics but also a victorious affirmation of life over death. Blindness, the psychic equivalent of castration, has been often described in literature as a punishment for masturbation, hostility or death wishes for the parents and for seeing forbidden sights, such as the primal scene (sexual intercourse between parents). Sight can be equated with love just as the eye is equated with the ego (and the penis).

Since ancient times, light and sun have been worshipped and deified as the embodiment of life. Both the Mayans and Egyptians identified the sun with God, and many more recent cults believed the sun to be the source of life. Current religions at times describe life after death as the "light of eternal life." Chadwick points to the symbol of the wide-open eye on the sarcophagus in early Egypt as a symbol of life. One well-respected theory among archaeologists is that the mummification of the bodies of pharaohs, their encasement in ornamented or gold coverings, and their eventual entombment in crypts and the pyramids with possessions and food were all a means of preparation for the return journey to the god of the sun and heavenly bodies. Shakespeare made extensive use of the identification of the sun with love in Romeo's soliloquy:

But soft! what light through yonder window breaks?
    It is the east, and Juliet is the sun!—Arise,
fair sun, and kill the envious moon, Who is already
    sick and pale with grief, That thou her maid
art far more fair than she. . .

Sight is one of the child's first means of contact with the world, even though the perceptual apparatus is not fully developed at birth. Making things appear and disappear by opening and shutting the eyes remains a part of the omnipotence of infancy. Children's first viewing of a corpse often leaves them with the impression that death is a state of permanent immobility with shut, sightless eyes, a state of profound sleep, or both. They may wonder why the dead person "is so still, can't move, or can't open his eyes." In religious hymns and prayers for the dead, death is portrayed as both "eternal sleep" and "perpetual darkness."

In light of these factors, unconscious fears of separation and death may be the dynamic underlying children's discomfort when banished from the presence of the parents for some misdeed with the phrase, "Get out of my sight." The visual properties of color, light, and movement, and their identification with life in nature, have long been a source of inspiration and subject matter for artists. Consider, for example, Claude Monet's *Water Lilies* and his visual obsession with the gardens at Giverny. The nuances of light, color, and technique blend flowers, water, air, and background into an integrated composition with the effect that portions of the canvas can be imagined to move in a flowing impressionistic celebration of life. Whatever the personally felt experience of anxiety about one's own death, from early childhood death achieves psychological representation as the loss of the self. Death fears arise in early object relations and they later symbolize fears about the self. It is the fear of the loss of the self that is most pertinent in the adult's neurotic fear of death. One theses of this work holds that death fears develop in childhood as expressions of depression and separation anxiety, only to be later integrated into characteristic personality trends that symbolize the individual's neurotic problems.

CHAPTER TWO

Death Anxiety in the Living and the Dying

Research concerning death and the fear of death has dealt with the psychological attitudes and needs of the terminally ill only in the last ten or fifteen years. There has been a more substantial and long-standing interest in death themes and fears in different types of psychopathology and in the relevance of death anxiety to personality dynamics. Death wishes or fears, the psychological implications of the death of important others and ambivalence about growth and a richer life experience are often important issues in psychotherapy. One indirect source of the current interest in death may lie in increased awareness of patient's and psychotherapist's conflicts about avoidance versus coming to grips with their own death fears and the personal implications of the recognition of one's own death. Furthermore, the experiemce of psychotherapy for both patient and therapist ordinarily occurs in a well-defined space and time with the implicit assumption that the therapeutic process, whether a brief encounter or an in-depth, intensive psychoanalysis, has a beginning period, a middle, and an end. The transitoriness of relationships, psychoterapeutic or otherwise, reflects, the transitoriness of life. That recognition can provide a glimpse of the existential orientation in realistic investigations of the fear of death, whether conducted in academic research or clinical practice. Aside from this existential dimension, the prevalence of the fear of death deserves scrutiny in terms of its relationship to religion, age, socioeconomic and demographic variables and developmental processes. Before establishing specific meanings of the fear of death, its prevalence and frequency need to be clarified and substantiated in relation to both the healthy and the terminally ill. A good deal of the psychological research literature supports my view of death anxiety, that it underlies and expresses the depression and separation anxiety inherent in neurotic charactor traits.

Historically, the psychological analysis of death anxiety began with Freud's second anxiety theory and his later writings on the relationship between psychoanalysis, social psychology, sociocultural issues, art, and, particularly, religion. The theology of Paul Tillich and the psychology of Carl Jung touched on the prevalance of the fear of death in terms of a refusal to accept life and a fear of living. The delineation of psychological factors in the etiology of death anxiety or its impact on neurotic functioning has been given relatively scant attention in the recent psychoanalytic literature. Aside from Freud's early treatment of death attitudes in obsessive-compulsive neurotics, little attention has been paid to the following questions: Who fears death the most? What accounts for such fears in physically healthy people who are not in danger of dying? Why might death anxiety become an obsession or a mainstay of neurotic character trends? Freud claimed that religion can serve as an effective defense against the fear of death and that religious ceremonies constitute elaborate equivalents to obsessional defenses that serve to ward off or protect a person from anxiety.[1] Many investigators have sought to test empirically whether religious people actually have more or less anxiety about death than non-religious people, but their results are confusing. Some of the evidence suggests that there is more fear of death among the spiritually oriented and thus that religion can be used as an effective defense against death anxiety, as Freud suggested. American soldiers, for example, have shown a strong connection between the vicissitudes of an interest in religion and their fear of death.

Herman Feifel has conducted many such research investigations concerning anxiety about death and personality traits, and he has written extensively on death anxiety and religion in the aged. Feifel believes that older people use religion to cope with fears of death and also that religious people see old age as the time when death is feared the most. In line with this view, one might assume that religious people are more afraid of death than non-religious people and more concerned about salvation and the possibility of life after death. Feifel suggested that a fear of death in an older person can represent a fear of annihilation and the loss of identity; but he also added the qualification that the specific importance of the role of religion in the older person's facing of death was not clear.[2]

In one relatively large survey of churchgoers only 10 percent of 210 subjects showed a strong fear of death. The more these subjects accepted fundamentalist religious ideas, the more they looked forward to death.[3] In contrast with this survey, another investigator found that a high degree of death anxiety among the aged was related to a lack of interest in reading the Bible and disbelief in life after death. However, when a more thorough study of geriatric patients was undertaken, no important relationship at all was found between religion and the fear of death.[4]

The source of the inconsistency in the research findings on the relationship between religion and fear of death will be identified in a later chapter. At present, there is no evidence to suggest that Jews, Protestants, Catholics, Buddhists, or any participants in organized religion differ in the degree of death anxiety according to their particular religious affiliation.

On a logical basis, it might be assumed that the aged, and people who have actually had close calls with death through accident, sudden illness, or their profession, would have a high degree of death anxiety; but this is not necessarily the case. Combat veterans of the Vietnam War who consistently faced death in battle or sneak attacks by an unseen enemy in guerrilla warfare very often do not fear death at all, according to Chaim Shatan and Robert Jay Lifton, both of whom have written extensively on the psychology of the Veitnam veteran. Depression, grief, mourning, depersonalization, the discharge of rage as a result of combat experience, and the erotic thrill of combat all may be much more important factors than a fear of personal death in combat.[5] According to these authors, the experience of basic training, the formation of a group identity and identification with one's unit or officers indirectly counter the threat of the loss of personal identity represented by death. Rather than necessarily experiencing a fear of personal death and then countering it by counter phobically attacking the enemy, the combat soldier may in fact be motivated much more by a drive for life through a universal need for "symbolic immortality," in Lifton's terms, and a kind of heroic transformation and identification with his national leader, nation, or countrymen.[6] In a study that typified one kind of research on death anxiety, John Hinton[7] interviewed over one hundred terminally ill patients who had only six months to live and compared the content of their interviews with a matched group of non-dying patients in the same hospital ward under the care of the same physicians. Three-quarters of the dying people were aware of their prognosis, and as a group they experienced much more anxiety and depression than the control group. However, anxiety in all of the patients was clearly related to physical suffering and particular symptoms that were difficult to relieve. Depression was the much more salient characteristic. The dying were more depressed and anxious than the non-dying, but they experienced much more depression than anxiety. My own theory which is supported by the research findings, involves an inherent interrelationship between depression, separation anxiety, and fear of death throughout life, not just at the approach of death.

The majority of people who have been "reprieved" from death do not universally report having a high fear of death at the time they were "saved." Richard Kalish studied over three hundred people who had close calls with death due to illness, drowning, car crashes, and a variety of other types of accidents.[8] Rather than being in a state of panic, 77 percent of the people reported that they did not feel fear; only 12 percent of the people stated that they had any kind of flashback or experience of reviewing their lives. Although a fear of death was part of their conscious stream of thought, it was not primary; thoughts about others, concern for family and loved ones, was often dominant. Even more to the point is

Daniel Cappon's finding that dying people don't necessarily have a strong fear of death and that the nearness of death does not drastically alter previous personality traits, but rather intensifies them.[9] An exception to this would hold in any case of physical trauma or illness affecting the brain or nervous system that has built-in, marked neurophysiological consequences (e.g., strokes often lead to depression as well as organic impairment).

When a group of twenty terminally ill patients in a general hospital were evaluated medically and psychiatrically and then compared with both a control group of physically ill people who were not dying and a third group of emotionally ill people, very little difference in personal death fears was found between the groups. Their reactions to the threat of death involved intensification of their habitual personality defenses, and very few of the "normal" people actually wanted to continue to live in their present state of suffering. The "strong" patients continued to be strong and the "weak" or passive ones continued to cling to their weakness or passivity as death approached. Rather than altering personality construction, it may be inferred that the nearness of death magnifies existing personality patterns (neurotic or healthy) in the direction of their characteristic bent. In other words, if generalization is possible, most people afflicted with terminal illness will respond to their own illness and death similarly to the way that they have responded to any emotional crisis in their life. The fear of death may be understood more adequately in the terminally ill as the simultaneous expression of the depression and separation anxiety inherent in their preexisting neurotic personality styles.

The fear of death itself has often not been clearly differentiated from the fear of dying, which itself has been the subject of exhaustive study in recent years by Elizabeth Kubler Ross, Avery Wiseman, Edwin Schneidman, and others. In the dying, a fear of psychic separation and anxiety about the impact of one's death on significant others become inseparable from the fear of death.

Since death represents not only the end of growth, pleasure, thought, consciousness, accomplishment, and striving of all kinds, it constitutes the final opportunity to experience the self, maintain self-esteem, relate to others, or care for loved ones. As a consequence, the extent of death anxiety and fear of the consequences of one's death have been shown to vary with age, sex, marital status, and most of the variables of adult life. The former dimension whereby death is defined as the loss of the self or as the end of human striving for personal emotional growth has not been fully addressed in either the research literature or in Freud's death instinct theory. The death instinct theory, according to which death is the aim of life and man is constantly pulled in opposing directions by the forces of life (Eros) and the forces of death (Thanatos),[10] has long been a source of psychoanalytic controversy. In a sense, the death instinct opposes all life instincts, including man's self-curative drive for psychological health, growth, and affirmation. People who fear death are those who fear to confront their unconscious conflicts and problems in living. "Death" is impossible to conceptualize, so it tends to be seen not only as the unknown but also as the unknown within the psyche—namely, the unconscious. Rather than expressing any specific fear of death, Hamlet's brooding and doubting reflected an ambivalence about death as self-lessness and a fear of the unconscious or his unconscious personality conflicts. Hamlet's depression separation conflicts, and ambivalence about death had not been brought to his full awareness or successfully resolved:

To die: to sleep.
To sleep? perchance to dream. Ay, there's the rub;
For in that sleep of death what dreams may come,
When we have shuffled off this mortal coil,
Must give us pause.

Camus' *The Stranger* also deals with ambivalence about death as a metaphor for healthy versus neurotic living in the last page of the book. As Meursault faces forthcoming execution, he feels exhilarated by the prospect because he has cleansed his spirit through an emotional cath-arsis and committed himself to living fully each remaining minute of life. When death attitudes disclose such unconscious components as ambiva-lent wishes for and fears of death, or the fear of the loss of the self, then the reliability and validity of much of the psychological research on death remains limited. The research conducted in this area does, in my opinion, lend support to the view that fear of death represents both the fear of life and the fear of growth and new experience, whether that ex-perience encompasses years or just a few moments of living.

Women and Death Anxiety

Whenever researchers have found differences between the sexes, women have consistently shown a higher fear of death than men. These findings have persisted in the literature without the emergence of any reasonable conclusive psychodynamic explanation. According to the present research findings it is clear that where significant differences are present, women at all ages fear death more than men. Women's greater susceptability to depression and depressive illness would be the most parsimonious explanation for these research results. There is a funda-mental relationship between depression and intense death anxiety that has been obscured in many of the experimental studies of death fears.

An attempt to find sex differences has been one of the frequent ap-proaches taken by investigators, but in the early studies of adults they found no sex differences in attitudes toward death. Similar results were reported by many researchers of death anxiety in elderly populations. However, death fears in males reflected concern with the impact of their death on their dependents, whereas death fears in females also reflected a higher fear of dissolution of the body.[12] When death themes have been compared between the sexes on psychological tests, sex differences were found relating to death concerns in Thematic Apperception Test (TAT) stories. (The TAT involves self-revelation through reactions to ambiguous pictures of interpersonal situations.) Males gave more death themes of violence, failure, and frustration, whereas females gave more themes of mourning and loss.[13] Lester, in his review of experimental and correlational studies, could report no definitive conclusions on sex differences in death anxiety.[14] However, when an objective personality test designed to study death anxiety was used on a variety of research samples, females had consistently higher death anxiety than males in all of the groups studied.[15]

These contradictory findings have led investigators both to provide some control for sex differences in research on death anxiety and to conclude that women's higher death anxiety reflects a generally higher anxiety level than is present in men. This explanation and quantitative approach to the question really explains very little. Feifel reported that women think about death a great deal more than men and suggested that the fear of life is much stronger in women than in men.[16] Rheingold has elaborated and developed this idea into a general theory of female psychology which has as its basis the castration complex and fear of maternal destructiveness.[17] Rheingold claims that unconscious maternal aggressive impulses (wishes to kill or mutilate the child) produce the fear of death, which he called the "catastrophic death complex." Maternal destructiveness engenders anxiety in the infant, which results in fears of mutilation or threats to body intactness as well as in specific fears of genital mutilation. Rheingold believes further that the destructiveness is transmitted from mother to daughter and that among psychiatrists there has been a strong reticence to trace the fear of death to maternal destructiveness.[18]

The basis for Rheingold's views are drawn from two sources: clinical data derived from psychotherapy with women and the biological foundations of the "death complex." Based on the connection in women between masochistic or hostile-dependent relationships with the mother and the fear of death, he cites a fear of mutilation as a punishment for a woman's erotic self-affirmation. The relationship between fear of mutilation or annihilation and menstruation and bodily functions is the second source of this theory. A great deal of evidence for a higher frequency and more overt death fear in women than in men has accrued, but the conclusion that women are more masochistic and make greater use of sadistic defenses than men seems hard to support. Many analysts of the culturalist school have pointed out that as children women especially are taught to please others and that their appearance and beauty is a large part of their ability to please. The fear of death, therefore, represents an additional threat to women's narcissism: and I believe that women's greater death anxiety can be understood in light of their greater susceptibility and depression. Women tend to show a conspicuous fear of death in adolescence, at the time of childbirth, and at menopause.[19] Rather than simply viewing each of these time periods as the height of fears of mutilation or bodily injury, they also may be considered times of great psychological change and possible threats to self-esteem. The fear of loss of love, self-love as well as the affection of important others, and the fear of not fulfilling adequately each particular feminine role represent much more universal sources of fear and fears of death. A direct generalizable connection between female biological experience and fear of death seems farfetched, whereas specific difficulty, such as adjusting to menstruation, might be indirectly related to death fears. Adolescence marks the beginning of maturity in sexual life and the integration of the psychological processes involved in establishing a feminine sexual identity. If an uninformed young girl's reaction to the onset of menstruation takes a negative form of "I'm bleeding, I must be injured" or "I might bleed to death," certainly a fear of death or loss of integrity of the body is plausible, particularly since previous associations with the loss of blood have involved cuts, scratches, punctures, and everyday minor injuries to the skin. However, adjustment to menstruation just as often involves pride and pleasure in a new-found femaleness that overrides discomfort. Adolescent boys have a similar preoccupation with their developing bodies and a similar tendency toward grandiosity or deflation, depending on the extent to which they resemble their ideal self-image. Biologically determined maturational timetables, sexual growth, sudden erections, intense sexual longing, fantasy, and wet dreams also represent dramatic challenges to psychological integration. In both adolescent girls and boys, death anxiety emerges with the depression that inevitably accompanies psychic separation and individuation from parents. Thoughts about death and the anxiety of individuation flourish in the turmoil of the adolescent's growth and need to master psychological developmental tasks. For women and men at any age individuation and psychological change may bring the neurotic fear of the loss of the self.

Age Differences

Research on death anxiety and age has most frequently dealt with young children or aged adults. Investigations of the fear of death among the aged have been more prolific and have involved attempts to answer the question: "Do older people fear death more than younger people?" None of the research is really sophisticated enough to determine what subtle psychological factors influence older people to accept death as a natural experience or to deny the inevitable, protest their helplessness, and feel rage, as Dylan Thomas observed, "against the dimming light."

As early as the nineteenth century scientific attempts to assess the degree of acceptance of death among the aged were commonplace. Interviews conducted with elderly institutionalized male patients noted a range of positive and negative attitudes in that death was frequently seen as either the beginning of a new life or as the end of everything.[20] Similar attitudes were also found among aged women. A stronger fear of death was reported among institutionalized females than among independent females who lived in apartments.[21] As activity increased among the aged in institutions, less fear of death was reported. Independence and the active pursuit of interests or hobbies decrease death fears in the elderly. All of the studies show that the amount of death anxiety among the aged is not dependent upon age, and, in fact, little or no relationship has been found between high death fears and age, sex, occupational status, marital status, or education.[22] Age, sex, source of income, and occupational status are not as related to fear of death among the aged as personality factors. Depression, a fear of abandonment, a fear of intrapsychic separation, and the degree of resourcefulness of the self seem the most pertinent factors, but none of these was carefully exposed to in-depth scrutiny.

When Jeffers, Nichols, and Eisdorfer studied the fear of death in a sample of people all of whom were over sixty years of age, they found that the fear of death was associated with feelings of rejection, depression, lower I.Q. scores, fewer Rorschach responses, less recreational activity, less belief in an afterlife, and less spiritual reading.[24] However, when geriatric psychiatric patients' fear of death was studied via word association tests, it was found that good versus poor health was the significant variable with respect to fear of death, and not age, sex, education, or religion. Most of the psychological research remains on this kind of superficial level and unfortunately denotes only surface differences between groups of people of different ages and in research samples of elderly people.

Several investigations have centerd around the development of fear of death as it begins in young children. Originally, small children's fears about death were thought to be basically a reflection of adult grief and mourning, and the imitation of adults. The child has progressively more realistic attitudes toward death as he develops cognitively, especially in terms of operational thinking and information-gathering skills.[24] Schilder and Wechsler[25] reported quite an interesting set of findings from interviews of children who were hospitalized for psychiatric disturbances. These children consistently saw death either as a deprivation and loss or as a hostile sadistic act to which they would be subjected. Depression and separation anxiety were not assessed in this early study, but the subjects did seem to fear death itself more than they feared being killed.

The most outstanding early research study on children's views of death was conducted by Maria Nagy[26] in a 1948 investigation of close to four hundred three- to ten-year-old children living in Budapest after the war. These children came from differrent religious and socioeconomic backgrounds and varied in intellectual levels from dull normal to superior. By means of their drawings, compositions, and discussions about their understanding of death, three distinct developmental stages were found, although there was some overlapping between the three. Between three and five years of age, children see death as a reversible departure in which no clear distinction is made between the living and the lifeless. Children at this age sometimes attribute life or animism to much of their environment, including toys, dolls, household objects, belongings, and inanimate objects of all kinds and sometimes worry about "their feelings." At this stage, their view of the world is egocentric and their cognitive skills are deficient in abstraction ability, so they really view the dead as "alive." In the second stage, from five to around nine years, children see death as a person who carries away living people. They may have fantasies about death; however, they don't see it as a universal personal experience but rather as an action that takes place outside them. Children sometimes also confuse dead people with "death" during this stage. After age nine or ten, during the third stage, children finally see death as a permanent, irreversible end that involves dissolution of the body and the end of all "living" processes. The conceptions of death and dying become much more realistic with the maturity of mental ability, and these stages of understanding of death correspond to Jean Piaget's stages of intellectual development.

Comparison studies across age groups would seem to be essential for a clear understanding of the relationship between death fears and age, but to date such investigations have been limited in scope and depth of focus. When personality tests were used with projective test responses in a comparison between sixteen- to twenty-one- and fifty-five to sixty-five-year-old subjects, more avoidance of death was seen in the older people. As noted above, death anxiety involves a threat to self-esteem, and the ability to care for dependents is a significant factor in the self-esteem of adults. Concern for dependents as a function of death fears reaches a peak in people from forty to fifty-four years of age.

Fear of death clearly becomes identified with concern about surviving family members and loved ones, which complicates the dimensions of the issue at stake in the research designs. Most of these studies ignore this point and have yielded very few insights of substance beyond statistical results. No general relationship between fear of death and age can be demonstrated, but there are specific relationships at various times in life that reflect deeper psychological processes.

In a more extensive recent study, a death anxiety scale was administered to upper- middle-class apartment dwellers from nineteen to eighty-five years of age; low-income aides in a state hospital who ranged in age from eighteen to sixty-one years; psychiatric patients from seventeen to fifty-nine years of age; and students from thirteen to twenty-one years of age.[28] In all of the groups there was no significant relationship between death anxiety and age.[29] Perhaps longitudinal studies, which involve following subjects' psychological changes over a period of time, might be employed to clear up the inconsistency in the literature on age and death anxiety. Some authors have speculated that the people who have a strong fear of death in old age may be the same people who had a strong fear of life in youth.[30] Fear of present and future experience, withdrawal from potentially anxiety-provoking situations, and living in the past all are common among the aged who fear death, and they are also characteristics of a neurotic tendency to fear life in younger people. All of the existentially oriented psychoanalytic writers on this subject have agreed that living fully demands awareness of and readiness for death. This spirit of awareness implies that at any age maturity demands living with death and ultimately dying with life.

In the language of legends and myth, heroism has often been defined as a strength of character, a freedom from anxiety and depression which involves their transformation into the heroic moment. The grace of the heroic gesture is particularly dramatic and compelling when it commands a slight of death anxiety. The transcendence of both the fear of death and powerful adversaries as a reflection of spiritual strength and cultural necessity often affirms the most salient traits of the hero. Orpheus, for example, received divine honors after his death not only because of his musical talent but also because his love for Eurydice compelled him to descend into the underworld to rescue her after her death. Orpheus challenged the king of the underworld and charmed him with his melodies to such an extent that after his death the nightingales built their nests near his tomb and his lyre became a heavenly constellation.

Socioeconomic, Demographic, and Educational Differences

Amount of education and level of intelligence generally have no direct influence on the fear of death. Among young, middle-aged, and aged adults the extent of education has no relationship to the fear of death.[31] Among geriatric patients, a limited intelligence has been correlated to some extent with higher death anxiety, perhaps because limited intelligence marks a limited capacity for the use of intellectual or philosophical defenses against death. Several authors have found that adolescents who have low academic achievement in school show higher death anxiety than students who are high achievers in school.

Among institutionalized adolescents, average or high I.Q. patients have less fear of death than low I.Q. patients and this difference is even more noticable in girls than in boys.[32] These findings can in no way be generalized to people living outside of institutions, and for the present no direct relationship can be demonstrated between I.Q. or education and death anxiety.

Research on cultural and socioeconomic variables and death anxiety has also been limited. Initially, some differences in death attitudes were reported across occupational groups, but no relationship has been shown to exist between the fear of death and occupational status, income, or urban versus rural location.[23] An additional note of caution must be observed here because almost all of this research on death anxiety has been carried out in the United States, and the conclusions cannot be applied to cultures or societies without supporting data. Even though there has been a deluge of written material, discussions, and seminars on death and dying, there is a natural resistance to openness about thoughts, feelings, and fears about death. This inhibition may have contributed to limiting the depth and scope of psychological and psychiatric research on death anxiety.

Emotional Disturbance and Depression

Many researchers have been interested in studying the relationship between death anxiety and types of psychopathology. After interviewing murderers, Schilder found much more preoccupation with death among the psychotic murderers than among those who had revealed a psychopathic character disorder.[34] Ideas about death have been reputed as persistent preoccupations among some neurotics, and they are frequent in psychotic hallucinations. Melanie Klein[35] maintained that fear of death accounted for the origin of all persecutory ideas, and a number of psychoanalytic theoreticians have claimed that the efficacy of electroconvulsive shock treatment with depressive patients lies in the stimulation of a death-rebirth fantasy.[36] The loss of consciousness due to the electrical shock therapy has been interpreted as a symbolic equivalent of death, and return to consciousness has been reported as a symbolic return to life. When ego strength and death fears were measured in schizophrenics, no correlation between death anxiety and general ego strength was found.

Paul Rhudick and Andrew Dibner[37] studied death anxiety in a group of healthy aged subjects by administering two very useful psychological tests: the Thematic Apperception Test (TAT) and the Minnesota Multiphasic Personality Inventory (MMPI). The latter text is a standardized, quantitatively scored, detailed, objective personality test that profiles personality variables. Demographic variables were not related to death anxiety in the results, but reports of physical and emotional symptoms were related to high concern about death. When all sixteen MMPI scales were studied, hypochondriasis was the only one very significantly related to death concerns; but hysteria, dependency and impulsivity were also related. In addition, the authors noted that depression, not fear or anxiety, was most clearly related to concerns about death and that demographic variables were unrelated to death concerns. The general conclusion that emerged from their findings was that the more neurotic the subject appeared to be, the more likely he or she was to have a high degree of concern about death. No other important relationship existed between death concerns and personality variables. Its relationship to depression supports my own view that fear of death can serve both as a defense against depression and as an expression of depression and specific neurotic conflicts.

Death anxiety has been shown to relate not only to depression but also to feelings of inadequacy, rejection, and lack of productivity on psychological tests that can register and diagnose depression.[38] Recent findings add support to the early studies which maintained that death fears are common among normals, neurotics, and psychotics, even though they have different meanings in different types of neurotic disorders.[39] However no general relationship has been proven between degree or type of mental disturbance and death anxiety.

Many investigators have suggested that depression increases with age, and Donald Templar was able to assess the relationship between age, depression, and death anxiety by means of a personality test called the Death Anxiety Scale (DAS). After administering the DAS, the MMPI, and the Cornell Medical Index, which reflects bodily or somatic preoccupation in neurosis, to retired adults aged fifty-one to ninety-two years, he found a positive correlation between death anxiety and depression.[40] Based on the positive association between death anxiety and depression, attempts have been made to alleviate death anxiety by treating depression psychopharmacologically. Ratings of death anxiety levels and extent of depression were obtained before and after antidepressant medication was administered to a group of hospitalized psychiatric patients suffering from a variety of emotional disorders with affective components including neurotic depressions, psychotic depressive reactions, schizophrenia, schizo-affective type, and manic depressive illness.[41] The antidepressant drugs lowered both depression and death anxiety, though the study did not go beyond symptom reduction and lacked controls, follow-up, and a well-constructed experimental design. These findings on increasing age, death anxiety, and depression are not conclusive or consistent with other research but are nevertheless interesting and lend support to the notion of an inherent psychological relationship between fear of death and depression.[42] The research data on the fear of death provides a body of support for modern psychoanalytic inquiries in the area, as does clinical data revealed in psychoanalytic psychotherapy. Only recently has any in-depth attempt been made to relate the fear of death to neurosis and depression in psychoanalytic theory.

In one such attempt, Stern[43] stressed the fear of death by emphasizing its frequency in neurotic disturbances and the extent to which preoccupation with death serves as a kind of storehouse of early psychological traumas and associated affects. Stern sees their origin as the young child's terrible fear of separation from and abandonment by the mother. In his view, which seems to me quite reasonable and clinically sound, working through the fear of death in psychoanalytic psychotherapy usually has the effect of unleashing considerable depression in the neurotic that derives from early disturbances in the mother-child relationship. Furthermore, instances of the patient's growth in psychoanalytic treatment often are accompanied by depression because of the fear of the loss of self in its intrapsychic attachment to the parents.

Differences have been found between "normal" adults and neurotics or psychotics in investigations on death, even though identical attitudes and fears about death can exist among all three categories of people. Fei-fel found that mentally ill people use much more denial as a defense against thoughts of death than "normal" subjects, and they also had a much greater tendency to imagine their own death as occuring through violence.[44] When asked what they would do if they could do only one more thing before dying, these normal subjects chose some pleasurable experience, whereas the mentally ill subjects tended to choose charitable or religious activities ("Get closer to God"). A third reported difference was that mentally ill subjects were more concerned about ideas of pun-ishment and failure in relation to death, whereas the more normal sub-jects were more concerned about loneliness and fears of the unknown. Denial is a primitive mechanism of defense that is relatively lacking in efficiency and sophistication, and its use is sometimes prevalent in psy-chotic or borderline psychotic people whose poorly functioning defenses reflect ego deficiencies. Ideas of guilt, punishment, and an unconscious need for punishment are all usually psychodynamic factors in depres-sion. Schizophrenics tend to have a decrease in death imagery after fail-ing in experimental tasks, while neurotic people show an increase in death imagery after they have experienced failure. This difference may also be due to the reltionship between failure, depression, and the fear of failure in neurotic living.

The research cited above confirms the view that depression is clearly related to death anxiety and the consistently higher levels of death anx-iety in women. The research also supports the hypothesis that neurotics who have an inordinately high fear of death often are experiencing de-pression.

It may not be coincidental that the popularity of the subject of death and dying emerged in American consciousness at the height of the Viet-nam War and in the early post-Vietnam years. Perhaps attention focused on death in popular American psychology reflects a national sense of loss and mourning not only for the victims but also for the survivors. Guilt and depression do play an important role in adjustment conflicts that involve the fear of death. According to psychoanalytic historians, the tragic losses and suffering that resulted from the first World War had a profound effect on the theoretical development of psychoanalysis. The war's destructiveness to humanity seemed to provide a context for Freud's development of the concept of the death instinct. At that time, there was an obvious need to reconcile the destruction and a drive for death with libido or sexual drive in the theoretical schema. Freud's feel-ings about the destruction of human life and his feelings about the war dead may have stimulated his theoretical interest in death.

Death Anxiety in the Dying

Research on death anxiety has recently been put into clinical practice with respect to the medical and psychological treatment of dying pa-tients. The psychological needs of patients who are about to die require different kinds of nontraditional psychotherapeutic interventions. The psychiatric problems of the chronically ill have begun to be addressed in conjunction with the treatment demands of total medical care, although the communality of depression in the chronically ill has long been recognized. One principal therapeutic task lies in helping dying patients explore and understand feelings and fantasies about their illness and approaching death where such psychotheraputic work is possible. Fantasies and fears about bodily changes resulting from chemotherapy, surgery, or life-threatening illness often have unconscious components and little systematic research has been done until recently in this area. Weisman and Kastenbaum's development of the Psychological Autopsy to assess the nature of psychological changes in geriatric patients before death and their reaction to the various phases of their illness represents one promising research tool.

The behavior of nurses and other hospital staff contributes greatly to the dying patient's comfort or anxiety, hostility, and regression. Humane and effective methods for treating the dying are also being developed with the movement for hostels for the terminally ill. Most workers emphasize the need for honest communication with the dying, if the patient's use of denial does not contraindicate it, and new psychotherapeutic approaches for dealing with impending death have recently been introduced.[45]

Physicians nurses, and therapists need to confront their own death anxiety in coping with the sensitivity, emotional pain, psychological problems, and enormous needs for attention, reassurance, and physical stroking of the terminally ill. Some dying patients regress not only because of pain, incapacity, and helplessness but also because of a wish for reunion and merger.[46,47] One of the tenets of ego psychology holds that the ongoing experience of struggle and adaptation to internal psychic actuality and external events in the world assumes the "prospect of pleasure." The mature ego's capacity to withstand pain and suffering has as its foundation the prospect of future pleasure. The emotional regression and associated feeling of helplessness involves the ego's inability to anticipate future pleasure for the chronically ill dying patient. The ecstasy of sexual orgasm has been described by ego psychologists as a momentary loss of the ego's efficiency in processing stimulation during which no future pleasure can be anticipated. Kurt Eissler suggested that death could therefore be accepted by the ego at such a moment. According to these principles, the dying patients' depression and separation anxiety need to be responded to with as much care as is taken in responding to their mere conscious concerns.

The role of the dying person's therapist has been depicted by a number of authors as involving a profoundly trusting relationship with the patient that revives early childhood nurturance and trust of the mother. In technical terms, the therapist encourages a dependent regressive transference in the patient and seems as nearly as possible, through the therapeutic alliance, to become the patient's mother so as to minimize suffering and pain. Eissler defined three specific functions of the psychotherapist under such conditions: (1) to accept the patient's regression and to reduce his or her anxiety about regression (and perhaps lowered self-esteem); (2) through the regressive transference to help the patient with the decathexis of love objects and coping with object loss.[48] What is implied here is that the terminally ill person who is aware of dying is actually losing the love and presence of all relatives, friends, and loved ones; this may entail the fear of abandonment by every important person in one's life, a realization that could depress any physically strong, healthy person, let alone a weak, suffering, frightened one); and (3) to present the patient with a "gift solution" that is a representation of mother's love so as to elicit the most gratifying childhood feeling of being loved. Actual gifts to the patient might be appropriate in accordance with this rationale, or the giving of gifts might be considered in terms of unlimited time availability, nurturing in the form of reading to the patient, touching, holding, and so on. Elizabeth Kubler Ross' recent case studies involve attempts at such treatment and Eissler's work based on the delineation of these parameters are quite moving contributions in themselves. Drugs cannot possibly replace the emotional support and comfort the dying person could potentially derive from psychotherapeutic relationships of this sort.

Summary

The suffering of the dying is augmented by the helplessness they feel in combating physical illness and in not being in control of the time and circumstance of their death. To interpersonal psychoanalytic theoreticians, this helplessness and fear of helplessness also plays a significant role in both the fear of death and neurosis. The psychic suffering, physical pain, and helplessness of the terminally ill have long been neglected therapeutically. The kindness, decency, and compassion involved in psychotherapeutic work with the dying renders it impervious to the criticism that it may constitute the acting out of a wish for merger. Here the wish for total gratification of one's emotional needs by a maternal figure may be imagined while one is mired in a state of utter passivity. Helping a dying person deal with the terror of abandonment and the pain of loss and separation when he or she actually falters on the brink of death constitutes a Herculean task. The interlocking fears of separation and abandonment stand forthrightly as really significant issues in death anxiety fantasies and their relationships to depression and neurotic personality traits. The inconsistent research findings on the frequency of death fears seldom penetrate to any of the above psychodynamic issues involved in either realistic or neurotic death anxiety.

The illusion that the therapist of the healthy but psychologically troubled patient has the capability of truely substituting for the parent of childhood under any circumstances supposes an altruistic conceit. This shared illusion might account for an opacity of therapeutic focus on unexplored symbiotic wishes and underlying unconscious needs for merger and fusion that penetrate to the very heart of the fear of death in many types of neurotic problems. The onset of life-threatening illness and realistic anxiety about death can bring to the surface inherent neurotic expressions of a deeper death anxiety, an anxiety about psychic growth and individuation that Erich Fromm described as the pain of "aloneness in the universe." The living, like the dying, do not just simply fear death as separation. Heightened death anxiety in neurosis conveys conflicting wishes for and fears of death in relation to ambivalence about separation- individuation from the internalized parents. Explicit depression and fears of abandonment may push into further unconscious obscurity representations of the patient's self as helpless in relation to parental images and in relation to the psychic demands of all separation experiences. In depth psychotherapy the fantasies and fears about the death of the self require investigation in juxtaposition with anxieties about separation from significant others and their internalized representations. Therapeutic work with both the living and the dying involves exploration and definition of the unconscious meanings of death associated with neurotic personality patterns. Furthermore, I will propose that the neurotic, like the terminally ill person, experiences and struggles against the depression and helplessness that accompanies the anticipated loss of the self.

CHAPTER THREE

Depression and the Fear of Death

Depression and Orality

The psychological and psychiatric literature touches very lightly on the relevance of death anxiety to depression. Karl Abraham described the relationship between grief and depression and Freud noted a number of reactions that are often common to both, including inhibition of activity, withdrawal, and decreased interest in work, social life, or love relationships.

The term *depression* implies normal affective responses that become a psychopathologic entity consisting of feeling states which range from sadness, dejection, and tearfulness to profound despair, pessimism, and self-hatred. Grief and mourning at the death or loss of a loved one involve similar affective experiences that may evolve into clinical depressive reactions. Neurotic depressive reactions, depressive character styles, and affective psychoses, however broad in their scope of symptoms, can all assemble unconscious processes in which the loss of the self is either wished for or feared in relation to a lost object. Self-critical ideas, feelings of guilt, hopelessness, and hostility predominate in depressions. Self-accusatory or self-critical thoughts frequent the depressed obsessional's ruminations. A wish for punishment and the conviction of one's worthlessness or inadequacy bristle vehemently in the conscious thoughts of the depressed person while fears of death lie in more unconscious obscurity. The ultimate expression of self-condemnation lies in suicidal gestures or attempts that express the unconscious wish for death. Although not all suicidal people are necessarily acutely depressed, as one might suspect, the research studies on successful and unsuccessful suicides confirm the important role of depression in suicide. Psychotherapists who work with depressed people cannot afford to overlook the significance of their patients' conscious and unconscious attitudes about death. The symbolism inherent in an individual's death attitudes betrays a psychodynamic relevance to his or her characterological problems and a framework in which to understand the significance of depression.

On a physical level, neurotic as well as more severe depressions often are accompanied by somatic distress. Loss of appetite or weight, lowering of the sexual drive, feelings of muscular weakness, sleeping disorders, constipation, menstrual disorders, and physical manifestations of anxiety are frequent. On a psychological level, hostility directed against the self and feelings of helplessness and pessimism about the future are commonplace. Aaron Beck suggested a "cognitive triad" of depression in which the core of depressive illness is represented by: lowered self-esteem or a negative view of the self; a negative view of the world; and a negative expectation for the future. In clinical cases of depression, that is an illness a psychotherapist encounters depressed affect, self-blame, and self-recrimination for one's failures and shortcomings (whether real or imagined inadequacies) and the consequent loss of self-esteem as deserved punishments. Lost self-esteem follows from some narcissistic insult such as the loss of a job or income, breaking up with a boyfriend or girlfriend, and failure in school or in business. These situations together with the death of a loved one typify the most frequent mechanisms that serve to trigger off acute depressions. When the underlying personality structures are predisposed, depressions result as frequently as with genetic predispostiions.

The interrelationship between these expressions of depression, death anxiety, and the underlying difficulty in psychological separation-individuation can be synthesized from research data and psychoanalytic studies, as well as from analyses of literature, folklore, and myths. The interplay between depression as an unfolding, evolving psychological character pattern and unconscious motivation involving death anxiety was insightfully depicted in the plot development of Joseph Conrad's *Lord Jim*. Helene Deutsch analyzed and interpreted Joseph Conrad's novel as a prose account of a search for lost self-esteem that portrays the unconscious psychodynamics of depression.[1] Deutsch's view of the book stressed the character Lord Jim's personal immaturity and predisposition to depression during his early period of competent performance at duties aboard ship. His successful engagement of the adult role was overshadowed by grandiose fantasies of heroic accomplishments and glorious triumphs in which Lord Jim would be showered with attention and praise by admirers. The moment of panic in which Lord Jim fled from his ship necessitated a fall from grace and the loss of self-esteem, which he spent the rest of his life trying to recover. When confronted with the single act of cowardice and panic, the triumphant, glorious hero in fantasy succumbed to a crippling depression. His depression was characterized by a complete loss of self-respect, a sense of worthlessness, self-hatred, and withdrawal from the world. The final phase of the novel's plot involved Jim's unconscious attempts to restore his lost self-esteem and grandiose self-image by traveling to increasingly more remote parts of the world in order to live among foreigners who could not know anything about his disgrace. Tortured by his own memories of disgrace and failure he was threatened by the chance comments of strangers whose innocent conversation awakened his fear of discovery and exposure. He then moved to an even more primitive region, where, as "Lord Jim," he became transformed into a fantasized version of his grandiose self. As he fled civilization, Jim moved further into a madness that allowed for an illusory restoration of his glorious triumphs and heroism. From the moment he deserted his duty until his death in the midst of his delusional state, Jim's behavior constituted a metaphor for the depressive process. Deutsch outlined as typical of depressives Lord Jim's use of the defense mechanisms of withdrawal, isolation, identification with the inflated ego ideal, and self-recrimination. The attempt to recover lost self-esteem in a process of making restitution also occupies the depressed person's ego in the struggle for recovery and health.

Reanalysis of Conrad's *Lord Jim* in light of the contributions of current analytic theory, and advances in the knowledge of early psychological development (principally Margaret Mahler's work on human symbiosis[2]) would add another dimension of understanding. Jim's delusional, psychotic state and the extreme grandiosity in his inflated, idealized image of himself as the hero suggest early disturbances in narcissism, an inflated grandiose self, and defensive splitting of the ego. Certainly Joseph Conrad must have experienced depression in order to write such an insightful description in the novel.

Conrad cleverly portrayed in *Lord Jim* the psychological relationship between depression, feelings of inadequacy, self-hatred, and the effects of disturbances in the sense of self during infancy and early childhood. Current psychoanalytic personality theory accounts for persistent depression and lack of feelings of self-worth in terms of disturbances in the sense of self or in self-esteem regulation in people with neurotic, narcissistic personality disturbances and borderline personality structures. The relationship between the separation-individuation phenomena, depression, and death anxiety can also be understood in terms of the fear of the loss of self. A fear of losing oneself correlates with depression and feelings of helplessness about oneself in the face of conflict.

In the character of Lord Jim, one might postulate a relationship between clinging to a grandiose, idealized self, a lack of adequate psychic separation from his parents, and his ego's turning of feelings of hate against itself. It is quite conceivable that along with Lord Jim's unconscious attempts at restoring himself to health and making restitution for his lost self-esteem, there existed an unconscious wish for death and punishment. Freud first described this defensive process of the ego's splitting and potential for sadistic attacks against itself in *Mourning and Melancholia*. Harry Stack Sullivan, Alfred Adler, and more recently Walter Boneim have added the significance of characterological problems to the psychodynamic understanding of all types of depression.

Boneim in particular has commented on the covert hostility, manipulativeness and need for constant gratification in the depressive.[3] Lord Jim's courageous struggle to the death with his enemy at the novel's end might amount to a counterphobic response to his depression and death anxiety. It was also a reversal of his previous panicked flight from responsibility as ship's officer. Jim's panic was not fully understandable in light of the storm and the fear of his fellow officers. It was an exaggerated anxiety beyond the realistic degree of danger. Hence, it could be considered as a metaphor for a phobic or death anxiety attack. The intense fear for his life and safety on a deeper level may have involved the fear of the loss of his self. The self this character feared losing was his grandiose self. We can imagine it masked a shaky sense of his true self, a tenuous realistic self-esteem, and a vulnerability to profound feelings of inadequacy and lack of self-worth. His grandiosity and need to be compensated for deprivations illustrate Boneim's observation that neurotic depression is essentially a characterological process. If this analysis is correct, then Lord Jim's death anxiety represented the top layer of the depressive pattern in a personality that was predisposed to depression and lack of self-esteem due to its psychologically immature narcissistic type of organization. His fear of death, and desertion of duty in light of death anxiety may have been influenced by an internal struggle between retaining and renouncing his grandiose self-image. The novel's plot illustrates the psychodynamic linkage between death anxiety and depressive characterological trends.

In my view, the fear of death is intimately tied to depression. Death anxiety represents both a defense against depression and an unconscious wish for death and punishment via the ego's passivity in the face of threat. As a particular, stressful life experience stimulates anxiety in a severe depressive, it mobilizes symbiotic like wishes which conflict with the fear of being devoured and destroyed. It is through the mouth that the infant takes in food, has contact with mother, feels her love, and makes contact with the world. The fear of the loss of the self by being eaten offers the psychological counterpart of the wish to eat, incorporate, or fuse symbiotically with the mother and the world. It is a defensive process related to the early oral phase of development that is found throughout neurotic disorders and in some psychotic affective disturbances to the extent that depression itself is found as a symptom throughout all psychological types of disturbances.

The fear of death can typically be found throughout neuroses and all types of depressions from neurotic to psychotic depression, manic-depressive psychoses, and schizo-affective schizophrenia because of its origin in infantile fears of the loss of the self. Just as the fear of death is essentially related to depression and separation anxiety, underlying separation-individuation problems are often involved as crucial ingredients in depressive reactions. Depressive affects have their origin in the period of the infant's separation from the mother, and the fear of the loss of the self emerges early on in relation to separation anxiety. This explanation relies on a synthesis of theoretical and clinical studies on depression and elation,[4] as well as on the developmental research on infant and toddler behavior.

In Melanie Klein's theoretical treatment of depression, she placed the notion of death anxiety within the framework of an "infantile depressive position." Mahler[5] reported the establishment of a "basic mood" in the infant during the separation- individuation process. A proclivity for depression arises through the infant's interplay with its mother in a distinct sequence. During the first subphase of differentiation, Mahler states that a "dialogue" is established with the mother. During the subphase of individuation from the mother, a basic mood of "elation" is characteristic of the young child because of the solid foundation of the dialogue with the mother. During the next subphase of "rapprochement" with the mother, Mahler found that the mother's lack of acceptance of the child can lead to ambivalence, lack of self-worth, aggression toward the parents, and feelings of helplessness in the child. These factors lead to the basic affect of depression.

This developmental position differs from Klein's theory in several key aspects. Klein posited an inherent fear of death as part of the so-called depressive position, but the Kleinian formulation of an inherent idea of death in infancy cannot be supported by current research findings on infantile mental development. It is more reasonable to assume that life stresses and conflicts revitalize depressive characterological trends that have as their basis oral conflicts and problems in separation-individuation. A second difference from Klein's view, and an advantage of stressing "depression-orality" factors underlying intense fears of death, lies in the relevance of death anxiety to separation-individuation problems throughout childhood and adolescence. The pioneering research of René Spitz[6] indicated that institutionalized infants who lacked adequate mothering care failed to develop adequately either physically or emotionally, and that their condition approached something akin to profound depression in an adult. Spitz followed 123 infants in the nursery and observed dramatic physical and emotional changes in them over a period of months. He called this occurrence "anaclitic depression" and attributed its origin to absence of a nurturing maternal figure to provide physical comfort and love for the infant. The effect of insufficient maternal care ranged from coma or the death of the infant following complete rejection to anaclitic depression in partial deprivation. Sptiz also correlated specific types of inappropriate maternal attitudes with specific types of somatic distress in infancy including colic, hyperrythmia, hypermobility, and dermatitis. In babies who had lost their mothers, anaclitic depression itself comprised a clinical state of depression consisting of: lack of responsiveness, sadness, apprehension, withdrawal, disinterest in the environment, lack of the capacity to smile, retardation in development and ability to react to stimuli, slowness of movement, insomnia, loss of appetite, refusal to eat, and weight loss. Child clinicians can now point to a body of literature on the effects of parental unavailability and depressive equivalents in childhood.

In non-institutionalized children who do have contact with their mothers, conflicts arising from pathological or extended symbiotic unions with mother, and problems in the young child's separation individuation from the mother, can often be expressed in terms of oral language and the fear of the loss of the self. The fear of being eaten by a witch, monster, ferocious wolf, wicked stepmother, or threatening animal has survived for centuries as a familiar theme in fairy tales and childhood fantasies. How many fairy tales involved a fear of helplessness and a fear of being eaten in a child who is alone and without the support of nurturing protecting adults? The practice of what Freud called "affectionate abuse"—the conveying of hidden messages of destruction embodied in adults' affectionate or endearing language with children—often involves elements of the threat of being eaten and the loss of the self. Without any harm being intended, adults at times announce to small children: "I'm going to eat you up," "I love you so much, I could eat you up," or "You're so cute or pretty, I could take a bite out of you." While not necessarily hostile or traumatic in themselves, these kinds of affectionate abuse can reinforce children's unconscious fears of death and feelings of helplessness that originate during the earliest period of psychological development. In the face of parental punishment, the very young child might unconsciously expect destruction through being devoured by angry parent figures, just as the depressed adult might expect a future of failure and disappointment. According to Fodor,[7] the fear of punishment and guilt feelings in children both give rise to unconscious fears of cannibalism. The open scolding mouth of the angry parent can seem to the child like a devouring mouth that threatens him with being eaten and swallowed. Fodor notes that "the ogres of the fairy tales" are not merely flights of fancy but the "objectification" of the child's panic. Parental terms of endearment such as "honey," "sugar," "sweety," etc., may rely on the communication of an alternate but related message, namely, that the good child, or lover to adults, deserves being eaten or incorporated out of love. The unconscious meaning can then be conveyed to the child in the height of praise or affection that love is the equivalent of being incorporated, being reunited, or fused with and literally becoming part of the loving mother and father.

Depression and the "Wolfman"

Freud's well-known account of the analysis of the "Wolfman" provides a telling illustration of the relationship of death anxiety to depression. The Wolfman's depression and death anxiety were not emphasized in the paper on the analysis of this famous patient's "infantile neurosis."[8] The Wolfman was a wealthy Russian man who had been terrified of wolves as a young child. He came to Freud for treatment as an adult with a variety of obsessive compulsive symptoms and hypochondriacal concerns about his body.

The "infantile neurosis" was the cornerstone of Freud's theory on the origin of adult neuroses. In the attempt to reconstruct and understand the etiology of this "infantile neurosis," great emphasis was placed on the analysis of this patient's childhood dream. In the dream the Wolfman saw a number of menacing, white wolves in the branches of a tree outside his window, and he became terrified of being eaten by the wolves. The young boy's terror of being devoured symbolized the principal affective statement in the manifest content of the dream. The terror of death later served as the Wolfman's first association to the dream during the analysis. Freud attributed the Wolfman's infantile neurosis to a mixture of castration anxiety, early seductions by adult females, and to the boy having witnessed the primal scene. The fear of the wolves had also reflected a series of childhood traumas in which the Wolfman's older sister had tormented him. When he was around four years of age, this sister repeatedly showed him illustrations of the frightening wolf in the story "Little Red Riding Hood" in Grimm's fairy tale. The wolves apparently came to represent the Wolfman's father, such that the phobia of wolves combined castration anxiety and fear of the boy's own passive sexual wishes in relation to the father. As interpretation gave rise to a working through of the infantile neurosis, the adult Wolfman's symptoms dissipated, and the treatment achieved a successful termination.

The Wolfman's intermittent periods of profound depression and his dependency on psychoanalytic treatment,[9] both of which lasted throughout his life, were touched on in his subsequent treatment by other analysts but not in the original analysis. Beneath the Wolfman's obsessive-compulsive symptoms and neurotic defenses existed a strong tendency to react to disappointment and frustration with moods of depression and despondency. The tendency toward depression and displeasure in the face of both positive and negative experience is a frequent faculty of neurotics in general and obsessive-compulsive personalities in particular. The Wolfman's case actually exemplifies the interplay between a fixation in the oral phase of development, depression, and problems in separation—individuation. His dream might be interpreted as documentation of the dynamic importance of death anxiety in neurosis and depression. The phobia of wolves in childhood might be understood in this sense as a literal fear of the loss of the body, and self via the terror of being devoured and annihilated. Freud conceptualized depression as often involving the identification with an introjected object as a source of self-esteem and the regulating of feelings of self-worth. Therefore, it is not difficult to take issue with the explanation of the Wolfman's life-long struggle with depression simply in terms of castration anxiety. The Wolfman's dream may be considered as a representation of conflict between the unconscious wish to incorporate or devour his mother and the wish to be devoured, taken in, or merged with his mother, with the threat of his own psychic and physical destruction as a consequence. His inability to enjoy a mature, symptom-free life without reliance on an analyst or substitute parent figure continued the Wolfman's attachment to an introjected parent figure. The Wolfman's need for Freud may have been not only a simple transference dependency but also an expression of the more deeply repressed wish for a symbiotic union with his childhood nurse, who had substituted for his mother. The meaning of the symptom of the wolf phobia was uncovered by Freud through the analytic investigation of several threads of association to the dream. First, the dream occurred the day before the Wolfman's birthday, which was Christmas day; and second, it brought to the Wolfman's mind associations to the stories of "Little Red Riding Hood" and "The Seven Little Goats." Both stories contain the symbolic equivalents of the fear of death and the loss of the self in the thematic form of children who have been eaten or threatened with being devoured. The time of the occurrence of the dream enabled Freud to speculate about the Wolfman's real or imagined observation of his parents' sexual intercourse, but the birth symbolism fits more succinctly with the above death anxiety point of view. The childhood terror could have also been associated with the birth of the Christ child and the Wolfman's own birth, therein symbolizing not simply the trauma of birth but also the trauma and fear of psychic separation. The Wolfman's fragile dalliance with health and his limited freedom from adjustment problems demonstrated the connection between death anxiety and separation anxiety in the fearful living of neurotic depression.

Death Anxiety and Childhood Depression

A number of writers have advanced theories on the origin of the fear of death that are similar to the present view of it as both a defense against and an expression of depression that has as its analogue oral conflicts and problems in separation-individuation. Grotjahn[10] concluded that very young children often fear annihilation, which they equate with being devoured, and that this presents a source of fears of death in later life. In Grotjahn's study dreams of reunion with mother showed the meaning of a fear of return to the helpless state of infancy. He notes that in dreams or fantasies the unconscious wish for reunion is overridden by the threat of the "annihilation of the ego" through the dreamer's regression to an early undifferentiated state. In this sense symbiotic merger with the parent or significant other has the further unconscious meaning of the loss of the self.

Stern presented a similar twofold thesis: that the fear of death arises at an early age as a repetition of "early biotraumatic states of object loss"; and that the inability to adapt to such terrors remains an integral part of all neuroses. Stern asserts that the fear of death must be worked through in psychoanalytic treatment.[11] He documented quite correctly the way in which neurotics cling to unconscious infantile wishes for symbiotic union, which are often expressed in the transference with the analyst as a mechanism for withdrawal from new experience. Stern saw depression and the fear of death as interrelated in the child's experience of night terrors, which he traced to early infantile "biotraumatic situations" such as the fear of annihilation or the loss of the mother. Although it does seem quite probable that the fear of death or "annihilation of the ego," as Grotjahn put it, originates in separation anxiety, there is no convincing evidence that neurosis has a biological origin. When the fear of death is viewed as neurotic depression and separation anxiety, given expression as the fear of the loss of the self, then there cannot be some vaguely defined developmental stage at which the fear of death is necessarily mastered in "normal" development. Both the psychoanalytic literature and psychological research studies show that the fear of death may or may not be present in neurosis, even though it can be found throughout all types of disturbances. In my opinion there is a much greater relationship between the fear of death and depression than between the fear of death and neurosis per se.

Rheingold[12] saw the child's wish to be eaten or incorporated as a result of the fear of being eaten or incorporated by a sadistic mother. In several early papers Sandor Rado stressed the craving for narcissistic gratification in people who are predisposed to depressions and the significance of the infant's "narcissistic bliss" in nursing at the mother's breast. Such narcissistic craving presented itself in drug intoxications, the psychological mood of elation or ecstasy and the intrapsychic reexperiencing of the infant's fusion with the mother while nursing.[13] Rado postulated a close alliance between drug addicition and depression or affective disturbances in which the drug high constitutes an artifically produced state of elation. The chemically induced elation overcomes depressions originating from narcissistic injuries and the predisposition to melancholia. According to Bertram Lewin,[14] the affective component of manic behavior is synonomous with elation, wherein the underlying recreation of an intrapsychic fusion with the mother can lead to either manic states or sleep. Oral satisfaction makes sleep possible for the baby, and the wish to sleep, together with the wish to devour and the wish to be devoured, form what Lewin called the "oral traid." In classical psychoanalytic theory, depressions may arise as reactivations of oral sadistic fantasies that may or may not originate in the nursing situation. Lewin demonstrated the common origin of the three wishes "to eat, be eaten, and to sleep" in the nursing situation, wherein the baby does not differentiate itself from the mother's breast and identifies itself with what is being eaten. Because of the common origin of the three wishes, the fear of death could be defined as both the fear of the loss of the self and the fear of being eaten. By the same token, the fear of sleep can be attributed to the fear of death and separation anxiety. Lewin interpreted the child's fear of being eaten as an expression of anxiety over a fear of falling asleep or a fear that the child will be "devoured into sleep." (Melaine

Klein also claimed that a fear of being eaten underlies manic behavior and fantasies, phobias and a variety of psychological disorders.) In carrying his theory through to its conclusion, Lewin attributed the fear of death to a fear of "bad sleep" or anxiety-filled, frightening, unpleasant sleep, away from the mother's breast. The content of some forms of suicidal fantasies in depressed people do contain such components. Death in fantasy and dream symbolism can alternately be viewed as "bad" or frightening, or "good," unending, blissfully happy, and a recreation of union with the "good mother."

Casual observations and scientific study both reveal the prevalence of such eating fantasies and oral themes in young children's games and fantasies. Psychological evaluation of children's fantasies has consistently shown that fears of being torn apart and eaten by witches, ghosts, or monsters are pervasive in preschool years and that children's play provides the mechanisms for adjustment to these fears. Their play and fantasies are not simply imaginative. Pretending and actually acting out games of being witches or other fairy tale characters provide the child with the means to adapt to and conquer the fears of being destroyed and devoured. The popularity of the story "Hansel and Gretel" documents the prevalence of children's unconscious fears of being eaten by the bad witch who puts small, helpless children into the oven and cooks them like food. I would imagine that its popularity and appeal attests to children's drive to master death and separation anxiety. This fairy tale most clearly illustrates the duality of symbolism in the depression-separation anxiety dimensions of the origins of death fears. The witch symbolizes mother in the story and the oven has often been interpreted as a symbol for the mother's womb or the inside of her body in literature and mythology. Thus small children who read "Hansel and Gretel" identify with their own fright and anxiety stemming from the psychic conflict between the wish to be eaten by mother—to return to her womb, to be incorporated into her—and the fear of being destroyed and eaten by mother. The threat of the annihilation of his own body, ego, and identity reverberates with the child's ambivalence about psychic separation from the mother and father.

The playhouse stories of preschoolers often involve dolls and babies who suffer being fed, cooked, and sometimes placed in an oven and eaten, only to reemerge unharmed. The drive for mastery compels children to watch television shows and movies about aggressive monsters and ghosts, in spite of their fear and death anxiety. The enormous popularity of the film *Jaws* among latency-age children may have had at its origin this same phenomenon. *Jaws* reflected the unconscious infantile fear of being devoured in juxtaposition with the corresponding wish to destroy and devour. Early elementary school age children who delighted in such play materials as in *Jaws* T-shirts and toy sharks demonstrated on one level their need to overcome their unconscious fears of death by being eaten and, on another level, their identification with the powerful, avenging, aggressive shark. The expression "the jaws of death" also identifies the fear of death as being synonymous with being eaten and annihilated, as does the content of the Old Testament story of Jonah and the whale.

Reevaluation of the research studies on death anxiety in light of its inherent relationship to depression and separation anxiety removes a good deal of the confusion and contradiction in the findings. For example, a recent study of the relationship between death anxiety and demographic variables in several hundred high school age adolescents showed some interesting results.[14] Although no clear differences on death anxiety existed for religious or socioeconomic variables, female subjects again showed consistently higher death anxiety than males. Adolescents who lived with only one parent had higher death anxiety scores than those who lived with both parents. Women's susceptibility to depression clearly lies at the root of their higher fear of death; issues of separation and independence from parental introjects underlies the fear of the adolescents who live with one parent. A predisposition to future depressions and anxiety about difficulty in autonomous growth and functioning underlie such adolescents' adjustment difficulties as well as adults' death fears.

Children who have lost one parent through death, divorce, or other separation undergo heightened ambivalent feelings about the lost parent, while at times, they unconsciously blame the present or surviving parent for their loss. Research done with children and young adolescents who have lost one parent through death confirms the susceptability of these children to depression and the difficulty they have in mourning for the lost parent.[15] Adolescents and younger children find great difficulty in overcoming the loss of a parent until they have reached the state of psychological growth when they are ready to mourn. Before this stage, denial of their loss may be the immediate response and the prolongation of severe bouts of depression the sequellae in adulthood. Until his grief and mourning has been resolved, the child suffers a pessimism akin to a repressed wish for death. Depressions in such cases simultaneously reflect intensified feelings of love and hate for the lost parent, an identification with the parent, and a dependency on, or intrapsychic clinging to, the internalized image of the parent.

Freud defined the conflict between the wish to kill and the wish to be killed in melancholic or depressed states as an outgrowth of ambivalence over lost objects (e.g., parents or other loved ones). The significance of a fear of being killed or devoured in depression extends the formulation that the wish to kill and the wish to be killed are inherent in depressive reactions. In children and adolescents who have lost a parent, the wish for death and the fear that this wish will be executed in reality essentially rely on three sources: a need for punishment for their having been abandoned, guilt over hostile wishes toward both parents, and a wish for reunion with the lost loved one. To the extent that their depression and death anxiety have shifted into long-standing problems of temperament, their psychological growth and mastery of their separation anxiety are held in suspension.

Experimental support for the existence of an inherent relationship between depression and death anxiety in adults comes from a 1974 study of depressed patients at a Western state hospital.[16] Because the study was based on the hypothesis that high death anxiety exists as a dimension of depression, it was expected that the symptomatic treatment of depression would lower death anxiety. Thirty-one patients diagnosed as suffering from neurotic depression; psychotic depression; schizo-affective schizophrenia, depressed type; and manic depressive psychosis, depressed type were administered the Death Anxiety Scale and a depression scale upon their admission to the hospital and again several days after their discharge. Significant reductions in death anxiety were accompanied by significant decreases in depression when the before and after hospitalization results were compared. Although this study was superficial, it did explore an experimental relationship between fear of death and depression that has been verified by other investigators.

The analysis of children's fantasies lends additional support to the fear of death-depression-separation anxiety thesis. Anthony[17] concluded, on the basis of children's psychological protocols, that normal children view death as either a painful separation or as a punishment, the result of some act of hostile aggression. Both depression and anxiety are frequent in neurotic or more disturbed children's fantasies and dreams that disclose partial solutions to developmental tasks and family problems.

As early as age two, children have dreams of being chased, attacked, and eaten by some frightening monster or animal.[18] This violent or sadistic dream content does not necessarily correlate with any specific traumatic event that could provide a rational or realistic basis for the child's fears. Violence and the fear of violent destruction are often also present in the anxious child's psychological projective tests, chiefly on the Rorschach and Thematic Apperception Test Responses. On test protocols children consistently identified death itself with punishment and violence. (In the early years they have no understanding of death as a natural process or as the culmination of the existence of all living things.) Paul Schilder's interviews with children confirmed this identification of death with violent destruction and punishment.[19] Guilt and the need for punishment of hostile thoughts and wishes play a role in children's unconscious death fears and in adult fears about death, as they frequently do in depressive reactions. Especially in very young children, who have not undergone the complete process of differentiating themselves from their mother, incomplete separation and differentiation exposes a threat of the loss of the mother, which also means loss of the self or death.

A variety of psychoanalysts have scrutinized the relationship between children's death fears and the terror of separation from the mother as symbolic of death and destruction. However, the connection between death fears, separation anxiety, and depression has not been emphasized sufficiently. The existence of such a relationship seems inescapable when studies on death fears and separation anxiety are integrated with those on death anxiety and depression. The research findings of the last two decades on children's responses to separation by Otto Rank's theories, particularly his statement that birth trauma was the prototype of separation or dependency problems in later life. For Rank life in-utero constituted safety and security. Birth represents its loss, and the trauma of birth was defined as the trauma of separation. For Rank the fear of separation from the mother, rather than the birth process, and the fear of independence lie at the root of the fear of death. Spitz's findings added support to the psychoanalysts' twofold assumption that depression can occur in the first year of life and the predisposition to depression lies in an oral fixation due to narcissistic shocks and maternal unavailability. These shocks were often related to the child's fear of death or fear of death of the love object.

It is a small plausable jump from the observable data—oral fixations, predisposition to depression, loss or death of the mother—to the dynamic level of the fear of separation from mother being equated with the fear of the child's own death. The possibility that complete reunion and merger with the mother also threatens the very existence of the child as a separate psychological person is the other side of the same unconscious dynamic. John Bowlby's research on mourning in children who have lost a parent provides still another basis of support for an integral relationship between depression, death anxiety, and separation anxiety. Bowlby presented ample evidence that infant's and young children's responses to the loss of mother are similar to those of adults who lose a loved one.[20] Once children have formed an intense tie to their mother in the first year of life, disruption of the tie produces separation anxiety and mourning. It predisposes the child to psychological disturbances as an adult. Throughout all of these research studies on early childhodd development, separation anxiety and the child's interchange with the mother are shown to provide the foundation for the affect of depression. Separation from the mother and terror of that prospect become equated with the child's own death. In the young child these fears are then externalized to the outside world, where they are transformed into the fear of being killed, usually by being attacked and devoured by some frightening animal or monstrous figure.

Suicide and the Fear of Death

Another clinical dimension of the fear of death-depression-separation anxiety formulation derives from research findings on the relationship between the wish for death, states of elation, and reunion fantasies. In one type of suicidally depressed person death can be experienced either as a peaceful nourishing sleep signifying a return to the mother's breast or as a psychic merger with mother. With this kind of uncon-

scious attitude toward death, suicide takes on the significance of a search
for peaceful surrender and reunion with mother. Suicidal fantasies disclose the wishes to sleep, to be fed, to give up the struggles of life for the
passivity and security of infancy. Abusive use of sleeping pills or alcohol
as the means for a suicide attempt might represent the passive giving up
of the self.

In Beck's survey of suicide attempts among hospitalized people, the
greatest risk of suicide was found to coincide with periods of separation
from the hospital (after discharge or on weekend passes). The separation
from hospitalization brings with it the demand for further independent
functioning. In my opinion, the suicidally depressed person often experiences separation anxiety, which becomes translated into a wish for death
and the surrender of the self. The self that is symbiotically attached to
the parent seems not to be lost as much as submerged and fused with the
other. Suicidal impulses may also arise from the sense of powerlessness
over the time and circumstances of one's death.[21] The fear of the uncertainty of death can engender a sense of helplessness in people who need
to maintain the illusion of perfect control over their lives. The fear of
death drives such people to suicide when their anxiety and loss of control feels intolerable. Under such circumstances, the act of suicide expresses a pseudo-victory over the fear of death and the sense of helplessness or powerlessness over fate.

As early as 1928 Sandor Rado identified, the wish for reconciliation
with a loving mother as a crucial underlying psychodynamic in suicidal
depression.[22] The depressed person is torn between wishing for such a
reconciliation and raging against the internalized parent-object who dis-
appointed him. The motivation for suicide therefore includes self-pun-
ishment, the wish for forgiveness, and the hope of reconciliation with
mother. Rado found a dual purpose behind depressed patients' rage:
first, destruction of the frustrating aspects of the disappointing mother;
second, and equally important, the retention of the loved "gratifying
mother." Suicidal rage was considered as unconscious "oral rage," with
the destructive power of biting and chewing directed against the mother
who was devoured.

Otto Fenichel equated severe depression with a lack of vital oral supplies in orally dependent people. He noted the frequency of cannibalistic
fantasies in melancholia and the prevalence of oral themes in less severe
depressions.[23] Depressed and normal children sometimes resort to
thumb-sucking and oral requests for nurturance at bedtime, when faced
with the prospect of separation from waking activity and when they experience other manifestations of death anxiety. Fenichel first noted in
print the very high frequency with which depressed children have suicidal fantasies in which reunion themes are couched in terms of resentment at parents. The suicidal child often fantasizes that the parents "will
be sorry, miss me and love me when I'm dead." Although these formulations underemphasize the primacy of aggression, guilt, and the emerging
characterological problems in childhood depression, my experience in

treating children suggests that they are clinically valid and practically universal in depressed children. The suicidally depressed child wishes for death to escape suffering in the hope of reunion with the lost good parent.

The fear of death-depression-separation anxiety thesis points to reunion fantasies within the cultural trappings of burial and funeral customs. In order to overcome the fear of separation from familiar sources of support and status, great efforts have been made to deny the meaning of death in funeral rituals. The excavations of the 5,000-year-old graves of royalty at Ur uncovered the carefully dressed bodies of as many as sixty-five people as well as wagons, supplies, animals, riches, and weapons buried with the dead king.[24] The fears of the unknown afterlife and separation from the world were reduced by the king's knowledge that he would be buried with his entire court and entourage. The elaborateness of caskets, floral arrangements, and mourning ceremonies not only obscure the finality and meaning of death but also serve to minimize the fear of death in the survivors. Freud identified the symbolism involved in the tomb-womb equation and in the lowering of the dead body into the ground as being a return to Mother Earth. Survivors often struggle with a combination of grief, ambivalent feelings about the dead person, feelings about separation from that person, and fears of their own death and separation from loved ones.

The theme of suicide as the wish for death—the joyful reunion with lost objects or the mother of infancy—abounds in the art and literature of Western culture. Much of the Romantic poetry on death can be classified thematically according to relative position between contrasting polarities. The fear of death-depression-separation anxiety cluster would fall at one end of the continuum. The wish for death-elation-reunion and themes of reconciliation with the lost good mother would fall at the other end. The themes of love, orality, death, and separation are interwoven over and over again in contemporary prose and the traditional arts of all media. Thomas Mann's *Death In Venice* has been interpreted as a tracing through the narrative of each of these themes. In *Death in Venice*, Aschenback's death occurred as a result of his eating contaminated food, which symbolized the interplay between love, sex, food, and death.[25] The alienation of death-in-life expressed in T.S. Eliot's "The Wasteland" provides a context for the poem's use of birth metaphors. Walt Whitman's expressions of joy in communion with nature extoll the view of death as a joyful celebration of life. In one poem, the romantic Whitman chanted in triumphant enthusiasm: "Death, Death, Death." D. H. Lawrence's prose and poetry stressed the relationship of love and death in the theme of surrender to sexuality. Lawrence eulogized sex as the height of natural experience, and death as the fulfillment of natural life. The loss of conscious control in sleep also parallels Lawrence's observations on the beauty of the momentary loss of control in sexual orgasm. The complete cessation of awareness in death finalizes the ultimate lack of control over the end of human destiny.

In the film *Elvira Madigan,* the main characters chose self-destruction as an alternative to starvation and pursuit by their adversaries. Their death symbolized retreat into a nourishing sleep of mutal love and union through death. Their suicide embodied a transcendence of separation anxiety and withdrawal from the painful conflicts of life. If death is viewed as positive or as a reunion in the unconscious, it can be wished for and sought after as the solution to intolerable conflict. It need not be experienced as annihilation or the end of suffering; it can serve as a return to a state of lost narcissism. Emma Bovary's suicide at the end of *Madame Bovary* may have included elements of both alternatives. Death itself can then be understood by some people not as an end but as a means for achieving the return of what has been lost in adulthood. Ernest Hemingway's suicide supplies another pertinent example. His son's recent biography solidifies the extent to which Hemingway equated his psychic self with sexual potency and creative ability. Throughout the Romantic Period, creativity was identified with life; death was considered by some writers as the only answer to creative blocks. Death itself became widely and highly romanticized, as A. Alvarez described, so that the death of creativity became grounds for suicide.[26] The early deaths of Keats, Shelley, and Byron reportedly capped their persistent anxieties that their intense creative feelings would not last into middle age. Baudelaire committed psychic-suicide for similar reasons, by an opium addiction that preceded his literal death by decades.

In Oscar Wilde's story *The Protrait of Dorian Grey,* the portrait became more hideous and frightening with the passage of time, whereas Grey's own face remained unblemished and youthfully attractive.[27] Just as Grey attached his murderous destructive feelings to the portrait, the person with intense death fear externalizes his own rage and destructiveness to the outside world and then becomes afraid of it. One could speculatively raise the possibility of a hidden sense of guilt in the character of Dorian Grey in which the split between his real self and the image of himself on canvas constituted a defense against depression and guilt. Fear of punishment can also play a role in the depressed person's fear of death. This is particularly so when the person's superego deems anger and rage unacceptable or when he believes in reward or punishment in the afterlife. The fear of punishment, like the fear of castration, can certainly be associated with a fear of death. Many different kinds of fears become attached to the fear of death, which itself is a normal universal part of life. The fear of punishment for loss of control and the fear of loss of control of sexual and hostile feelings clearly constitute two such combinations.

The Death of the Self

Otto Rank's *The Trauma of Birth*[28] constituted a significant departure from Freudian theory in its deemphasis of instinctual conflict as the source of neurotic anxiety. Rank saw intrauterine life as a psychic state akin to a blissful Garden of Eden. It is so satisfying that throughout his life man unconsciously strives to return to the womb. The birth process itself, hazardous though it may be, does not achieve a significance equal to that of the trauma of separation from the womb. Rank called the psychic pain of this separation "primal anxiety;" this was the origin of all anxiety. Such pain motivates man in a sense that is entirely different from Freud's drive for Thanatos. Rank defined neurosis as the unsuccessful attempt to resolve the birth trauma and anxiety as the signal of the reapperance of trauma. Ranks theory relied on Ovid's version of the Narcissus myth and the original version of the Oedipus myth. He formulated a cohesive set of interpretations for both myths that augmented the view of death anxiety as the fear of the loss of the self. Freud developed the Oedipus myth into the Oedipal complex as a means of understanding childhood psychological phenomena. The myth itself recorded a sophisticated composition that far exceded the simple murder of Oedipus' father and the incestuous marriage with his mother. The essence of the first part of the myth lay in the ability of Oedipus to solve the riddle of the Sphinx: "What animal walks on four legs, then two legs, then three legs?" The Sphinx swallowed all the men who unsuccessfully tried to solve the riddle. Oedipus did solve the riddle and, according to the Greek legend, thereby assumed his throne. Oedipus guessed correctly that the animal was "Man as a baby, an adult, and in old age with the aid of a staff." Rank traced the Sphinx to a mother symbol and suggested that the Oedipal drama was a sexual repetition of the primal anxiety. Through the act of sexual intercourse, Oedipus unconsciously sought to undo the primal trauma and reenter his mother's body. The wish to return into the mother was transformed into the fear of being swallowed by the Sphinx. In the original legend the god Juno sent the half-human, half-animal Sphinx as a punishment. A great many men were devoured before Oedipus rescued his countrymen by defeating the sphinx.

For Rank the Sphinx legend thus symbolized the fear of death and the contrasting wish for death via return to psychological union with the mother. It predated by a millennium the psychological research on death and reunion fantasies. The riddle of the Sphinx stood for the early childhood conflict between the wish to be devoured, incorporated into mother, and remain fused with her versus the fear of being devoured, killed, and engulfed by the mother's ego and identity. Rank understood the fear of death as having two functions: the alleviation of primal anxiety and the attempt to recapture the tensionless pleasant state of life in the womb.

Although it is quite unlikely that birth itself provides the origin of all anxiety in childhood, birth and separation themes do override children's imagery of death.[29] Rank did not connect the fear of death with depression but saw it rather as a struggle over primal anxiety. It is in a sense this struggle that entangles man in the conflict between the fear of life and the fear of death. In depression and suicide there is often an ambivalence about biological and psychological death. The depressed resourceless self that is rendered ineffectual by psychic conflict is given up or surrendered in suicide. In Rank's alternative explanation of the Narcissus myth he espoused a view of psychic life and the self that put him at variance with Freud's usage of the myth. The myth itself tells the story of the young beautiful Narcissus who fell in love with his own reflection in the water. In Freudian theory, Narcissus has come to stand not so much for self-centeredness or self-love in the parochial sense as for a type of object choice. Narcissism is love that is based on a representation of the self. This kind of involvement with "self" is appropriate in childhood, whereas it signifies an arrest in emotional development when it characterizes an adult's emotional life. In Rank's uncovering of Ovid's version of the myth, Narcissus' self-love resulted from the death of his identical twin sister.[30] Her death forced Narcissus to find a means of overcoming grief and finding consolation for his painful loss. At that point only did he turn to his own image reflected in the river, and he remained fascinated by this reflection. His self-love and self-absorption sprang from the wish for immortality, which was transformed into the love of his own image. To Rank the identical twin of Narcissus symbolized the feminine side of his own personality and, therefore, the bisexual substrate of all human personality. More importantly, the identical twin symbolized "The Double"—man's immortal self—or the soul. Primitive man feared the loss of the double in death. Protection from exposure to evil forces could obviate any threat to the loss of this immortal self. Modern man attempts to overcome the fear of death not so much by perpetuating the double or the hidden bisexual side of his personality as by defending against death anxiety. The twin theme expressed in *The Prince and the Pauper,* and even more dramatically in *Dr. Jekyll and Mr. Hyde,* carried the dual aspects of the self one step further. The double or self that could be lost and annihilated secures sanctuary by being split in half. The danger of death menaces with less ferocity when it is experienced as under ones own central. The threatened split self is divided into one that is socialized and pleasant and one that is bad or even monstrous and evil. In some suicidal adults death simultaneously achieves annihilation of the bad monstrous self and salvation of the good self through renewed union with the last good parent. In others suicide represents revenge and retaliation against the internalized bad parent for a perceived rejection of the depressed helpless self.

Rainer Rilke's sonnet to Narcissus captured this Rankian version of the myth by describing Narcissus' mirror image in feminine terms as "almost a maid" who could both possess the world in her sleep and sleep in his ear. Hers was a "perfect" sleep that continued after she awakened, and left the stricken Narcissus wondering about the possibility of her death. Here again, the perfect sleep of the twin represented the peacefulness and safety of union with the mother in death, the state of being taken in or reincorporated into the mother's body and psyche. I have previously stated that these themes are commonplace in suicidal children and adolescents. In the young child, the mirror image originally appears to be an independent entity existing in the world and gradually becomes integrated into the self as its external representation. Mirror play and play with imaginary companions, whether animal or human, serve the function of assisting in the process of differentiation of the self from the mother. In this process, the integration of representations of the self assists the child. It provides a means for overcoming loneliness or anxiety about individuation in a foreign world of social relations. The fear of death, the potential for depression, and the struggle for separation in the child all vary with the solidity and permanence of such self-representations.

The integrity and wholeness of the self strongly correlate with the image of one's body during early childhood. In most psychoanalytic theories, the body image and the self are said to have boundaries that distinguish and differentiate it from the outside world and other people. In the child, the intactness and health of the body is equated with the intactness of the self. A deep fear of dissolution of the self sometimes lies hidden beneath anxiety about physical injury or sickness. Similarly in schizophrenia, close intimate contact with another person may be avoided if it presents the threat of death anxiety. Relatedness may threaten the schizophrenic with the possibility of invasion of the boundaries of the self. The anxiety a schizophrenic experiences in the ego's defensive struggle to ward off a psychotic break with reality may partially express a fear of dissolution of the self in response to some interpersonal or intrapsychic stress. The normal developing infant discovers different body parts, their function and interrelationship, and later integrates the configuration into the body image and later the self. The schizophrenic who experiences strong feelings of depersonalization may talk of a body part becoming strange, unfamiliar, or apart from the rest of the body. Edith Jacobson and other clinicians have described quite vividly regressed schizophrenic states in which the person's self had decomposed to the point where they felt that they had died or lost their identity. Jacobson has also documented the resourcelessness and separation problems of the severe depressive.

In Freudian theory the self-image depends on memory traces. The possible loss or extinction of the self-image becomes associated in the infant with psychic representations of the excreted feces.[31] The one-and-a-half to two-year-old child undergoing toilet training at times experiences upset at the loss of his stool and enjoys playing with the stool, potty, and toilet. In the classical psychoanalytic model, obsessional neurotic states that involve strong fears of death were seen essentially as problems related to anality. The death fear was reportedly due to retention of the memory trace of a threat to the self-image representation. In contempory psychoanalytic theory there is an emphasis on characterological mechanisms for countering threats to the self. Thus, some fears of injury to body parts, sense organs, or the fear of blindness can stand for anxiety over a loss of the self, or a nuerotic fear of helplessness as well as castration anxiety. The rock opera *Tommy* elaborates this theme through the character of the "deaf, dumb and blind boy" who is cut off from the world (dead), helpless, and in need of rebirth.

Summary

The fear of the loss of self unquestionably finds expression in psychological manifestations of depression. The case of the panicky, anxiety-ridden person who develops an intense fear of being killed can be understood as a real struggle with separation-individuation conflicts as well as the depression inherent in the fear of the loss of the psychological self. The phobic who is terrified of being run over in the street, or of rapidly developing an incurable illness though in good health may display a core neurotic problem similar to those of the suicidal depressive. Two key factors have been stressed in depressions: first, the resourcelessness of the self in separation problems, and second, the connection between the depressive fear of the loss of the self and wish to give up the self.

A variety of the early psychoanalytic papers on depression were compared in terms of the position on death anxiety. Lewin's theory of the "oral triad" related the infantile feelings of elation, security and joy in nursing to the later unconscious fantasies of depressives that contrast with their hopelessness. The interrelationship between the components of the "oral triad"—the wish to sleep, the wish to eat and the wish to be eaten—was closely tied to the psychodynamic connections between the wish for death, joy, and reunion with the mother. Drug usage was related by Rado to a sense of the thrill of the "high," and to the equivalent of being fed by the nurturing, protective, good mother.

Another aspect of the fear of death theory that was reported in relation to depression involved a fear of one's own sexual and aggressive impulses. Finichel stated that the fear of death may evolve more fully in a person who is afraid of his or her own sexual excitement. This fear includes an intense panic about the loss of self-control, whereby dying becomes equated with panic or orgasm with death. In such a situation, the person will fear death when another person in the same situation might eagerly anticipate sexual pleasure. In this state of affairs proposed by Fenichel, a specific sequence of psychic events could be identified that underscored the neurotics feeling of helplessness and anxiety over loss of control. Death anxiety, could then be said to have the further twofold meaning of fear of orgasm and fear of loss of conscious ego controls.

The single most dangerous period in the hospital treatment of suicidally depressed people has been determined to be at the end of their hospital stay. In out-patient psychotherapy, the greatest danger is also at the point when they appear less depressed, more energetic and most hopeful about their recovery and future life. One possible explanation for this puzzling phenomenon can be derived from the individual's attitudes about death and problems in separation-individuation. Once the decision for suicide has been irrevocably made, the self-torture and intra-primitive rage of the depressed person ceases. There is an unconscious surrender of the self. The anticipation of reunion with a lost significant other brings the prospect of a pleasurable feeling. That pleasure consists of "peace of mind," the "giving up of hope," or feelings associated with passivity. There may be a giving up of the self in the fantasy of a return to an imagined, less troubled, less painful time of nurturance and unconditional love. The ultimate expression of these largely unconscious processes shifts the understanding of one type of suicide to the reexperiencing of the relative safety and security of a child's symbiotic reunion with the mother. Quite often surviving relatives and friends of successful suicides lament about why they committed suicide when they finally seemed "peaceful," "happy," or "had so much to live for."

The deemphasis on the view of death as a destruction or an annihilation, or as the end of life, and the emphasis on covert themes of joyful reunion are conventional aspects of various religious death and burial rituals. In a variety of Christian theologies, heaven is often refered to as a state of reunion with God and associated joy in union with the souls of the redeemed.

Current neo-Freudian analytic theory stresses the character flaws that grow from feelings about childhood deprivations in the depressive. The present view holds that death anxiety is an expression of depression in the adult. Both find concrete expression in anxiety about independence in the process of psychological growth. Childhood depression can also arise originally in part as a concomitant to the separation-individuation process. The depressed person remains vulnerable to feelings of hopelessness and quite anxious about the loss of the self. At times, this death fear can reach the degree of feeling "paralyzed"—"unable to move a muscle," or "having one's feet glued to the sidewalk." Seidenberg has called such death anxiety attacks "existential agoraphobia" because of the relevance of the problem of finding one's own identity and self-worth within the problem of existence.[32] In this existential sense, the depressives fear of death expresses a fear of psychological death more than biological death. The fear of death and the intense death anxiety attack can be found throughout all problems in neurotic living and growth. The knowledge of death and death anxiety are to some extent universal. In intense fears of death, the fear of the loss of the self is either projected and experienced as a fear of being killed or modified by a dissasociation of the self into good and bad fragments. The fear of the loss of the self expresses the neurotic's feeling of helplessness and lack of self-worth. In this existential framework, fears of death are easily understood as an expression of depression and separation anxiety. The fears are of not really experiencing life due to either the person's own emotional limitations or restrictions imposed by socioeconomic and cultural conditions.

CHAPTER FOUR

Adjustment Problems and the Fear of Death

Mental Development, Denial and Individuation

In Goethe's version of Faust, an atmosphere of gloom pervaded Faust's study in the darkest part of the night. As he realized that he had grown old, after spending an empty life pursuing knowledge that seemed trivial, Faust became obsessed with the need for love and renewed youth. Vulnerability and disappointment drove Faust into a bargain with Mephistopheles. The thought of death led him to depression, but not simply because of a fear of the prospect of nothingness; Faust suffered equally from painful regret that he had not lived a truly meaningful inner directed life. The loss of his soul to the devil seemed to be a reasonable exchange for a second youth, with its fantasy of a joyous encounter with a beautiful young girl. The gloominess of Dr. Faust's internal psychic state stemmed from his realization of the inevitability of death and the shallowness of his life. His despair reconciled the expression of death anxiety in depression with the neurotic's conviction of hopelessness about emotional salvation.

In D.H. Lawrence's poetry, knowledge about one's death took on a tangible essence. It came close to resembling an enormous sea of darkness from which the artist proceeded in making statements about life. In the "Hymn to Priapus" in particular, Lawrence dedicated himself to remembering that his own personal life was like a "stream in darkness" set toward death.[1] Although the waters might have ebbed and flowed in transverse patterns, the current was always "deathward" bound.

These dual themes of confrontation with despair and the hope for a renewal of life in the face of death anxiety have found a permanent place in literature and in social scientists' persual of contemporary customs and societal taboos. Both conflicting fears and wishes for death and the denial of fears about death have both often been dominant cultural motifs. The use of denial as a defense against death fears has been universally recorded. In general, it seems as though life proceeds from an unconscious conviction of personal immortality. Without that belief, perhaps man tends to withdraw from taking risks and thereby impoverishes the experience of finding meaning in living. The search for knowledge about the relation of death anxiety to depression and separation anxiety has not been a popular subject in the psychological literature. A historical survey of the significance of death anxiety will emphasize its expression in depression and separation anxiety.

In the earliest psychological treatises on the subject, Freud looked at death anxiety in the light of his instinctual and economic theories. Freud found that primitive man's attitudes toward death differed according to his relationship to the deceased.[2] The death of an enemy or a stranger caused no suffering. In fact, the need to kill enemies was well recognized and culturally rewarded. Freud noted the extent to which primitive history, as well as Greek and Roman mythology, was replete with numerous murders. The death of a kinsman, however, caused primitive man much anguish. He defended himself against this anxiety by a cognitive set that ignored the abstraction that death was final or irreversible. Grief and loss were not always the felt experiences of primitive man at the death of a loved one. In *Totem and Taboo* Freud highlighted this inconsistency of attitude about death in a statement that remains as accurate a description of current American mores as it was of prehistoric conditions. In Freud's view the death of the stranger is not felt personally and, therefore, it may go unnoticed or perhaps even seem unreal. The death or serious illness of a loved one, on the other hand, engenders the defensive use of denial, heightens ambivalence, and awakens the fear of death. Freud believed primitive man's attitude about death to be entirely reasonable and consistent with the importance of what he called "primal guilt." Patricide and Oedipal guilt became mainstays in the psychoanalytic approach to the thematic interpretation of culture and literature. Early psychoanalytic theory predated the current work on the origin of the self and the ego psychologists emphasis on psychic structure in the theory of the mind. The early analytic emphasis on psychodynamics also typified the scope of explorations on the fear of death.

For example, Freud interpreted Dostoevski's epileptic seizures as death anxiety related hysterical conversion attacks.[3] The attacks, he speculated, arose from an unconscious sense of guilt related to the murder of Dostoevski's father when the author was eighteen years old. Freud also thought that the duality of attitudes about death are the source for the creation of ghost and spirit legends as well as a major source of interest in theater. On the stage, the actors in a play dramatize the audience's conflicts about life and death. The death of a character in a play provides an opportunity for the audience to project its feelings onto the characters. The dramatization achieves a point of focus for the viewer's empathy, denial, or hidden anxiety about death. However, the distance between the stage and the audience may be sufficient to hold any intense personal reactions to death anxiety in check.

Much of the American way of death superimposes on the survivors a structure for dealing with both grief and death fears. We may suppose that the more elaborate the ritualistic aspects of the funeral, the greater the need to deal with death fears and unresolved feelings about the dead person. On January 31, 1977, *The New York Times* reported one of the latest "advances" in funeral homes that far surpasses the whimsical excesses of Forest Lawn Cemetery. A funeral home in Louisiana had built a window in the side of the building that allowed motorists to drive up in their cars and view the coffin; the mourners "pay their respects," sign the guest register, and drive off in several minutes. The reporter stated that the concept of the drive-in funeral parlor had not caught on widely in other areas. Yet one wonders if the future might bring videotaped funeral services that could be played on home television sets for mourners who are too busy to attend funerals.

The denial of death anxiety tends to correlate directly with the fear of death in many different cultures. The Hopi Indians are reported to have been extremely fearful about death and very uninterested in recalling the memory of the dead person.[4] Their funerals were small private affairs that allowed for a minimum of mourning and outward display of feelings about the dead person. Opposite elements have been observed by investigators of the funeral rites of the people of the Hebrides island of Barra . The Barra islanders embellish elaborate social customs to mark mourning rituals for relatives and friends of the deceased.[5] Grief and feelings about death are dxpressed more openly, with a minimum of denial and avoidance. Because death fears don't dominate the survivors, their mourning process is accelerated, and the adjustment to death seems relatively smooth. The openness and emotional availability of the group in this culture provides enormous psychological support for the surviving loved ones. Another, related reason for the variety of attitudes about death and related death fears is the primitiveness of modern man's unconscious feelings about death.

A sharp contrast is possible between unconsciously held thoughts and feelings and unconscious attitudes about one's own death and the death of others. Some remnants of primitive man's attitudes remain in the unconscious mind of modern man. The fear of the Hopi Indians and the detachment of the drive-in funeral-home mourners present elements of the same fear of death and the defensive denial of its reality. The individual's ambivalence about the death of others and the fear of his or her own death remain as the cornerstones of cultural attitudes about death.

Freud first suggested that the unconscious does not accept the idea of death and that the creation of ghosts, witches, and spirits has become the battleground for working out conflicting attitudes about death. Since young children lack the developed psychological resources of adults, they use imaginative play and games to master these phenomena. The holiday of Halloween galvanizes children's fears about death and spirits, as Freud observed. For one day's play, in a kind of reversal and reaction formation, children become the ghosts, witches, bandits, pirates and goblins they usually fear the rest of the year. In the current psychoanalytic model of development and adjustment, a gradual shaping of the ego's capacity for integration is said to take place. Separation anxiety is inherent in developmental tasks. There is a process of differentiation of feelings about death from feelings about separation from parents. Some researchers have suggested that there is actually a developmental stage at which death anxiety is mastered by the child. The present view holds death anxiety to be more general and pervasive. It has been described on two levels as being closely tied to depression and separation anxiety, and as an important influence on neurotic character trends. In clinical work with patients who report death anxiety, it can be particularly useful to think of it as the fear of the loss of the self.

The child's games, stories, and flights of fancy contain disguised statements about castration fears, separation anxiety and related issues. If children's fears about death are viewed not only as castration anxiety but as fundamentally oral fears associated with separation-individuation, then death fears assume a more reasonable developmental perspective. The demons or witches in children's nightmares represent their own transformed aggressive conflicts and fears about the loss of the self in its internalized attachment to the parents. The wish to devour and become reincorporated into mother and the fear of being killed when separated from her are behind most children's death fears and a good many of the myths and fairy tales that are their equivalent. The inherent relationship between death anxiety, depression, and separation anxiety clarifies mythological and biblical death themes. Symbolic statements of the struggle of the self for individuation were frequently interwoven with the more obvious dramatic and religious content.

Death Fears and Separation Anxiety

According to psychoanalytic anthropologist Geza Roheim, various mythologies are replete with tales of mortals and gods who lived in terror of some monster or demon, until the strongest of their lot destroyed the monster with a symbolic phallus.[6] The prototype of the demon has been interpreted analytically as the expression of oral aggression and oral-aggressive conflicts that are resolved by genital wishes. The witch or demon outside the child's bedroom window or the monster who, despite parental reassurance to the contrary, relishes hiding in closets and under beds embody the child's own oral-aggressive feelings. On a deeper psychological level, conflicting fears and wishes about separation from the protecting parents are at the root of the oral issues. Roheim saw oral-aggressive conflicts as the origin of the myth of the vampire—the ghoulish demon who kills by sucking out his victim's blood. The stake through the corpse that kills the vampire in the legend reportedly stands for the dawning of genital sexuality in the child. The vampire's thirst for blood symbolizes the magnitude of the child's oral-aggressive feelings and need for dependency. In Arthurian legends, the knights' ritual slaying of the fire-breathing dragons can be understood in similar terms.

The child's oral aggression and dependency needs conflict with his emerging independence and genital sexuality. In the healthy child, some kind of psychological movement is necessary for emotional growth beyond that point. In the neurotic child, death fears manifest in depression and separation anxiety retard such movements in the transition through the developmental stages. The young princess of the castle tower in medieval legends, who lives in fear of the dragon, represents the dependent needy part of the child's personality that fears autonomy and further craves parental protection. The ferocious dragon symbolizes both the child's own oral-aggressive feelings and the fear of the parents' oral aggression as punishment for either prolonged symbiosis or individuation. The valorous young knight who slays the dragon can be understood not just in Freudian terms as genital sexuality or as an Oedipal victory but also as the assertive, independent, autonomous part of the same child's ego. Such legends portray a struggle for mastery parallel to the child's struggle to overcome the fear of death in relation to oral conflicts and separation anxiety from the parents.

In the old English legend of Sir Gawain and the Green Knight, Gawain's adventures can be seen as the simultaneous portrayal of two themes: the overcoming of the Oedipal conflict and its relation to the fear of death manifest in separation and dependency problems. As a test of courage, the chivalrous Gawain must journey to a forest where he has to confront the Green Knight in spite of his fear that the Green Knight may behead him. On the way to the forest, Gawain is invited to spend the evening in the castle of a beautiful young woman who tries to seduce him three times. After his initial reserve is warmed by her charm, Gawain feels aroused but he resists her advances and, duty-bound, proceeds to meet the Green Knight. One imagines that in the legend the Green Knight personifies death even though, as it turns out, he is the husband of the young woman. Because of his fortitude in withstanding temptation, Gawain receives only a slight cut on the neck by the knight. All of the other young men before him had been slain, but Gawain achieves his victory. The legend might depict the young boy's fear of punishment from father via castration as punishment for sexual desires for his mother. Leaving the safety of the parent's side or separating from internal intrapsychic representations of the parents foreshadows death for the child. The symbiotically attached self faces the danger of extinction either through annihilation or abandonment by the significant other. Separation from parental love and protection can thus be unconsciously sensed by the child as mortal danger. In the Gawain legend, autonomous self-reliance brought the possible threat of death as punishment. By pursuing the chivalrous task which proved his valor, Gawain escaped over-involvement with the good-mother and achieved individuation. The fear

of death and the fear of abandonment lie at the bottom of the child's passivity and reluctance to venture out of parental reach. The wish to devour and the fear of being devoured correspond to Gawain's fear of
decapitation. The loss of the penis or decapitation, its equivalent, doesn't
serve as the only important thematic statement in the legend as much as
it symbolizes the fear of the loss of the self in the quest for separation
and independence. Here again the fear of death-depression-separation
anxiety complex apparently fits the evidence derived from myths, legends, and clinical research more fully than the simple notion of castration anxiety.

The Old Testament Book of Jonah benefits from loose interpretation
as one of the earliest treatments of the relationship between death fears
and separation-individuation. Excessive dependency in adult relationships closely allies depression and anxiety about separation. The text of
Jonah first recorded the symbolic dramatic treatment of the connection
between depression, the fear of death, and separation anxiety.

According to the King James Bible, a defiant Jonah fled from the Lord
on a ship bound for Tarshish. The ships' crew cast Jonah into the sea after he had revealed himself to be a Hebrew. When Jonah was swallowed
by a whale, the tempestuous sea calmed. The Lord heard Jonah's pleas
for salvation made during three days spent in the whale's belly, and he
told the whale to vomit Jonah onto dry land. The repentant Jonah later
converted the sinful people of Nineveh and saved them from God's ven-
geance. Even though the city was mercifully spared, Jonah became angry
and deeply despondent. In a state of utter despair, Jonah finally begged
God to take his life. When Jonah cried out: "It is better for me to die than
to live," God was unable to deliver him from "his grief." The despondent
Jonah continued to wish for death in spite of God's pleasure at the redemption of the city of thousands.

What was the source of Jonah's depression, if not the failure of his
rebellion against "The Father" and a capitulation that turned the fear
into the wish for death? Perhaps the act of defiance to the will of God
symbolized the young child's wish for independence and autonomy. The
child's inherent need to say "no" to their parents persists in the service
of their own psychological independence. The flight by ship, the casting
of Jonah into the sea, and the swallowing of Jonah by the whale all reiterated the theme of the child's fear of death via being devoured by angry
parent figures.

In the child, death anxiety develops in the context of the wish to be
incorporated or returned to the safety of the womb or the protecting
arms of the parents. Jonah's restful sleep aboard ship was short-lived.
His simultaneous fall into the sea and ingestion by the whale symbolized a punishemnt that resulted in a return to the safety of the young
child's symbiotic attachment. The days and nights in the whale's belly
clearly signified both pregnancy and the prolonged childhood period of
dependence on parents. Jonah's being vomited onto "dry land" couldn't
be a more direct translation of birth, the expulsion of the wet, helpless

newborn from the womb into the unfamiliar world. The image of the fragile ship, tossed by the high wind and tumultuous seas in the tempest, presents a compelling metaphor for the fear of death and a foreshadowing of the child's sense of danger in the psychic struggle to separate from the parents. Jonah's depression marked a failure in separation and a submission to parental authority that grew out of the terror of death. It has been argued repeatedly that death anxiety often finds a fertile medium for expression in depression. If the Book of Jonah is looked at as a myth, it provides further documentation of the psychodynamic link between the fear of death, depression, and separation anxiety. On a second level, Jonah's depression reflected the vacillation between the fear of being devoured by an angry frustrated parent and the wish to be devoured or transformed intrapsychically into the inner state of symbiosis with the parent. On a third level, it dramatized the child's fear of the loss of the self in the quest for autonomy.

The Greek myth of Prometheus adds even further documentation to the interconnections between death fears and the child's separation conflicts. According to legend,[7] the mortal Prometheus ridiculed the god Jupiter by offering him a dead stuffed bull as a sacrifice instead of a living one. Jupiter punished Prometheus by taking fire from the earth. Prometheus retaliated by climbing to the heavens to steal fire from the chariot of the sun and carrying it back to earth on the end of a ferula. Jupiter next sent a woman, named Pandora, to Prometheus with a box full of valuable objects. Prometheus spurned Pandora, and persuaded his brother, Epimetheus, to marry her. These actions so enraged Jupiter that he had Prometheus tied to a rock on the top of a mountain where he remained powerless to fend off a vulture that dined on his liver. The vulture continued to eat his liver, which was undiminished in size, for 30,000 years, until Hercules finally killed the bird. Prometheus was revered by his descendents not only because he brought fire to the earth but also because he brought the first man and woman to life by breathing fire into them. The Greeks celebrated his fetes by a race in the Olympiad between contestants who vied to carry the burning torch without extinguishing the flame.

Part of this legend addressed the same theme as did the Book of Jonah. Because of his rebelliousness and disobedience to the father god, Prometheus faced the punishment of the endless fear of being devoured. If one thinks of the theft of fire as a symbol not of castration but of the thriving of the autonomous ego or of independent life, then the crime of Prometheus acquires newfold meaning. By establishing his own life and identity on earth, he had challenged and diminished the power of the gods (parents) and had to be punished. Pandora's box has always been understood by investigators as a symbol of the vagina or the womb. The literary device of the identification of part of the body with the soul or the mind dates back to the Bible and Greek mythology. It seems to me that the legend depicted the child's conflict with the authority of father and simultaneous fear of and wish for return to the mother's womb. The vulture's daily assault and feeding on Prometheus' liver parallels the child's persistent struggle for independence in the face of the fear of death and the unconscious fear of being devoured. The liver represented the child's body and ego, which stood at the center of the conflicting needs, wishes, and fears. In children's fantasies, these psychic phenomena are externalized to the devouring vulture, monster, or demon who threatens the passive child with death. The tribute to Prometheus at the onset of the ancient Greek Olympiad celebrated this victorious struggle for life. Prometheus' fate symbolized the adult's death anxiety in psychological individuation and the child's death anxiety in coping with developmental tasks. In this sense, Promethean man escapes death via transcendence and the terror of separation by healthy autonomous risk-taking.

Separation Anxiety In Childhood and Adolescence

If myths and legends reflect the emotional struggles of childhood, then one would expect to find death fears and depression in youngsters with severe dependency problems. This is precisely the finding of child psychiatrists and child psychologists who treat children with school phobias and adjustment problems that exceed the normal developmental limits. For example, sleep disturbances in children before and after the Oedipal period frequently involve fears of death and injury. Analysis of children's anxiety dreams and nightmares reveal not only projections of children's own aggressive feelings but also their separation fears and dependency needs. Most of these fears can be classified on a surface level into two categories according to their latent content. First, "If I am attacked, kidnapped, injured, or threatened with death, will mommy and daddy take care of me and protect me?" "Will I be all alone or protected?" Second, "If mommy or daddy is hurt or killed, will I be alone?" "Can I survive without them? Who will take care of me?" Frightening fantasies and dreams about death synthesize the young child's feeling's of helplessness and ambivalence about separation. A five-year-old boy who exhibited a very poor adjustment to the first year of school reported having a dream of being chased by a ferocious lion that threatened to eat him. The hungry lion in the dream combined the child's own oral-aggressive wishes to bite, eat, and devour with the fear of being devoured by punishing parents. The boy's fear of the social demands of the school day reawakened a wish to merge, to be devoured by the good, nurturing, protective mother. The relationship between sleep disturbances, anxiety dreams, and the child's disguised feelings about separation from the mother extends back to infancy. Sleeping problems in children not accounted for on the basis of neurological anomalies or somatic distress may be a reflection of a great many developmental problems that center on familial discord and parental conflicts.

The research on early infancy clearly establishes the mother's relationship to the child to be essential to the development of normal rhythmic sleep patterns. A sufficient amount of positive interaction between mother and infant facilitates the development of an appropriate sleep rhythm.[8] Disturbances in the pattern of a child's sleep activity varies as to its psychological meaning depending on the child's age, physical state and his particular developmental level. Sleeping difficulties can often accompany the child's experience of intense anxiety. Occasionally, as symptom choice occurs, the child's sleeplessness becomes organized into persistent sleeping disorders during the latency period. The significance of teething, walking, weaning, oral conflicts, anxiety about toilet training and fecal play, and concern about genital stimulation is understood in neo-Freudian analytic theory in terms of the child's relationships and internal object relations. To the extent that these occurrences are interpersonal, they contribute to an experience of the self in what Sullivan called "reflected appraisals." The presence of anxiety about school and fear of going to school also often relate to the influence of death fears and the interplay of separation conflicts.

A psychological inquiry into the meaning of anxiety about going to school or an actual school phobia very often discloses fears that either the child will be hurt or killed or that his parents will be hurt or killed. The fear of death or the fear of the death of the parent expressed in separation anxiety occupies the child as a continuous source of worry, which becomes translated into anxiety about school. Traditionally, psychoanalysts looked at the fear of school in children as the result of masturbation conflicts, castration anxiety, and difficulty with aggressive feelings toward parents.[9] School failures were originally attributed primarily to sexual guilt and concern about the loss of love. Whether Oedipal problems play a primary role in school phobias or not, the child's unrecognized death fears almost always do. In severe phobias the young child's fear of death arises not just out of a need for punishment or guilt but because he or she depends on and identifies with the parent. To this extent, the child may view himself or herself as a psychological extension of the parent. Anxiety about separation-individuation underlies the fear of school to the extent that the child is overwhelmed with helplessness in dealing with school and the separation. With older children and adolescents who suffer excessive separation anxiety, greater opportunity occurs for displacement of these intrapsychic struggles onto school-related problems. Pressures for academic performance, fear of punishment, or fear of social and school failure serve to augment and localize the more pervasive underlying anxieties. Once school attendance becomes the focus of the child's separation anxiety, overt test anxiety, somatic complaints, or behavior problems express and attempt to lower anxiety about individuation. The school-phobic child becomes unable to withstand the pressures of the school day, as the unconscious conflicts escalate and insure the need for further dependence on parental support. The conscious school fears intensify the unconscious conflict between the child's wish for a symbioticlike dependence versus his wish to achieve independent mastery of his difficulties. If the situation escalates to the point where separation from mother to attend school signifies abandonment or death to the child, then independent activity can bring guilt, or be experienced as a threat to the life of the self. When leaving mother's side can bring such intense anxiety, her vigilant presence feels necessary for lowering anxiety and securing the survival of the self.

Children ordinarily overcome separation anxiety gradually in the toddler years so that separation causes less anxiety as they mature. Ambivalence about autonomous functioning and dependency needs continually to be reconciled with the developing child's ego functions and increased tolerance for ambivalence. The variety of avenues for expression of children's separation problems are not easily exhausted by their temperamental differences. In children with a predisposition for psychophysiological disorders, separation anxiety can be expressed in psychosomatic communication. For example, gastric ulcers in children have been shown to derive from dependency conflicts (death anxiety) and separation problems. One thorough study of ulcer-prone children documented the constant battle they wage to achieve some measure of independent function in spite of an impaired capacity for independence.[10] Maternal overprotection of these patients contributed to their rage, which when repressed contributed to failures in independent behavior. As the child's attempts to become successful while independent fail, a great deal of hostility is generated against the mother that runs counter to the child's continuing need for safety and protection. The gastric ulcer has therefore been portrayed as the result of the interplay of the child's hostility, dependency, and separation anxiety.

For the adolescent struggling with identity formation, depression and death anxiety can be renewed as his developmental problems give rise to separation anxiety. Developmentally oriented psychoanalysts, such as Peter Blos, have recorded the adolescent's emotional push for separation from the internalized parents in the complicated end of the magical childhood symbiosis. The adolescent's rebelliousness and need for experimentation mark a struggle for more complete individuation. Physical and sexual changes demand new modes of psychological adjustment. The adolescent's sensitivity, feelings of loneliness, and thoughts about death are often the accompaniments of this individuation from the parents.[11] Depression and anxiety result from the necessity of giving up the protecting powerful parents of childhood in the face of the flimsiness of the adolescent's sense of self and emerging identity. The end of childhood, with its necessity for more fully establishing a sense of self, insures an adolescent emotional turmoil in which separations may become quite painful and concerns about death predominate. The adolescent's brooding, introspectiveness, sensitivity, and normal lability of affect testify to the complexity of the adolescent process of integration of "self" experiences. Leaving home to attend college typically brings to the forefront separation conflicts that the middle-class adolescent harbors. A fascination with death and the unconscious fear of death express both the adolescent depression and separation fears.

For adults who have been unable to separate psychologically from their families, concerns about death and dying can also emerge as foci for the expression of the fear of the loss of the self. Especially in people who lack firmly established ego boundaries, separation anxiety in adult functioning can augment the perceived threat to their psychological survival. Death anxiety becomes the price paid for individuation. In truly symbiotic attachments between parents and their adult offspring, a mutual interdependency is overdetermined by the integral part each plays in maintaining the other's mental equilibrium. Independence for either partner threatens the self with the loss of a part of the shared inner psychic structure. The successful mastery of career choice or any of the tasks of adulthood can then imply the threat of abandonment or disintegration through to loss of the self. Separation only feels subjectively like the threat of annihilation in such relationships. Consider, for example, a mother's comments upon interview by the admitting nurse when her 20 yr old daughter was being screened for admission to a psychiatric hospital. Throughout the meeting, the mother gave her daughter necklaces, and bracelets she was wearing, which the girl hesitated to put on or accept. Noting the girl's reluctance, the mother said repeatedly, "If you stay in the hospital I'll never see you again. I'll never visit you." Even though she had herself asked for the admission the physical and psychological separation triggered an intense anxiety akin to the fear of death.

Giving her daughter her own jewelry exemplified the woman's separation anxiety and confusion about a lack of psychic differentiation between herself and her daughter. Perhaps the jewelry was not a genuine gift as much as an expression of the woman's own fear of being abandoned by her daughter and her need to reaffirm their symbiotic union. The mother's statement expressed annoyance at the prospect of their separation. It also revealed a less overt fear of the psychological death of either mother or daughter that might be the result of separation. The mother's subsequent rage at the nurse and hospital for imposing the separation she feared was in part displaced from her daughter. These reactions coincided with the mother's depression, and they would be likely to induce feelings of guilt, helplessness, and anxiety in the daughter who was also ambivalent about her survival without her mother. The separation for a period of hospitalization seemed to have the meaning of death or abandonment for both. The rage reaffirmed the attachment that negated their mutual fear of death without the other. In this case, the hidden message contained in the mother's interaction with her daughter could be oversimplified to read: "I'm furious at you for thinking of leaving me. You'll be sorry; I'll die without you" or, "You won't be able to live without me."

Neurotic Helplessness and Death Anxiety

The psychological and psychiatric literature on specific death fears is remarkably sparse. The specific content of death fears varies with the individual's characterological problems and the conscious or unconscious dimensions of the fear of the loss of the self. Although fears of injury through assaults and violent crimes grow with the increase of violence in our cities, one's persistent worry about being killed does not necessarily correspond to external dangers. When specific fears of death are differentiated from abstract fears about being dead, unique constellations of personality factors cluster around the fears. Even though specific fears of death arise from unique life experiences, psychodynamic sources of anxiety-laden fantasies about death often contain portraits of the person as a passive victim. Fears of a potentially fatal attack, illness, or accident augment a more basic childhood fear of helplessness and passivity in the face of stress. As specific fears of death become interwoven with neurotic conflicts and character defenses, these feelings of helplessness and passivity manifest themselves in the adult's anxiety dreams about falling or flying and in children's anxiety dream's about being chased by monsters or criminals.

Edgar Allan Poe's short stories presented this terror and helplessness of the neurotic fear of the loss of the self. Poe admitted that his plots attempted to capture terror "of the soul" in the guise of horror tales. The sorry state of Roderick Usher in "the Fall of the House of Usher" depicted death anxiety in graphic imagery. Poe's victims often succumbed in a helpless surrender to death insured by his dramatic contrivances. In anxiety dreams about falling and crashing, the dreamer may be portrayed in a parallel way—as the helpless victim who struggles unsuccessfully without assistance against the forces of gravity. The atmosphere surrounds and controls the dreamer's body as it is hurled through space. In dreams of falling, the wind and the air envelop the body of the dreamer just as the earth threatens to immobilize the body in fantasies of the fear of burial. The fear of drowning and the fear of death by fire have similar thematic components. One imagines the possibility of a fight for air and a flight from the flames or the deadly pull of the water. In the midst of a nightmare about dying, the dreamer-victim may be surrounded by water or perhaps trapped by flames. In many of these kinds of fears, the sea or the flames envelop the body while the defeated victim succumbs to death. The expressions "swallowed by the sea" or "consumed by the flames" also convey a similar intent. In the surface content of these fears, the body is imagined to be enclosed and rendered helpless by earth, air, wind, or fire. These fears partly derive from the infantile fear of helplessness and the terror of vulnerability in separation from the parents.

Freedom from harm and discomfort is intimately tied to the infant's security. The infant's and toddler's dependency on parental protection is central in the continuity of what Erikson has called "basic trust." This dependency, at the earliest ages due to physical immaturity and the lack of judgment, ego maturity, reasoning ability, or other cognitive skills, does truly render the infant helpless. The adult's fears of drowning, burning, falling, and being buried alive or suffocating have their common origin in the representation of the independent self as a helpless object of attack. The elements threaten the self or the body with being controlled and destroyed. This threat can again symbolically represent the fear of the loss of the self disguised as the terror of abandonment or engulfment by the parent. In such anxiety dreams or neurotic fantasies, death results from the disintegration of the body on one level and the loss of the self on a deeper, intrapsychic level. The healthy resourceful adult who becomes subject to intense fears of drowning or falling or being killed experiences the revival of early childhood fears of separation and depressed feelings of helplessness. However, these dual aspects of death anxiety should no longer present a great threat to the adult ego. In spite of the anxiety, the adult, in fact, is not helpless or lacking in resources or the aid of significant others. In intense death fears, nevertheless, the adult experiences feelings of dependency and helplessness that seem to be current statements about the "self" in the present. Compulsive fears about infections or hypochondriacal preoccupation in healthy people can often be traced to similar origins. Take, for example, the diction of the person with a fever who speaks of "being burned up," or the infection or sickness that is referred to as "eating someone up." Depression accompanying ordinary colds and bouts with mild flus or minor illness may similarily generate from the unconscious notion that the illness is an external, foreign object that has entered the body and is rendering the ego weak or helpless.

The dreamer who awakens to shudder at the thought of his own death experiences a depressed reawakening of these early childhood fears of genuine helplessness. The very young child's inability to cope with dangers and external as well as psychological conflict places him in a position similar to that of the passive Prometheus as he awaited the attack of the vulture. Prometheus had no choice but to petition Jupiter and depend on the gods to free him from danger. The baby in the nursery, too, needs only to cry in order to be picked up, fed, or removed from discomfort. Parents are the gods who dismiss danger and provide security from threats to physical safety and emotional survival. The parents' powers might seem to the child on a par with those of the Greek gods who could instantly destroy, reward, and punish without warning. The child's dependence stands in sharp contrast to the perceived magical power of the parents.

In summary, the functioning adult who becomes overly fearful about death when not in any physical danger experiences a reawakening of the conflicts involving passivity, depression, and separation anxiety. Death anxiety becomes the neurotic consequence of some new form of living more fully. In neurosis, the fear of death is manifested in the fear of creative living, relatedness, and adult productivity, as Erich Fromm observed

in *Man for Himself*. Depression and the revitalization of separation conflicts are magnified as the neurotic obsesses on thoughts about death.
When, for example, ordinary concerns about one's safety when swimming or flying under "safe" circumstances grow to the point of prolonged intense anxiety, the painfulness of the feelings derive from childhood death fears and anxieties about helplessness. Much of the
experimental data on death anxiety corroborates the existence of a causal
relationship between the degree of death anxiety and a person's general
sense of competence. People with a high degree of anxiety about death
don't necessarily show a generally high anxiety level, but they have a low
opinion of their own competence and resourcefulness.[12] Given a low
sense of competence and feelings of helplessness, specific and intense
fears of death augment the person's helpless and panicky feelings. A pattern of associative linkage of death fears can evolve in which exaggerated
fears of swimming or flying may escalate to become larger death threats.
In this respect, death fears are quite similar to other kinds of neurotic
fears. The neurotic fears the helplessness of the experiencing self.

Passivity and Specific Death Fears

Fears about death express the secondary fear of helplessness as they
become evident in specific neurotic conflicts. In the early psychoanalytic
inquiries before the contributions on the psychology of the self, attitudes
toward death were related to a variety of specific neurotic symptoms.
Bromberg and Schilder undertook several comparative studies of death
attitudes in accordance with their belief that the fear of death was
equivalent to the anticipated loss of enjoyment and the fear of castration.[13] Common themes in their interviews included death as a punishment and death as a deprivation that was feared for its own sake. Anticipation of the loss of pleasure and equating death with punishment were
consistently in the evidence. These investigations of the 1930s fore-
shadowed later work on the relationship between the fear of death and
aggression. Throughout the psychological research literature on death
anxiety and neurosis, castration anxiety was studied as the essential phenomenon. The rationale for this singularity of focus relied on the variety
of possible forms of unconscious expression of castration anxiety. Men
have differing degrees of castration anxiety, in the Freudian view, depending on childhood experiences. Overt or disguised threats of castration in childhood predispose one toward the unconscious fear of castration in adulthood. In such individuals, unconscious castration fears can
be shown in a variety of conscious fears including fear of bodily injury,
disease, or ultimately death. This line of thought becomes unreasonable
only when extended to encompass all death fears in their characterological complexity. Individuals who have high levels of castration anxiety have shown increases in death fears after being exposed to sexually
arousing stimuli. In typical experimental studies of this sort, male college

students' psychological reactions would be measured when they were shown photographs of naked women; their fear of death and castration anxiety were then assessed by objective personality tests.[14] As interesting as such studies might be, they do not fully explain the origin of the fear of death or its diverse meanings in neurotic conflicts. I submit that the neurotic's death anxiety expresses the depression and separation anxiety of the fear of the loss of the self. The neurotic fears the passivity of the threatened self; while the psychotic experiences the disintegrating self.

The early psychoanalytic approach also traced the source of anxiety in neurotic death fears to anxiety in childhood about witnessing sexual scenes between adults. This "primal scene" is supposed to create the impression in the child that sexuality is aggressive and dangerous.[15] In theory, this association predisposes the child to a fear of sexual excitement so that anxiety about death and sleep emerge at physical maturity. The child is excluded from what Freud called the "primal scene" except as an observer and is flooded with tension that cannot be discharged. Here again, the child's helplessness and fear of separation stand out as fundamental in the adjustment conflicts. Freud attributed death fears to separation anxiety but saw castration anxiety as a much more important agent. If one believes that childhood Oedipal conflicts and castration anxiety are always the sole bases for neurotic symptoms, then it follows that castration anxiety is assumed to be the basis for death fears. However, the fear of death is a universal and much more complicated statement about intrapsychic conflict.[16] Understanding fears of death as an extension of depression, separation conflicts, and the fear of helplessness seems more consistent with the current knowledge of developmental psychology.

By defining death fears as manifestations of a neurotic fear of the loss of the self, characterological problems can be viewed as central aspects of anxiety. Depression, passivity. withdrawal and counter phobic aggression can all be discerned in death fears and understood as consistent with the "human" model of neurotic conflict. Neurotics really fear dying and living fully because healthy growth threatens their characterological defenses to the point of an exaggerated anticipated annihilation of the self. The fear of death constitutes one of many sources of neurotic anxiety that arise in the context of early interpersonal relationships. As death anxiety increases in intensity for the neurotic, concomitant feelings of depession and helplessness may also increase. The person in the midst of a death anxiety attack typically becomes afraid of his own anxiety and helplessness. He fears his own projected feelings of hostility and destructiveness as much as the loss of the self in response to resourceless passivity.

Franz Kafka's short story "The Vulture" quite succinctly exemplifies this post-Freudian view of death anxiety as depression and helplessness.[17] A vulture is hacking at the unidentified narrator's feet as he feebly attempts to fend it off. A passerby inquires why this torture is allowed to continue, and the narrator replies, "I'm helpless," adding that the vulture is so strong that he has decided to sacrifice his feet to spare his face. The passerby leaves to get a gun to use on the vulture. As he leaves, the vulture attacks the narrator quite viciously and kills him. This tale encapsulates an unambiguous metaphor of neurotic helplessness in relation to death anxiety. The narrator's helplessness exemplifies the genuinely neurotic component of the conflict. Rather than the narrator experiencing himself in a real struggle in which the vulture could be engaged in fierce combat, his passivity precipitated his death. The vulture also stands for the narrator's own destructive feelings and wish to devour the passerby's strength. As the narrator's defenses were stripped away, he grew more anxious and unable to defend himself against his own destructiveness and childhood fears. He relied on the passerby rather than use his own resourcefulness in fighting the vulture, just as children rely on their parents to combat death anxiety. The vulture's final attack represented the culmination of the child's fears of being devoured *and* the partial wish to be devoured and reunited with the mothering person. The narrator's sacrifice of his feet to save his face recalls one essential aspect of neurotic death fears: Remaining passive and preoccupied with death in the face of life's stresses leaves one depressed and powerless. Active enjoyment and autonomous responses can bring the anxiety that accompanies relinquishment of a passive position.

The active engagement of life challenges neurotic defensive operations when the fear of death is intense. One paradox of the death anxiety complex lies in the passive acceptance of the finality of death. The physically healthy person who persists in fantasizing about death or possible sickness can be conceptualizing the moment of death as a passive giving in. Otto Fenichel pointed out that the moment of death, like the onset of sleep, implies a loss of conscious control over one's thoughts and body. That loss of control can confirm a sense of passivity. The emotionally healthy person combats the fear of death in a working through of a fear of passivity and helplessness. If one imagines being conscious and aware at the moment of death, then the anticipated loss of self-control recapitulates the feelings of helplessness and fear of loss of control over bodily functions common to childhood.

The identification of body parts with the "self" compounds the search for a one-dimensional account of the neurotic's fear of death. If the fear of death really represents a fear of loss of the self, and the ego and self are characterized by the body image, then the location of death fears becomes a viable question. Physical abilities and body parts are invested with different emotional valences by different people. Just as the terminally ill person may query, "Where is the me that is dying?" the neurotic may question, "Where is the me that I am afraid is going to die?" The greatest anxiety about loss of function or injury concerns the threat to bodily parts that are unconsciously deemed most important. The athlete who lives in fear of traumatic injury to the legs, the painter who fears blindness, and the neurotic who fears cancer or coronaries

may be making a multileveled unconscious statement about the definition of self. The more that the child in the adult feels the early terror of
helplessness and separation anxiety in the present, the more powerful
the impact of the anxiety about death.

Kafka again reiterated this theme of passivity and the fear of the loss
of the self in his story "The Dream of Josef K":[18] During a pleasant walk
on a beautiful day, K is compelled by some force to go to a fresh mound
of earth in a cemetery. With no apparent warning, K is magnetized to
that spot and falls to his knees by a graveside. Here he sees two men
raise a blank tombstone up above the ground and then quite suddenly
cement it to the earth. An artist mysteriously appears and paints the
words "Here Lies" on the tombstone. K starts to sob and feels himself
driven by some mad compulsion to dive into the mound of earth. It gives
way quite easily and K feels himself being pulled into the earth. As a big
hole opens up, K sinks further into the earth. As K is received into the
depths, his neck strains upward to see his own name appear on the
tombstone before him. "Enchanted" by the sight, he then wakes up in
improved spirits.

K's feelings of terror and helplessness in his dream could easily symbolize repetitions of children's feelings about death. As in Kafka's story
of "The Vulture," K passively succumbs to death in the dream. K experienced himself as powerless, and he was taken into the earth without offering any resistance to physical (or psychological) forces. In fact, he
woke up feeling "enchanted" at the certainty of death, perhaps because
it realized an end to his suffering and neurotic struggling. The "self" K
feared losing in the dream was surely a representation of himself as a depressed, passive, impotent victim who would delight in the giving up of
the self. His fascination with cemeteries and his experiencing an uncanny
sense of fear masked the child's terror and helplessness in experiencing
the possibility of personal death. The fear of death seemed to fascinate K
just as much as passivity permeated his dream. In giving in to death anxiety and surrendering his body to the earth, K "successfully" resolved
the perpetual burden of his neurotic conflicts. Rather than experience
life, he found security in the passivity of death anxiety and comfort in
the helplessness that, paradoxically, he feared. This paradox has very realistic origins in early childhood, but it should be improved upon without that degree of difficulty in the resourceful adult. K's fear of being annihilated in the earth alternated with the wish to be buried alive. One
supposes here the wish to be magically catapulted into the childhood
state of symbiosis and reunion with omnipotent parental figures. To the
extent that "The Dream of Josef K" projected autobiographical statements about Franz Kafka, K's affective experience in the dream fits the
emotional fabric of Kafka's death anxiety, morbid sense of doom, and
depressed view of helplessness in the world.

The force that drove K to the cemetery and compelled him to grovel
at the grave site surely came from within. The tears K wept seemed
likely to have come from the depression connected with his own fear of

death and sense of powerlessness. What glued K to the spot in passive resignaion and exhorted him to wait for the artist to paint his premature epitaph? Why did he not flee rather than succumb to death anxiety? Was it not the conflict between "aloneness" and the fear of death versus a suicidal wish for death from which K could not free himself? At age two or three, the child's fears of separation from the parents can quickly escalate into the fear of death, if the child's own ego is inadequate to meet internal and environmental dangers. If parents are necessary for one's very survival, separation from their protection readily equates with death. The retention of these feelings from childhood stifled K's independence and capacity to combat death anxiety as an adult. Unlike the child, K was, in fact, free to struggle at that instant in his dream and, if need be, to suffer with the psychological conflicts that surround activity in the daily problems of living. The fact that he cooperated fully with death, and with a feeling of enchanment, presents to the reader the fundamental elements of K's neurotic death anxiety. K, like many people who are completely enmeshed in neurotic conflicts, feared death at the same time that he was afraid to live life.

Sex, Love, and Ambivalence

The adult experience of intimacy and sexual contact can evoke fears of death for three reasons. In the first place, unconscious connections exist between adult sexuality and early childhood feelings about parents. The interplay of the couples neurotic problems may insure that each partner can provoke the other's psychological survival issues. Second, intimate relationships stimulate intense feelings of ambivalence that can be connected to thoughts about death. Third, intimate relationships inevitably present for the couple problems about self-definition versus dependence upon the partner. These challenges to adult's maturity and flexibility are met with either buoyancy and growth, or regression and defensiveness. The adults' experience in the present thereby reawakens the childhood fear of death via depression-separation anxiety without the person's clear awareness of anything except anxiety. Sex, love, and death have often been linked together thematically in a variety of human experiences that encapsulate the fear of death.

Shakespeare's Hamlet demonstrated all three dimensions of death anxiety in the plot relationship between sex, intimacy, and death. Hamlet's prolonged obsessional doubting illustrates the fear of death as a punishment for freedom as well as for Oedipal's wishes. In his psychoanalytic interpretation of Hamlet, Theodor Reik[19] stressed Gertrude's fear of being killed by her son. For both Freud and Ernest Jones, Hamlet could be accurately interpreted only as the ultimate Oedipal drama. Hamlet's indecision, brooding, and doubting were understood as an outgrowth of unconscious guilt over hostility toward his father and sexual longings for his mother, the queen. The death of Ophelia added greatly to Hamlet's torment, but his feeling of helplessness and inability to act added to his depression.

Ophelia's death redoubled the intensity of Hamlet's unconscious strivings for his mother. One supposes that the king's death could have been experienced by Hamlet at some psychic level as a triumph over his father, but can it be simply guilt that explains Hamlet's obsession with death?

In the churchyard scene, Hamlet's annoyance at the clown who dug Ophelia's grave may have protested his own uneasiness about death brought to the surface by the clown's song of love and death. Hamlet could only speculate about death in a very intellectual way. The gravedigger seemed to taunt Hamlet with an experiental knowledge of death:

In youth, when I did love, did love,
Methought it was very sweet
To contract—on—the time, for—ah—my behove,
O methought there—ah—was nothing —ah—meet.
But age, with his stealing steps,
Hath claw'd me in his clutch,
And hath shipp'd me until the land,
As if I had never been such.

When the clown threw Yorick's skull, Hamlet was confronted with his own death anxiety and ambivalent feelings about death. The clown may also have brought closer to awareness the connections between Hamlet's anxieties about love, and autonomy. Hamlet's disdain for women derived in part from his attachment to his mother and his unconscious rage at her for the remarriage to his uncle. To Hamlet, Gertrude's marriage was "an act that blurs the grace and blush of modesty," and his sense of his mother's commitment to him was: "'tis brief...as woman's love." This antagonism toward her smacked of feelings of rejection and betrayal. In Reik's paper on the importance of the mechanism of reaction formation, Hamlet's relentless criticism of Gertrude covered the reversal of his love and desire for her. The prince of Denmark's depressive brooding and philosophical introspectiveness overlay deeply passive, suicidal wishes:

To die: to sleep.
No more; and by a sleep to say we end
The heart-ache and the thousand natural shocks
That flesh is heir to: 'tis a consummation
Devoutly to be wish'd.

At the Oedipal level of his conflict, Hamlet seemed tormented by jealousy and guilt over his father's death as well as by his unsuccessful attempt at replacing him in his mother's affections. Unable to avenge his father's death or bring his unacknowledged courting to fruition, Hamlet's depressions, inhibition, indecisiveness, and feelings of outrage crippled him. Hamlet's depression and suicidal thoughts ran parallel to his procrastination and ambivalence about whether or not to kill his uncle, the new king. In one critical view of the play, Hamlet's depression reflected Shakespeare's wish to present the essential view of melancholia prevalent in the sixteenth century.[20] Hamlet's fear of death and depressive thoughts began with the first soliloquy and remained in full force until the denouement of the tragedy was reached with Hamlet's death.

The prince of Denmark, clearly a grown man of at least twenty-five or more in Shakespeare's play, remained preoccupied with his mother in a way that resembled common neurotic Oedipal attachments. His failure with Ophelia and his flight to England may have stemmed from his inability to separate from his attachment to his mother and achieve autonomous independence as an adult. If one of Gertrude's lines is closely examined in juxtaposition with those of Hamlet, her attitudes seem to be a reflection of Hamlet's unconscious feelings. Gertrude was also afraid of death and Hamlet's violent feelings, as much as she felt hurt by his critical attacks. Hamlet's suicidal longings that "this too too solid flesh would melt" counterbalanced his own feelings of betrayal and fear of taking action of any kind. Hamlet's painful ramblings typify obsessional rumination in which the primary problem is the inability to divorce himself from childhood feelings about parents. Hamlet never resolved either the Oedipal conflict or his need for and dependency on his mother. His fear of death involved the fear of dissociating himself from his mother and the ghost's command that he avenge his father. The death anxiety he felt found expression in depression and separation anxiety that enriched the characterization of his guilt. Hamlet's doubt ridden introspections and his unrelatedness exemplified a combination of Oedipal conflicts with the fear of death and depression . Hamlet's prolonged attachment to his mother and his consequent wish for a "sleep of death" clearly illustrate the process by which entrapment in death anxiety interferes with adult maintenance of intimacy in interpersonal relationships.

Furthermore, the continuance of Hamlet's unconscious, incestuous ties to his mother can be understood in relation to the threat of death as a punishment for partial separation. Gertrude's fear of death expressed a conscious fear of Hamlet's rage with the less conscious fear of his sexual advances. The interplay of their possible unconscious sexual feelings for each other contributed directly to Hamlet's depression and fear of death. Aside from this Oedipal element, Hamlet's personality portrayed in dramatic terms the connection between neurotic separation anxiety, love, and death.

Hamlet's feelings of rejection and hatred disguised a neurotic attachment manifest in the constant criticism of his mother and the fear that he would kill her. He felt both the need for revenge and the need to resolve feelings of guilt over having wished for his father's death. Caught up in these conflicting feelings of guilt and attachment to his mother, Hamlet steeled himself from a deep commitment to Ophelia or any woman. For Hamlet, any decisive action was risky since it insured an intense threat to the self. In ordinary neurotic emotional communication, the wife or husband projects onto the other childhood feelings about the parents that were closely tied to threats to the self. Although this degree of Oedipal entanglement is not universal in love relationships, some degree of ambivalent feelings are universal among couples who are in love.

Freud placed the tolerance for ambivalence at the highest order of conditions necessary for the continuance of an adult love relationship. Even though love dominates hate, some negative feelings about the beloved person are inevitable, even if unrecognized. Husbands, wives, parents, and children all vary in their ability to tolerate their own hateful feelings and those of their loved ones. Paradoxically, the closer and more loving the relationship, the greater the potential for hateful feelings. Freud also stressed the conversion of narcissistic instinctual libido into object libido as essential in love. The neo-Freudians on the other hand emphasized the primacy of unconscious neurotic needs and distortions in the inability to develop or mature in love relationships.

The recognition of ambivalence presents a serious threat to psychological security and a positive self-image. The lack of tolerance for ambivalence also places a consistent strain on both of the people in the relationship, if hostility remains disguised, covertly expressed, or denied. In normal psychological development, children adopt characteristic modes for dealing with their hostility toward mother and father as well as for dealing with their own hostility. Ordinarily, good parents put up with some measure of angry outbursts and temper tantrums during early childhood and at times have the patience to accept adolescent rebelliousness, mood swings, and negativism during the teenage years. Through some partly verbal and partly nonverbal process, young children learn to discriminate and tolerate the specific meanings and intensity of mother's and father's angry reactions to them. Sullivan noted that with overly defensive, rigid, or punitive parenting, the child may dissociate parental anger from full awareness. The less able the parents are to tolerate ambivalence and anger in their children, the more difficulty the child might have in coping with his or her anger. As the child's anger is in turn defended against by means of denial, repression, displacement, or any possible variety of security mechanisms, the whole system of family interaction may carry with it a sense of terrible danger that is communicated to the child. In the context of this kind of a neurotic family structure, perhaps young children may really be unable to discriminate their parents' hostility from the fear of death. If this family pattern of hidden hostility gets perpetuated, it often is unconsciously recreated by the adult in contemporary love and family relationships. Typically, children do learn at an early age, as they become increasingly effective in their communication skills, to distinguish parental anger or annoyance from hatred, displeasure, or some other affective message of disapproval. The frequent declarations children exchange that "I'm going to kill you" are not usually problematic. If a particular child has a deficiency in discriminating between varieties and degrees of expressions of anger or has grown up in the kind of family noted above, then expressions of rage can be quite frightening. Declarations of anger can reinforce unconscious connections in the child's mind between anger, the fear of death, and ambivalence about separation-individuation.

When these unconscious attitudes extend into maturity, couples can fall prey to great difficulty in dealing with both their partner's anger and sexuality. The interconnections between sex and death anxiety in Hamlet's personality serve as a model for the fullest kind of difficulty people can experience in intimate relationships. When sexual intercourse has the unconscious emotional meaning of death and anger at one's lover, it signifies the threat of death.[21] The stability of the relationship becomes threatened by the drive to avoid death anxiety and to minimize the other's power in eliciting threats to the self. Both the man and the woman deprive themselves of the enjoyment of sexual life and close emotional contact by the transferential projection onto the partner of the parents' power to stimulate and give protection from death anxiety. The very experience of intimacy and mutual sharing of feelings, perceptions, and wishes ends up in unsatisfying neurotic discourse. The sexual and emotional needs of the couple overlay their need of each other for self-definition, acceptance, and reaffirmation of personal worth. The experience of intimacy in living together in close emotional contact thus separates lovers as it awakens their fear of death. Sexual contact for the undifferentiated self brings the experience of a severe threat. It drives a couple further apart in the pursuit of a fleeting sense of security. The neurotic need for distance from husband, wife, or lover often evidences itself in fears of sex and intimacy that reawaken the fear of the loss of the self. Although "Oedipal" elements may be present, the fear of death as it arises in relationship problems cannot be simply reduced to Oedipal fears and conflicts. For that matter, Oedipal conflicts that arise in relationships cannot always be explained simply as the emergence of the fear of death. Conflicts in marriage about sex, the failure of need satisfaction, and closeness versus emotional distance that are brought into psychotherapy need to be examined for the particularly private and interpersonal meanings of the conflict. Hamlet's guilt and Oedipal strivings stood in contrast to K's inner emptiness and passivity; they both shared a depressed sense of futility as well as a fear of and fascination with death. The relevance of death anxiety to a person's unique neurotic difficulties deserves elucidation in whatever form it takes. The fear of the loss of the self can be seen clearly in defensiveness with intimacy.

The identification of sexual intercourse with the loss of the self in death can also stem from childhood fears of disapproval or fantasies about the dangerousness of sexuality. To small children, adults' sexuality perhaps conveys a mysterious air of the forbidden, and danger from which they are excluded. The adult who has a disguised or unrecognized fear of the opposite sex may harbor this equation of sexuality with death. The unconscious image of the opposite sex as a destroyer or potential murderer has been described by many psychoanalytic writers beginning with Melanie Klein and Freud. Freud interpreted the theme of the three caskets in *The Merchant of Venice* and the three daughters of King Lear as symbols for the three modes of women's relations to men as "mothers, lovers, and destroyers."[22] Freud presumed that the adult man's fear of women becomes evident in relation to this threefold image of woman as death, lover, and "Mother Earth." The preadolescent male fantasy of self-sufficiency in a world without women follows from this unconscious belief in women as murderous and powerful. Fragments of this notion can be noted in DeFoe's *Robinson Crusoe* and especially in the glamorous myth of the freedom of the American cowboy. The fear of women's hidden, destructive power urged Hamlet to condemn Ophelia for the "power of beauty" and the Greeks to memorialize Helen of Troy. In the Freudian system, the adult woman's fear of men has been understood similarly as originating in childhood sexual wishes for the father that are accompanied by unconscious fears of punishment and death. The little girl's unconscious wish for the father's penis conveys a sense of danger that can become transformed into the adult woman's fear of death. Deutsch compared the woman's fear of male sexual power with the unconscious need to see all men as attackers and murderers. The young adolescent girl's crushes on movie stars, rock singers, or other remote male figures serve to mitigate such fear while providing transitions to later relationships with men. The childhood fear of and wish for the father's penis can, in some although not all women, lead to strong unconscious fears of men or sexual fantasies in which the fear becomes eroticized.

When young children are punished severely or frightened about masturbation, the presence of this fear is reinforced. Prepubescent girls who are filled with exaggerated statements about the discomforts of menstruation may experience a greater than average amount of anxiety at their menarche. Folklore, religious teachings and family myths, about the dangers of masturbation may contribute to intense anxiety in adolescents who are conflicted about masturbation and intense sexual longings and fantasies. Stories about the incredible pain of childbirth that young girls may overhear do little to alleviate the fear of adult sexuality or further sexual development. Overcoming anxiety about menstruation, masturbation, and sexual contact remains a developmental task of adolescence. In spite of the so-called sexual revolution, the adolescent's anxiety about sex persists. Mothers' and fathers' unconscious perceptions about their sexuality and sexual identity continue to make significant impressions on their children.

Helene Deutsch wrote extensively about such unconscious links between sex and death fears in a Freudian elaboration of female psychosexual development. Through decades of psychoanalytic work with patients, Deutsch observed the frequency with which fears of sexual intercourse in women implied a fear of injury and ultimately of death.[23] In this theoretical framework, the injury was always attributed to castration whereas I attribute it to threats to the self. Deutsch believed that the fear of castration, masochistic fantasies, and destructive feelings would be mixed with sexual desire in women and then the combination transformed into the fear of death. Furthermore, in this system, women's fear of death in childbirth arises from similar psychodynamic origins. According to Deutsch, death also reaches its fullest unconscious symbolism in the rape fantasies. Deutsch especially stressed the importance of the superego in masochistic fantasies about violation or prostitution and the role of the girl's death wishes for her mother in the development of later death anxiety. Death anxiety in men was explained similarly within this Freudian model as the transformation of castration anxiety and the boy's fear of the loss of his masculinity as it is attached to his genitals. Deutsch's consistently tracing the fear of death in women to fantasies about rape during adolescence overlooked the importance of social learning, familial and characterological variables.

However, in recent years, more careful attention has been paid in the psychoanalytic literature to disorders of the self in sexual fears, dysfunctions and especially in sexual perversions. Sexual perversions, such as fetishes, and sexual fantasies in both men and women encapsulate and reiterate injuries to the self. Sexual intercourse and orgasm may either threaten the self or reaffirm its reality and vitality. If masculinity and femininity are affirmed in orgasm then sexual activity strengthens the self and the sexual identity. Sexual dysfunctions that are debilitating may contain statements about the person's self, the partner and the true nature of the emotional entanglements in the relationship. Sexual dysfunctions often involve neurotic problems sometimes evidenced in semiconscious sexual fantasies and feelings about the partner during intercourse.

While acknowledgeing the theoretical contribution of the notions of female masochism and penis envy, their universal validity have been refuted by Karen Horney, Clara Thompson, and other neo-Freudian theoreticians. Despite the best parenting, the very nature of childhood insures that development through life will demand coming to grips with both sex and death fears. Mature sexuality in the face of death anxiety may have been symbolized as the "Albatross" around every man's neck that Coleridge described in "The Rime of the Ancient Mariner." Intimacy, emotional closeness, and sex can be anxiety-arousing in their own right without any psychological connection to death or the fear of death. Sullivan wrote very cogent clinical and developmental descriptions of the eventful clashes between the need for intimacy and the need for sex. The result of the clash was that feelings and pleasurable experiences of intimacy could be dissociated from a person's awareness.[24] Sexual and emotional intimacy can thereby represent threats to the self. If sexual experience presents the possibility of a disintegration or loss of the self, then mature heterosexuality elicits a profound kind of anxiety. The struggle against this death anxiety encompasses much more than a defense against penis envy or castration anxiety. If intercourse and orgasm are accompanied by merger fantasies, then the person may experience a more serious survival threat. If sexual experience brings neurotic guilt, then the fear of the loss of the self also serves as a punishment. Psychological defeat at the juncture between sex, and death anxiety, leaves little room for the neurotic person to experience himself as truly sexual or engaged in the present. The neurotic keeps mature related orgiastic sexuality and love at a distance to the extent that they evoke anxiety and particularly death anxiety.

Summary

One of the paradoxes of adult life holds fast to the extent to which people try heedlessly to overcome the fear of death through love. Love's revival of childhood patterns for countering death anxiety rests on the arousal of the individual's characteristic defenses and unconscious reactions to death. From Gershwin and Cole Porter to the Beatles, popular music has idealized love as the solution to fears of living. If "Love is a Many Splendid Thing," "All We Need Is Love," and "Love Is the Answer," then anxiety about existential living and dying can more easily be kept at arm's length until circumstances thrust them into awareness with sudden recognition. For example, prolonged idealization of the loved one in childhood feelings, adolescent hero worship, crushes, and beyond to adult love yields some protection from the recognition of death anxiety. Perhaps the fear of death or the need to transcend it stand high on the list of unconscious motives that dictate the decision of couples to have children. The subtleties of the interaction of a couple's neurotic character traits may yield further protection from the fear of death. However, neither affectionate amiability nor unbridled passion may be sufficiently strong to fully quelch death anxiety. If one ruthlessly seeks to find in the other an answer to his or her own death anxiety and depression failure is preordered. The mutual sharing and relatedness can turn into early childhoodlike dependency on the partner to compensate for fears of the loss of the self. Neurotic disillusionment with a basically healthy marital relationship because a husband or wife "doesn't really understand me" or "doesn't love me enough" can stem from a failure in individuation, an unacknowledged depression and from death anxiety. Maintaining a sense of autonomous adaptability and individual identity in the midst of a close emotional involvement would be the ideal. Across the spectrum of psychoanalytic personality theory, the capacity for mature love and sexual fulfillment has been given its brightest clarity when it is defined in terms of recognition of the boundaries of two distinct personalities that recognize each other's uniqueness. Overcoming the fear of death by definition encompasses personal individuation manifest at different stages in life. It remains a solitary process valued in significant others. The course of this psychic struggle can either bring a couple to a deeper attachment or drive them into mutual flight. The juxtaposition of emotional forces and interconnections between love and the fear of death were fully captured by William Blake's poem "For the Sexes: The Gates of Paradise":

...I rent the veil where the dead dwell;
When weary man enters his cave;
He meets his savior in the grave;
Some find a female garment there;
And some a male, woven with care;
Lest the sexual garments sweet
Should grow a devouring winding sheet.
One dies! Alas! The living and dead!
One is slain! and one is fled!...
The son of death I open found;
Throw'st my mother, from the womb;
Wife, sister, daughter, to the tomb;
Weaving to dreams the sexual strife,
And weeping over the Web of Live.[25]

Freud's description of primitive man's mental states, in particular the use of magical thinking and denial, has been applied to modern man's neurotic responses to the anticipation of personal death. Death anxiety has been described further as a subspecies of the basic insecurity beneath the neurotic's experience of helplessness and passivity. The experience of the self as resourceless and helpless underlies the neurotic's defensive character movements in unsuccessfully grappling with death anxiety. Like Kafka's K and Prometheus the neurotic fears the loss of the self in living fully in the present. Based on current psychoanalytic theories it has been hypothesized that the fear of the loss of the self often finds expression in depression and disguised derivatives of separation anxiety. Thus the brooding Hamlet, the overly dependent adolescent and the adult neurotic reluctantly acquire "devouring winding sheets" of defensiveness.

Finding authenticity in relating and security in loving constitute the adult existential challenge of men and women. The projection onto the husband, wife, or lover or the parents' power to elicit and lower death anxiety complicates authentic involvement. The honest sharing of the possibilities of emotional experience occur throughout life in the face of the certainty of death. The thought of death provides part of the context for the growth of love. The fear of love and the fear of death in adults arise from similar distortions, unconscious processes, and threats to the self.

CHAPTER FIVE

Religion and the Fear of Death

Religious Experience and Freudian Theory

Religious rhetoric, more than a genuine spiritual commitment, helps the neurotic form a steadfast line of defense against his fear of the loss of the self. The three dimensions of death anxiety have not been subject to detailed analysis in the history of the psychology of religion. Erich Fromm's observations on the types of religious experience seem to come closest to sifting the true value of authentic religions from the self-serving facade of pseudoreligion. Neurotic religiosity confers a conservative, aspect of defensiveness on the worshiper's involvement. It can be a highly effective defense even if it is not altogether urbane.

To Freud and the early Freudian theoreticians, the relationship between religion and death fears stemmed from an essential connection between early man's belief in God and unconscious feelings toward the father. Primitive man accrued a montage out of alternate images of God's benevolent protection and punitive authority. In Freud's history of society, the second source early death attitudes in religious thought lay in the similarity between the minds of children and the mental operations of primitive man. Freud defined religion as the aggregate projections of the child's emotional relationship to the father. Thus the mental exercises common to both primitive man and children could be traced in the history of religious practices. A brief summary of Freud's religious writings will readily serve to pinpoint the basis of the child's emotional relationship to the "heavenly" father in the need for protection from the fear of death.

Primitive man feared God as the omnipotent being who provided safety from danger. Freud similarly reasoned that the young child's physical survival depended upon the parents' supervision and protection. For an older child, their physical presence may not be actually necessary to assuage fears. Internalized images or memories of the omnipotent parent of infancy or the good parent of childhood suffice when the child's own psychological security system does not. One supposes that to the degree that early dependency needs persist, religious experience reinforces the adolescent's or adult's need for God as the parent at the same time that it reduces anxiety about death.

It will be alleged that the more dependent the person's unconscious attachment to childhood parental images, the clearer the fear of death becomes. Death anxiety is generally given ample room for disguise in the neurotic use of spirituality and religion. Religious prayer and worship have the potential to both perpetuate and alleviate the fear of death-depression-separation anxiety complex in several ways. First, as Freud suggested, religion fosters denial of death fears by means of identification with God, the omnipotent father. Second, religious ceremonies can lower death fears via the person's identification with the religious community. Prayer that focuses solely on personal spiritual fulfillment certainly differs from liturgical prayer or worship in which the prayer asks God for favors, forgiveness, blessings, or support in some human undertaking. Petitions of this second type can maintain the dependent subservient position. One could argue that such religious practices renew dependence upon the benevolent father, who is viewed as the source of human happiness or as the all-powerful protector. On the other hand the Judeo-Christian ethical tradition of striving for a just moral life in the hope of a reward in heaven provides more of a framework for the continuity of life. As Fromm put it, religion in this sense can be said to mitigate man's sense of "aloneness". Might a spiritual union with God lower anxiety about being an autonomous independent individual who is troubled with the anxieties of a complicated life in an insecure world? I am suggesting here that neurotic commitment to religion shifts the focus of religious activities from genuine spirituality to a fascination with attachment. This fascination intensifies neurotic defensiveness by contributing to the struggle against death anxiety. Perhaps the neurotic's religious and emotional connections to God also combat a susceptibility to depression.

According to Freud, a close relationship was apparent between religion, obsessional neurosis, and the use of magical thinking. Belief in God dismantled uncertainty through submission to the father's authority and reliance on him for daily survival. Freud noted the repetitive, ritualistic aspects of religious services, and he discerned close parallels to the child's compulsive security rituals. Childhood rites convey a sense of the power to reduce fears of death. The child's games and ceremonies cannot be dismissed as purely neurotic since they are appropriate defensive attempts at mastery. The continual repetition of prayers and worship also protects the worshiper by assuring him a measure of safety from psychological danger due to his alliance with God.

Charles Wahl carefully documented the importance of magical thinking and the retention of omnipotent feelings in children's dealing with thoughts about death.[1] Because of the prelogical thought processes and inability to understand cause and effect, young children can confuse parental anger or angry feelings toward parents with mortal threats to the body and self. If thoughts, feelings, and actions cannot be fully distinguished, then subtle interpretations of emotional communications are difficult. In children, anxiety about hostile wishes toward parents generates death anxiety, which can be counteracted by rituals or obsessional thinking. Bedtime rituals magically protect the child from hostile attacks during the night by some imaginary, predatory animal, hostile monster, or ghost. Such fears have been described in earlier chapters as arising from fears of separation, hostility and the loss of the self. The preschooler's bedtime rituals serve as a means of retaliation against avenging monsters or ghosts. They simultaneously help the child to disguise the powerful affects that may need to be expressed. The familiar early childhood fear of dying in one's sleep during the night can also be diminished through the child's incantation of "Now I lay me down to sleep." Clutching the teddy bear to cushion the separation from the parents and from waking conscious life alters the child's vulnerability to the fear of the loss of the self.

By active use of the mechanism of projection in these situations the child internalizes conflicts and painful affects within the psyche and then attributes them to the external world. The defensive use of the mechanism of introjection implies that someone absorb into the self the attitudes, affects, or personal characteristics of another and then react accordingly to external events. In normal ego development, children differ as in the extent of their internalization and the completeness of their introjections. Developmental psychoanlysts have studied the individual differences in the child's internalization and introjection of parts of their parents' personalities.

The psychological history of religious experience has noted worship's evolution in terms of an integration of projections, introjections, and magical thinking with the demands of cultural conditions. The intellectual sophistication of a given cultural period is evident in the intermingling of these mental operations in relation to attitudes about God and death. For example, the ancient Aztec worship of the sun in bloodletting and sacrificial rites thematically and structurally resembled the ritual magic of early childhood. According to the Aztec legends a small, unworthy, leprous god sacrificed himself at Teotihuacán on a bed of blazing coals and thereby transformed himself into the sun.[2] This sun remained so weak and invisible to man that other gods immolated themselves to enable the sun-god to acquire strength from their death. In the legend, the sun thereby gained mobility and acquired its capacity to traverse the sky. The essential need for the Aztecs' human sacrifices stemmed from their fear that the sun would stop moving. Their ritual sacrifices squelched the terror of death, the darkness that would blanket the earth. As a result, atop the pinnacle of their highest pyramid, the Aztec high priest would sacrifice daily a human heart, still dripping with the victim's blood. Immediately after the heart had been torn from the victim's chest, the high priest placed it in a special vessel of the sun. This gesture seemingly insured the return of daylight and prevented disaster from befalling the world. The Aztecs' equation of death with darkness and immobility dramatized the young child's equivalent literal-mindedness. The Aztec assumption of a casual connection between the sacrifices, divine protection, and the sun's brightness or movement predated logical operational thinking. Magical thinking inherent in the prayers of some young children also relies on obsessive compulsive devices in rescuing the child or his parents from danger.

Scholars view introjection as the essential aspect of mental development in early religious experience. Its functional relevance has been well indexed in the account of Hebrew prophets, medieval sorcerers, and Christian saints.[3] For Freudian scholars, the prophet receiving the word of God was considered less puzzling because of the process of introjection-projection. Primitive man was said to have introjected a powerful father figure and then to have been overwhelmed by feelings of safety and security as part of the internalization.[4] The experience was said to have been given verbal organization and symbolic representation as the next step of the historical reconstruction. The introjection would have been labeled a religious experience and then the "train of associations reversed" or projected onto God. In Freudian theory, the magical omnipotence of God's words and the strength of their impact arose from the powerful influence and awe of the original introjects. Finally, the worship of God and the reverence of his image was understood by Freud to have developed from the worship of the parental introjects. Early man's fear of punishment by God reflected the durability of the introjects and the drive to retain them as a source of comfort. At the earliest stages of moral development children lack an innate sense of right or wrong. Their knowledge of safe, socially acceptable behavior and the norms of ethical conduct directly reflect parental modeling. The preschooler's reliance on the parents' moral authority has been described by several investigators as akin to man's reliance on the prophets' holy words. With the repetition of parental commands, children begin to assimilate not only their parents' words but also their feeling tones associated with correct or improper behavior. Eventually, the preschooler repeats the phrases and experiences them as part of the self when tempted to participate in some naughty or anti-social behavior. Once inhibitions and moral values have been internalized, moral danger, like physical danger, no longer demands the parents' presence.

Forceful arguments have been raised against this Freudian analysis of introjective processes in the role of religious attitudes. A number of authors have attacked its presumption of a universal patriarchal society and its ignorance of the role of sociocultural factors. In spite of these criticisms, Freud pursued the historical associations between the role of the father and religious ceremonies, based on his premise that God is the "magnified father."

In the practice of circumcision, for example, Freud saw a partial castration of the infant boy by the father or his representative as a means of forestalling the child's incestuous wishes and his potential role as a rival for the mother's affection.[5] In his last published treatise on religion, *Moses and Monotheism,* Freud speculated that because the history of the human race has paralleled the developmental course of human life, mankind must have passed through a stage of sexual aggressiveness. He argued that the "primeval horde's" murder of their father epitomized that primitive epoch.

Freud's final contribution on the subject was to define religion as a logical outgrowth of the ancient family history of man and of the attempt of later societies to overcome unconscious guilt feelings. Man's full expressions of "primal guilt" were recorded in the foundations of both Judaism and Christianity. The revival and expiation of guilt in religious worship evolved from this primeval murder. Freud believed that Moses and Christ assumed the guilt of the murdering horde, and that their deaths served as a communal atonement for the guilt. Inherent in all of these formulations was a central notion that religion demonstrated a collective neurosis that had its basis in the Oedipal conflict.

Much of Freud's analysis of religious experience was published in *Totem and Taboo* in 1913 and in *The Future of an Illusion* in 1927. The latter work hypothesized an illusory quality of religion. The credence placed in dogmas or beliefs about the nature of reality that man could not come to by himself seemed illogical to Freud. The illusion lay in the wish for protection in the face of the cruel trials of life in the modern world and the perversity of human nature. Primitive man ingeniously devised this psychic protection to counteract his helplessness in an uncomprehensible and terrifying world. Mankind projects the infantile relationship with the father onto God to sustain the attention of an ever-vigilant, exalted protector. Only such an omniscient, powerful parent could fully understand the needs of daughters and sons or be moved by their prayers and feelings of remorse. The more intellectually primitive and ignorant early man was, the greater his experience of helplessness. At this point, one could emphasize the role of "the Father" in protection against the ultimate fear—the fear of death. The young child's death fears persist and vary in degree with the extent of his or her sophistication and maturing capacity for defense under emotional and environmental stress.

In *Totem and Taboo,* Freud based the relationship between religious services and the Oedipal drama on the early triumph of the "murdering horde." Totemism was portrayed as a major source of religions, and its relation to the Oedipus complex accounted for the origin of culture and civilization. The standards of the tribe and their religious sacrifices grew out of this concept. To Freud, the history of Christianity embodied the symbolism of the murdered father-totem and it reinstitutionalized the ritual of sacrifice. Since Christ redeemed man by sacrificing his own life, Freud also interpreted original sin as an offense against the father, most likely his murder. Freud reasoned that by Christs' sacrificing his own life, he himself became God and took the Father's place. For Freud, the Christian eucharist reiterated both the animal sacrifice of the totem and

Christ's human sacrifice. Christian communion was interpreted by him as an expression of ambivalence to the Father through repetition of the crime, the punishment of the slain Christ, and the triumph over the Father. In totemic societies, the ritual sacrifice freed the members from their collective guilt, just as the eucharist freed the Christian from the subservience to the Father. Freud argued that the Christian mass evolved from the ritual of sacrifice of primitive religions and mythologies in which the slaying of the totem animal had itself replaced the slaughter of a human sacrifice. Sacrifice reunited the totem or slain human member with the community and its god. It thus reestablished the psychological bonds of worship and dependency.

Freud based many of these theories on anthropological studies and the revolutionary work of Charles Darwin. He also utilized his own psychoanalytical methodology in the analysis of culture and religion. He reasoned that murderous impulses lie in modern man's unconscious, thinly veiled by the trappings of civilization and easily stirred by war and combat. The powerful prohibition "Thou Shalt Not Kill" was evidence, Freud felt, that we sprang from blood-lusting, murderous ancestors. The ritual sacrifices and later Christian eucharistic feasts emphasized ambivalence about the Father. They celebrated the triumph over the Father in his symbolic murder. They also reiterated a sharing in his power through the communal feast, a relieving of guilt, and a petition for forgiveness.

The same view of religious beliefs and ceremonies was Freuds' key to understanding men's attitudes toward the devil. Fear of the devil's influence on man stemmed from the unconscious projection of a negative demonic father figure who was as powerful as God. In his paper on demonic possession in the seventeenth century, Freud identified cases of demonic possession with the present-day neuroses. He linked evil spirits with the projected derivatives of repressed evil wishes.[5B] In the study of an early manuscript about the possession of the painter Christopher Haizmann, Freud formulated the psychic dynamics of demonic phenomena and actually identified separation anxiety with the fear of death. According to his diary, Haizmann had struck a bargin with the devil out of despondency about his art. He had pledged to give his body and soul to the devil at the end of nine years but then tried to escape the contract. Haizmann was given refuge with priests at the shrine of Mary at Mariazell, where on several occasions the devil appeared to him in a vision. Freud noted that Haizmann's pact with the devil grew out of depression and despondency over the death of his father, as much as it was provoked by the need for the devil as a substitute father. Haizmann's despair over an inability to work and his impotence were the cause of his belief in the curative powers of the Satanic pact.

Freud embellished his conjecture about Haizmann's feelings about his father into the notion that the devil represents the child's projections of negative aspects of the father's personality. Haizmann's visions, seizures, and melancholia were said to originate from a mixture of hateful and loving feelings toward his dead father. The demonic neurosis and visions of possession substituted for these conflicts with an intense defensive flair. Herein Freud came closest to linking depression and separation anxiety with neurotic death anxiety. The demonic possession solved Haizmann's difficulty in working at his art. At the same time, his depression rendered him passive and dependent upon the devil as a replacement for his father. The implication was clearly present that Haizmann's depression embraced prolonged separation anxiety from his father. Possession by the devil graced Haizmann with the strategy to surrender to the "father's" destructive power. It undermined his anxiety about further psychological separation and calmed his fear of living. In Freud's theory, the fear of God and the devil found its clearest rationale in the fear of castration, whereas in the present view, the fear of both is comprised mainly of the fear of helplessness in the face of death anxiety and the uncertainty of the human will.

Freud drew many analogies between religious practices and the symptoms of obsessional neurosis in his earliest papers on religion. He in fact defined obsessional neurosis as a kind of private religion. Religion approached the status of a universal obsessional neurosis that obviated the individual's need for a private, more personal one. The religious practices left intact the observer's psychological armor against the expression of some unacceptable unconscious impulse. From a contemporary psychoanalytic viewpoint, unconscious sexual or aggressive energies simply don't account for the complexity of characterological strategies in this defensive process. Depression and the unconscious fear of separation seem to provide a more richly appointed context for the individual's fears of death and of life. Freud's position in his essay on "The Future of an Illusion" ingeniously associated man's continuous longing for father's protection with the need to combat helplessness and the memory of the helplessness of childhood. The transformation of the forces of nature into gods by the ancients was described parallel to the later repressions of civilization. This change yielded further safety from the fear of death. The development of monotheism was also traced by Freud to the need to reexperience the child's feelings of intimacy with the father. Belief in some form of life after death continued the promise of a compensation beyond what was earthly possible because of the cruelties of civilization and fate. In this conceptual framework, it followed that Christianity and other religious systems arose from the ancient need for self-defense against the forces of nature. Religious beliefs realized particular manifestations of this world view.

In summary, Freud based these views of religion on a composite of mankind's wishes to be ruled, controlled, and made comfortable. Freud suggested that religion arose as the universal neurosis due to ubiquitous Oedipal conflicts. The origin of formal religions coincided with mankind's passage through a developmental stage that resembled obsessional neurosis. The positive aspects of religion were overshadowed in this theory by the emphasis of its role in the avoidance of punishment for Oedipal strivings. Religious beliefs and ceremonies were said to fend off the hostile feelings toward God and to promise his protection from Oedipal punishment and the violence of nature. Freud conceptualized primitive man's creation of the gods because of the deeply felt need for them to exist. Modern man's creation of religion was characterized as an attempted resolution of his longing for the father and his archaic feelings of helplessness.

Religious Experience and the Fear of Death Complex

William James' lectures on the *Varieties of Religious Experience,* published in 1902, conveyed the most serious and best known early treatment of these issues aside from Freud's.[6] Through extensive case histories and philosophical arguements, James assessed "religious geniuses" in their "encounters with religion without regard to the influence of their psychopathology." James tried to reduce religion to its lowest common denominators in an attempted reconciliation of human reason with belief in God. Through psychological inquiry into the lives of Tolstoy, Henry Alline (a Nova Scotian evangelist), and others, James concluded that the essential elements of religion were obvious in the extreme, most exaggerated instances of religious experience. James urged that the importance of this category could not be dismissed even if it was contaminated by visions, hallucinations, melancholia, or pathological obsessions. "Sick souls" were contrasted with the "healthy minded" as antagonistic poles of religious experience in the Jamesian position of an apologia of faith. Religion approached the totality of the individuals' actions, feelings, and experiences with a "religious happiness" unparalleled in the possibilities of human experience. The religious life stood on the basis of three characteristic beliefs for James. First, the significance of the world lies in its participation in a spiritual universe. Second, man's true purpose is envisioned in the harmonious union with the spirit, or God. Third, prayer lingers as an open-ended process of communion and energy flow from God; it vitalizes and changes phenomenological experience. Spiritual happiness necessitated surrender of one's will to the divine. A life of sacrifice gives the firm impression of a renewed sense of power and freedom from tension, dejection, and loneliness. The ultimate religious happiness assembles an absolute transcendence of human fear with graceful moments of joyful self-abandonment. This religious self-awareness extends an inner self-consciousness whose authenticity cannot be doubted as a source of knowledge. The height of the religious happiness appears as a kind of new, or second, birth. In its ideal form it satisfies man's metaphysical curiosity and reconciles inner struggles with the outer universe. Religion's self-awareness accomplishes this tranquil harmony in spite of the conflicting impulses toward good and evil. Once it has imbued man with a sense of psychological safety and feelings of love for others, human nature does not deter his earnest enthusiasm to life. What

James called the religion of "healthy mindedness" sees all things as good without puzzlement. The goodness of life and the goodness of the universe are without exception the most essential aspects of being. Walt Whitman's poetry exemplified this inability to feel evil as present in the world.

The fundamentalist zest for righteousness and the Catholic practice of confession keep healthy mindedness in the foreground of religious attitudes. A soul that adheres to the presence of evil or the negative aspects of the universe deprives itself of the joy of the healthy minded. What James called the "sick soul" finds its end in sadness. The "sick soul" ignores goodness while lying in wait for the mental agonies of melancholia. Its anguish bears the mental qualities of self-doubt, despair, irritation, suspiciousness, anxiety, and fear. James identified the lot of the "sick soul" as perpetual "religious melancholia." The ultimate type of this melancholia occurred in the form of a "panic fear" that amounted to paralyzing horror of one's own existence. This intense fear of the universe and heightened sense of guilt and sin debilitates meaningful life.

James foresaw the inevitability of the breakdown of healthy mindedness. Some melancholia creeps into unconsciousness, even if only from the recognition of the brutality of nature and the inhumanity of war. Since evil does exist as part of human nature, religion needs to reconcile evil and death with the righteousness of the healthy minded. Therefore, James considered Buddhism and Christianity the "completest religions" because of their message of the deliverance of man in second birth. After life on earth, James argued, man must be born again to escape unscathed from the melancholy and pessimism of his age. Supernatural religions of salvation thus solved "panic fear" and the human entanglement in morbidity. In Jamesian theory, the twice-born character possesses a native discordance of will that seeks unification via religious conversion. Tolstoy repeatedly found relief from his depression in the gradual recognition of the infinity of the soul, which led to his rejection of an "artificial" quest for earthly happiness. James concluded that Tolstoy's salvation from madness came about through faith and his embracing of God. A schematic overview of his writings makes it clear that William James focused more directly on spiritual experience than did Freud. Freud's early psychoanalytic writings on dogma, beliefs, and rituals reflected his interest in the more formal aspects of religion.

Without so identifying it, James, like Freud, was grappling with defining the dimensions of death anxiety. The inherent relationship between the fear of death, depression, and separation anxiety was depicted by James in the dilemma of the "divided soul." Religious conversion and second birth might assure a means for deliverance from the fear of death. The "sick soul" in James' schema runs parallel to the depressed, anxious suffering of the neurotic who is overwhelmed by the fear of death. In fact, the terrors of the "panic fear" seem rooted in this ultimate fear. The emotional experience of "religious melancholia" seems analogous to the neurotic's depression and death anxiety stated in religious or philosophical terms. The idealist who becomes overly depressed about the evils of the world and metaphysical anomalies may protest too much. A more personal and neurotic substratum of insecurity and despair may be expressed in brooding about religious issues. It has been well known since Freud's initial efforts that religion can be the matrix for the expression of a host of neurotic entanglements. Intense, tortured involvement in religion, therefore, can be a symptom of unrecognized and unresolved entrapment in the fear of death, depression, and separation anxiety. One supposes that religions emphasizing a centrality of guilt, obsessional ritualistic practice, and codified prohibitions can function smoothly as media for neurotic fears.

Religion offers ample opportunity for solutions to the fear of death to those whose character problems combine a religious upbringing with pressing neurotic needs. However, few would agree with Freud's allegation that all religious involvements are by definition automatically neurotic. The religious melancholia that James delineated gives the appearance of the neurotic expression of the fear of death in religious terms. Healthy mindedness via communion with God offers a diversity of psychological postures, including a non-neurotic spirituality. Positive emotional attitudes and some measure of "self"-integration can surely be formed, in religious commitment. Freud's view, however, was a rather negative indictment of religious experience. He portrayed the Christian rite of communion as the reintegration of the worshipper into the unconscious dependency on the parents. The eating of the symbolic representation of Christ's body and drinking of his blood metamorphosed the individual in a mystical union with God as one continuous spiritual entity. Freud believed that such spiritual reunion with God was generally more neurotic than spiritual. For the neurotic, union with God has its counterpart in the child-parent relationship. To the extent that this spiritual union symbolizes symbiotic merger, it could be used to cover normal anxiety about separation-individuation.

Separation, death anxiety, and depression can be put off as psychological realities through any neurotic attachment that symbolizes symbiotic union. Blind adherence to religious teachings and blind obedience to imposed codes of moral values might reflect neurotic defensiveness. To the extent that these attitudes keep the worshiper, as the child, in the subservient dependent relationship on God and the minister, they can mask anxiety about autonomy. The young child's immaturity excuses and makes charming his wholesale mimicry and absolute obedience to the parents. Fromm assumed that the more authoritarian and rigid a religion, the greater the potential conflicts unveiled in the adult's blind obedience to it. Let us also assume that the more neurotic one's religious commitment is, the more the involvement counters death anxiety and threats to the self.

Modern man's "religious melancholia" seems as much a reflection of death anxiety as was primitive man's need for mythology. Greek mythological motifs and ancient religions dwelled on themes of rebirth and transformation of man into animal and divine form. The delight in sustaining a "new" life in Christ has persisted as a central motif in Christianity since the first century, A.D. Carried to an extreme, religious fervor brings an irrepressible panache to the task of maintaining defenses against death anxiety.

St. Paul of Tarsus defined the Christian's lot as one of becoming a "new man" who was "born again" through faith. The doctrine of the Resurrection of Christ, the central tenent of Christianity, denotes a symbolic restatement of triumph over the fear of death. Since Christ rose from the dead, the Christian who shares in the body of Christ has the capacity to rise from the dead at his second coming. The Christian need not fear death, since the Resurrection provided the verification of regeneration. The earliest Western myths of rebirth and reincarnation conferred some measure of immunity from death anxiety. Freud first noted that the religious person has a transferential relationship with God that has dual purposes. First, a subservient submission to God's unambiguous guidance, or the Father's authority. Second, identification with God as an immortal, almighty, and powerful being provides ample grounds for man's security. One shares in God's power over life and death as a Catholic via participation in the "mystical body of Christ." The function of funeral services revolves around smoothing the transition of the dead person into a fuller participation with God as a spirit in heaven. The proximity of heaven offers great consolation to the religious person when death is near. In some religious cultures, the triumph over death anxiety and the emphasis on reunion makes the mourning period a joyful celebration of faith. Less ambivalence and hesitation in giving up and severing of ties with the dead person persists in such cultures. Communion with God can be used to ward off the depression and anxiety which accompanies adult individuation.

The psychotherapist who listens to a patient's complaints about religious doubts or brooding about philosophical issues often hears the influence of depression. Depression and the individual's characteristic defenses can be beneath what may be a legitimate concern. Absorption in countering death anxiety brings theological pursuits to the brink of neurotic self-deception. Further investigation of the individual's religious and philosophical doubts might also reveal an overt fear of death and separation conflicts. The intellectual espousal of beliefs and the execution of rituals in religious services doubtless reduce anxiety in the neurotic. Let us assume that both fill the worshipper with a subjective feeling of good that could counterbalance depression.

Psychoanalyst Gregory Zilboorg alleged that Freud's own passionate concern about religion resulted from his fear of death. Freud seemed to be obsessed with the thought of his own death. According to his biographer, Ernest Jones, it was, Freud's wont to frequently predict the actual date of his death. The source of his assertion that all religious experience could be relegated to the realm of neurosis has often been called into question.

The ancient Greek myth of Adonis, like the life of Christ, reiterated early integrations of "religious melancholia" with death anxiety. The legendary Adonis was beloved by the goddess Venus, who warned him repeatedly to be careful when hunting. Ignoring her advice, Adonis was bitten by a wild boar. The wound proved fatal, thereby substantiating Venus' worst fear. Venus was so distraught by his death that she changed Adonis into a flower. Proserpine, goddess of the underworld, then restored Adonis to life so that he could spend half of each year with her rival, Venus. The Greek ceremonies held in honor of Adonis symbolized the change of seasons from winter to summer. What began with tearful mourning ended with joyful celebration as the festivals celebrated Adonis' return to life.

This myth suggested themes implied in the Christian dogmas of communion and Christ's Crucifixion and Resurrection. Adonis' fear of death was given substance by the envy and scorn of Venus. His rebirth mitigated her depression and prevented their separation. Adonis' death following the wild boar's attack also symbolized the early childhood fear of being eaten. This fear has been described in an earlier chapter as the counterpart of the wish to be eaten or reincorporated into mother and more succinctly as the fear of the loss of the self. Death and rebirth imagery give concrete form to the psychological demands of separation-individuation experiences. In both the Greek legend and Christian liturgy, the believer achieves some reintegration into the parental image.

Ernest Jones was the first to observe that death and the admission to heaven gratified the child's wish to return to the mother's womb. Adonis and Christ conferred symbolic victory over death and provided a model for mankind's wish for immortality. In this sense, the Greek rituals and Christian eucharistic feasts confer on the participants a symbolic triumph over the fear of death complex by satisfying dependency needs, reducing separation anxiety and depression, and defying the finality of death. The reborn, resurrected Christian apparently does not give countenance to the fear of death. Religious conversion stamps the soul with the characteristics of being "twice born," in William James' terms. Perhaps conversion fortifies behavior against the fear of death, depression, and separation anxiety. If this is true, then the security derived from prayer and religious services superimposes additional gains on the individual's needs for an organized religion.

The lives of several Christian saints portray such conversions as a complete transformation of both the soul and the personality in response to death fears. St. Francis Borgia, apparently resolved his fear of death in a counterphobic way by keeping a coffin in his room. It reminded him of the certainty of death and the unreasonableness of death anxiety. The polemics of St. Jerome revealed his keeping a skull on a table, and the charity of St. Vincent was unveiled in his walking among the sickest of the terminally ill tuberculosis patients. A fear of death did not emerge into later consciousness after these saints' commitment to God since they lived with his grace and protection. Veneration of saints and religious leaders such as Moses, Luther, Wesley, and Gandhi provides the faithful with identity models. Following their teachings provides direction for living. A religious purpose in life outweighs the need for reassurance against the fear of death.

Obsessive-compulsive rituals that have a religious content can so fully absorb the individual as to indefinitely hold insecurity and fears in abeyance. Striving for holiness or righteousness in the neurotic may raise rigidity to the height of moral principle. At the very least the worship of God may obscure the fleeting passage of time and remove the neurotic's horror of death. St. Paul, originally named Saul, described his own conversion as a total transformation in which he no longer lived as himself. His previous frivolity was unbalanced with the knowledge that it was "Christ who was in me." His new self was directed by God. The identity change so completely altered his old self that he gave up the name Saul and named the new self Paul.

The Christian practice of baptism signals a similar symbolic rebirth. Baptism banishes original sin by imbuing the baptized person with God's grace so as to set it apart from the former natural self. The conferring of the Christian name in baptism seals this transformation. When the child's first name is that of a saint, he or she is provided with a lifelong model to imitate.

Humanistic Religion

Erich Fromm's metapsychology has touched directly on the religious aspect of the fear of death complex. Fromm pointed to the origin of religion in man's helplessness in the face of internal instinctual forces and the external forces of nature. He characterized the anxiety of such helplessness as an essential aspect of human neurosis in *Psychoanalysis and Religion*. Fromm reversed Freud's position that all religion really constitutes a private type of neurosis.[7] Religion instead served the primary function of stopping man's regression to ancestral worship and totemism. It was Fromm's view that the neurotic lives out private rituals as a kind of ancestral worship of the parents. The neurotic fails in achieving independence and integration of the self as an adult.

A related issue stems from the neurotic's choice between what Fromm termed "authoritarian" and "non-authoritarian" religions. In authoritarian religions, man escapes isolation by surrender to a powerful transcending figure who, in turn, provides the illusion of protection in exchange for obedience. Fromm observed that authoritarian religions command obedience and submission whether they are theistic, like Calvinism, or secular, like fascism. In humanistic religious experience, the identity of man and God is affirmed out of love, not power. Fromm found elements of this humanism in early Christianity, Protestant sects, Buddhism, and Jewish history. Here God could be understood as a symbol of man's higher self, power, and capacity for self-realization. The more authoritarian the religion, Fromm alleged, the more man projects onto God the richest possibilities of his own nature. This submission dictates man's "alienation from himself."

In Fromm's view, the humanistic psychotherapist can neither be the enemy nor the ally of religion, since the therapeutic role is to cut through theology to the essential characteristic nature of man. A huministic psychoanalyst assists the patient in learning about the presence and meaning of the private neurotic rituals. The Oedipal complex gains meaning in Frommian and neo-Freudian theory when seen as the adult's longing to remain a child in the context of interpersonal relationships. Incestuous relationships with parents do not have to be sexual. In Fromm's view, an adult who remains overly attached to his parents avoids the anxiety inherent in the awareness of living as a distinct, separate entity. Man feels insecure and defensive to the degree that he remains dependent on his parents. Man fails to be truly human, in Frommian theory, by remaining protected, submissive, and undifferentiated. To the extent that these psychological events are essentially tied to religion, religious faith cannot be fully distinguished from neurosis. The greater the tendency for one's neurosis to become a private religion, the stronger is the need for religion to counteract the fear of death. In carrying Fromm's work one step further, intermittent bouts with death anxiety seem an inevitable outgrowth of the self-alienation he has described. A central implication of his work puts the Freudian notion of guilt in perspective.

Religious guilt does not simply present elements of Oedipal conflicts displaced onto God. It arises perhaps intertwined with death anxiety as a result of the lack of differentiation. The role that religion plays in absolving guilt feelings does not rely on man's sexual conflicts. For Fromm, guilt is mobilized with the genuine failure of the person to attain independence and autonomy in interpersonal relationships. Religious worship for Freud derived from the effects of repressed instinctual conflicts. Fromm, however, believed that religious practices can be used to hide a failure to achieve independent adulthood. Freud sought to explain the similarities between the "observances of the pious" and neurotic rituals of obsessionals that arise from their need to ward off anxiety. He assigned religious ceremonies to the categories of sublimations or defensive rituals to control Oedipal wishes and sexual and aggressive libido. Thus repression assumed the highest importance as a virtuous reaction formation against the expression of the forbidden. Fromm contended, on the other hand, that the type of religious experience was crucial. In "humanistic" religious worship, the similarities between ritual and defense can be superficial and insubstantial.

The real nature of a person's faith and motivations for religious practices may be lost in the tracing of reaction formations. Fromm's point was evident in the claim that agnostic neurotics can be as much a victims of "submissive docility" and "ancestor worship" as the most committed practicing Christian, Protestant, or Jew. The "authoritarian religious" follower remains satisfied with obedience to God, whereas the "humanistic religious" person fully develops the capacity for emotional growth through self-actualization and love for other people. Maturity with achievement of success in love, interpersonal relationships, and work depends on adult emotional integration and independence regardless of one's particular religious orientation.

Death Anxiety and Type of Religious Experience

Fromm's humanistic religious type seemed quite sytonic with Victor Frankl's suggestion that a spiritual life of religious commitment constituted one of the most authentic ways of maintaining an existential purpose in life. Fromm elegantly dichotimized the two simple possibilities of adult emotional response into autonomy and health versus regression and despondency. This division seems also congruent with William James' view that religious experience is composed of the life of the "healthy minded" or the "sick soul." One-half of the research study detailed below was based on the assumption that a high purpose in life would accompany low death anxiety. On a logical basis it appeared that a highly developed sense of purpose in life would tend to make death meaningful. Gordon Allport's psychological research studies fell within the humanistic tradition of Fromm. Allport was the first investigator to extend the relationship between death anxiety and religion into the arena of social-psychological research. He had speculated that the fear of death might not be intense among people who had a strongly internalized "intrinsic" commitment to religion.

Allport distinguished between people who have "intrinsic religious" values—mainly, those that are integrated and comprehensive ends in themselves and those with "extrinsic religious" values—those that are "escapist and ethnocentric"[8] Allport was first intrigued with the meaning of religious outlooks as a result of the finding that high religiosity was prevalent among very prejudiced people. Racial prejudice and ethnocentrism were linked to the extrinsic religious outlook in which church membership was based on allegiance to a powerful, socially approved "in-group." Church members with the interiorized religious outlook believed in the religious ideals of their churches, and they did not tend to be significantly prejudiced or ethnocentric. I believe that the self-serving, power- and security-conscious extrinsic religious outlook appeared to be quite similar to Fromm's notion of the authoritarian religious experience. The intrinsic religious outlook seems to encompass Fromm's humanistic religious experience. The intrinsically religious were described in the research as more involved with the love of neighbor than power and security. They appeared to place a greater emphasis on helping others as a priority in their religious attitudes and were more tolerant of racial and religious differences among poeple. Allport developed a Religious Orientation Scale (ROS) to measure the degree of intrinsic versus extrinsic religious orientation after criticizing the previous instruments that had been devised to study religious outlook. Although the extent of research on religious variables was limited up to that time, the research consistently had shown that there was no real difference in the fear of death among various religious denominations. Factor analytic studies and validation studies authenticated the use of the ROS and its general reliability and validity for research.

Research Findings: Religious Orientation and the Fear of Death

Experiments with the ROS supported Allport's hypothesis that the extrinsically motivated person uses religion to provide security, status, self-justification, and social approval. This finding made it seem even more likely that extrinsic religious affiliation captured the defensiveness, depression, and separation anxiety inherent in the neurotic fear of death. On the basis of Allport's division of religious outlook, the type of religious orientation was included as one of the three major variables in the research design of my 1973 study of the fear of death. Three factors were assessed in the study in relation to their effect on death anxiety: (1) religious versus lay groups; (2) intrinsic versus extrinsic religious orientation; and (3) purpose in life. The initial division of the three hundred subjects in the study was made on the basis of Allport's criteria for intrinsic versus extrinsic orientations on the ROS. One hundred and sixty of the three-hundred subjects met the test criteria for selection into intrinsic and extrinsic religious orientation groups and high and low purpose in life groups. Thus there were eighty religious subjects and eighty non-religious subjects whose death anxiety scores were organized according to the above experimental design. All of the subjects in the study were pursuing a bachelor's degree when tested and had completed from a minimum of two years to a maximum of three years of college credits. The religious subjects ranged in age from twenty to fifty-six years, and the non-religious female subjects ranged in age from nineteen to forty years. The mean age of the nuns was thirty-five; the mean age of the lay subjects was twenty-one years. A brief summary of some of the findings of the study will be reviewed to support the importance of religious orientations impact on death anxiety. The three hundred female college students had been administered the following psychological tests: The Death Anxiety Scale, the Purpose in Life Test, the Religious Orientation Survey, and the Social Desirability Scale. Only women were used as subjects because of the sex differences in death fears reported by the research studies on death attitudes. One hundred and fifty of the subjects were Roman Catholic nuns and one hundred and fifty were single female undergraduate students who, by their own report, were actively participating in the Catholic religion. All of these people volunteered for an 'attitude survey' of college students and listed their age, number of years of college completed, and number of years in the religious order or years of regular church attendance.

In an earlier unpublished study of Roman Catholic nuns, I found that intensity of religious participation did have a significant effect in lowering death anxiety. The study was designed to assess the interrelationship between the fear of death, purpose in life, and extrinsic versus intrinsic religious orientation.[9] Based on Frankl's supposition that existential purpose in life lowers fear of death, it was expected that its presence would vary with type of religious orientation. Based on Allport's research on religious orientation and Fromm's distinction between authoritarian and humanistic religious outlooks, it was expected that the intrinsically religious would have less fear of death than the extrinsically religious. Although the experimentation did not pursue the matter further, it was also speculated that the intrinsically would show less depression and less neurotic investment in religion.

The first two hypotheses drawn in the study stated that intrinsically religious subjects would have lower death anxiety than extrinsically religious subjects and would have a higher sense of purpose in life than extrinsically religious subjects. Generally, for most but not all of the subject groups, these hypotheses had to be rejected. Where there was a difference in death anxiety between intrinsically religious and extrinsically religious subjects, it was not as meaningful as the differences within the intrinsic and extrinsic groups. In light of the rejection of the second hypothesis, Frankl's concept of existential purpose or meaning in life could not be identified with intrinsic or extrinsic religious orientaion. Its rejection did, however, support Allport's notion that an extrinsic religious orientation constitutes a defense against anxiety or that, in motivational terms, it serves needs for security, status, and self-esteem. The study did not support Allport's contention that people with an intrinsic religious orientation would be less afraid of death than those with an extrinsic religious orientation. The rejection of Hypothesis One was consistent with the psychological and psychiatric literature on death anxiety and religion in which no consistent relationship between the two had been reported.

Hypothesis Three stated that "intrinsically religious people, with a high sense of purpose in life, would have lower death anxiety than intrinsically religious people who have a low purpose in life." Hypothesis Four stated that "extrinsically religious subjects with a low purpose in life would have a higher death anxiety than those with a high purpose in life." Both of these hypotheses were generally accepted in the study. Their acceptance suggested that purpose in life does play a crucial role in reducing the fear of death if the type of religious orientation is taken into account. Hypothesis Five stated that "Roman Catholic sisters who have an intrinsic religious orientation would not differ from intrinsically religious Roman Catholic women either in death anxiety or purpose in life."

Hypothesis Five was only partially accepted. The differences in death anxiety between intrinsically religious nuns and lay subjects were not significant for either high or low purpose in life groups. However, intrinsically religious nuns did have significantly higher purpose in life scores than intrinsically religious lay subjects. Hypothesis Five was drawn in light of Allport's contention that religious participation per se was not as meaningful a variable with respect to death anxiety as is type of religious orientation.

The intrinsically religious nuns did not differ from the intrinsically religious lay subjects in death anxiety, nor were the formers' length of time in a religious order a significant factor. The significant correlation between length of time in the religious life and purpose in life was congruent with the finding that intrinsically religious nuns had significantly higher purpose in life scores than intrinsically religious lay subjects. This latter finding, however, was considered to be an artifact of the age differences between religious and lay groups. On the basis of these results, little could be inferred about the existence of a general relationship between length of time in a religious community and extrinsic religious orientation.

One note of caution in interpreting these results is that extrinsic and intrinsic religious orientation seemed to represent entirely different personality traits rather than the extremes of a unidimensional trait. Expected differences between intrinsically religious and extrinsically religious subjects were not found for either death anxiety or purpose in life. The contention that there would be a relationship between intrinsic religion and low fear of death, which I based on the work of Fromm and Allport, was not supported. The contention that intrinsic religion would be related to high purpose in life was not supported either. The results indicated an interesting relationship between length of time of membership in a religious order, age, and extrinsic religious orientation. However, hypotheses drawn on the basis of Frankl's point of view were generally verified and support was provided for his theory. High purpose in life subjects had less death anxiety than low purpose in life subjects for intrinsically religious nuns. For extrinsically religious lay subjects, the differences were in the expected direction, but the results were not significant. Intrinsically religious nuns were not found to differ in death anxiety from intrinsically religious lay subjects. After statistical adjustments were made for the subjects' age differences, intrinsically religious nuns did not have significantly higher purpose in life scores than intrinsically religious lay subjects.

Within both the intrinsic and extrinsic groups, there was a direct correlation between degree of death anxiety and lack of purpose in life. This particular finding supported the speculation that religion is only one of many possible lines of defense against the neurotic's fear of death. Within religious groups' psychological variables are more crucial to the degree of death anxiety than differences between religious groups.

Summary

Beginning with primitive man's need for protection from natural forces, religion has supplied multileveled opportunities for the securing of a firm foothold against death anxiety. Freud speculated about primitive man's dependence on the father to lower the fear of death. Since his contributions, investigators have stressed the primary roles of introjection and unconscious communication in religious worship and dogma. To the extent that the defensive aspect of religious commitment motivates the individual's faith and observances, religion has been described as being more neurotic than genuine. The repetition of prayers and participation in church or synagogue services leave the participant with a subjective feeling of good. The person who suffers from the fear of death complex to a neurotic degree thereby gains relief from depression and anxiety over separation and "aloneness." The worshipper's internal reunion with God through spiritual communication is reinforced in this endeavor by the group process. Freud's early definition of religion emphasized the defensive projection of the infantile relationship to the father. The group process inherent in religious services and the internal struggle for communication with God mutually reinforce each other. The worshippers are placed in a dependent or subservient position to the authority, whether priest, rabbi, or teacher in one type of arrangement. The repetition of the parental relationship may counter early childhood feelings of helplessness in the face of death anxiety. Vocalized prayers, religious gestures, the singing of hymns, and the playing of liturgical music add to these effects by uniting the group in a solidarity of purpose. The variable of type of religious orientation has been taken into account in relation to death anxiety. It had been hypothesized that the more dogmatic and authoritarian the religion, the greater is the potential use of the religious participation as the means of coping with the fear of death complex. The prevalence of resurrection, second birth, and reunion themes have been cited as an indication of the validity of these claims.

Freud's religious theories were briefly summarized and compared with several tenets in the writings of William James and Erich Fromm. Freud stressed the infantile relationship to the father and the Oedipal complex in his outline of religion from totemism to monotheism. Fromm saw man's early helplessness as the source of religion. He defined neurosis as the adult's lack of autonomy and capitulation to the anxiety and helplessness of childhood. Fromm's distinction between authoritarian versus humanistic religion remains a key point in the understanding how religious strategies counter death anxiety. Allport's distinction between intrinsic versus extrinsic type of religions gave the appearance of covering similar theoretical ground. The experimental design that assessed some of these theoretical conceptions was based on Frankl's notion of the centrality of having a purpose in life. Part of the rationale for these assumptions was that an inner-directed, humanitarian, and more religious outlook would be less involved with death anxiety. It seemed logical that an intrinsic outlook would reflect greater security against the threat of the loss of the self.

The concept of extrinsic versus intrinsic religious orientation was the particular dimension of religion that was studied experimentally in relation to death anxiety. There seemed to be a logical relationship between intrinsic orientation and a high purpose in life. None of these interrelationships had been previously empirically tested. In spite of the limitations of the above study, it did provide definitive support for the notion that purpose in life is intimately related to handling the reality of oncoming death. One of the most productive topics for future research would be the more direct assessment of depression in relation to all types of religious experience. Not all intrinsically religious or humanistically religious people fear death. Those people with an intrinsic or humanistic type of religious attitude who are depressed should also show a high fear of death. This effect would be expected to be based on the acceptance of Hypotheses Three and Four in the study. The diverse body of research and clinical evidence on the interrelationship between death fears, depression, and separation anxiety needs to be studied further in relation to religion. The religious neurotic who is terrified of death seems not to have achieved in old age what Erikson has called "integrity," as opposed to despair at life's missed opportunities.

The research suggested that there are many deep-seated and not necessarly negative reasons for the involvement in religion. The mystery of death compels, even if life is thought of as eternal and an afterlife is believed to be certain. The human mixture of body and soul raises questions about the meaning of salvation and the terror of death. Since the prehistorical totem worship described by Freud, religious rituals have provided a definite medium for dismissing threats to the self. If death is grasped as nothingness or ceasing to exist, then its terror in the modern person may not be mitigated even by the most sincere religious beliefs or commitment to humanistic religious practices. When religious experience fails to provide a person with a solution to the fear of death, depression and a conscious fear of death may result. Religious commitment thus adds a new level of meaning to the child's fear of the world and the neurotic's fear of the loss of the self.

Death Anxiety In Neurosis and Psychotherapy

CHAPTER SIX

Children and the Fear of Death

Separation, Depression, and Cognition in Children's Death Attitudes

Children's death fears arise at the point of intersection between two psychological vectors: the fear of death-depression-separation anxiety conflicts and the phase specific developmental tasks of childhood. When anxiety is experienced by a child in accomplishing developmental tasks, it may activate the fear of death, and, conversely, the arousal of death anxiety interferes with the mastery of developmental tasks. A brief review of psychoanalytic theory will provide the rationale for this assertion.

In infancy, death is initially sensed by the child in nonverbal, non-cognitive terms as either the equivalent of separation from the mother or of psychic engulfment by her. The fear of death and depression both have their origin during the first year of life in what Mahler called the "normal symbiosis." The initial maternal role in monitoring and effecting the infant's mood in the symbiotic union can account for the early genesis of depression. The exact process by which the fear of death becomes interwoven with separation anxiety and depression has been sketched in greater detail in earlier chapters. The key point in regard to later developmental problems concerns the foundation of the self in the first year, along with the potential for separation anxiety and depressed moods. Death anxiety persists with the emergence of the self and the fear of the loss of the self underlies many aspects of children's developmental problems.

The emergence of the self from the symbiotic union does not fully protect the child from psychological threats. According to object relations and classical psychoanalytic theory, this infantile vulnerability is more complicated than the lack of the establishment of "basic trust." The differentiation of self from other and the origin of early patterns of defense both imply the importance of the mother's role in the development of the child's ego and self. Melanie Klein's theories and Edith Jacobson's contributions on infancy formulated the early origins of the self and depression from the object relations point of view. Klein's notion of the infantile depressive position held that the child's fear of his own aggressive and hostile impulses threatens him with the loss of the object, which creates a predisposition for depression. On the basis of Mahler's infancy research and Spitz's findings, it was argued in an earlier chapter that classical psychoanalytic theory had oversimplified the explanation of death anxiety. Death anxiety was attributed in classical theory to anal events, castration anxiety, and the lack of object constancy. The infant's symbiotic dependence on the mother for security and emotional survival determines an inherent interrelationship between separation problems, depression, and ambivalence about death that evolves into death anxiety. This dependency on the mother persists beyond the development of object constancy. The connections between dependence, depression, and separation anxiety have been shown to persist as a consistent psychodynamic pattern in children's adjustment. A potential for depression and separation anxiety persists as an important psychodynamic factor in children's unconscious fears and wishes about death throughout childhood.

The infant's conflicting wish to devour mother and fear of being devoured by her corresponds to the wish and fear of merger with her. The young child's depression and fear of the loss of the self are therefore expressed primarily in oral terms. Threats to the self are handled by either the mother or child as they arise in the course of what Mahler termed "rapproachment." In summary, the origins of infantile death fears have been traced in psychoanalytic theory to the infant's total helplessness and state of normal psychological symbiosis with the mother. Development of "security" in the protective warmth of the mother's presence allows for the continuance in the child of a sense of magical control and shared omnipotent power with the mother. Melanie Klein described the fear of death as having arisen from the infant's ambivalence toward the mother and cannibalistic fantasies toward her. The early origin of the fear of death can be more easily understood as a result of the child's helplessness, complete dependency and oneness with the mother. The remnants of infantile omnipotence and realistic trust in the parents enable the child to later defend against anxiety in general and death anxiety in particular. Although it continues its unconscious influence on the personality of the developing child, death anxiety can become conscious at times or at least revealed in dreams. The development of the child's depressive moods in relation to separation-individuation phenomena has been noted by the developmentalists, and this finding can be understood with greater clarity than Klein's concept of a universal "infantile depressive position." Given the infantile connection between separation from mother, death anxiety, and a potential for depression, psychoanalytic theory suggests the possibility of their continued influence on a variety of developmental problems. Inherent in Sullivan's developmental schema, Freud's psychosexual development, and Erikson's psychosocial epigenesis lie intrapsychic and psychosocial tasks that may all evoke and become intertwined with the child's death fears. Although the psychological tasks of these stages are distinct, the child's conflicts in the pursuit of emotional growth retain ubiquitous expressions of the fear of death.

For example, the appealing charm of the principal character in *The Adventures of Tom Sawyer* fails to obscure the impact of the fear of death complex in the preadolescent period. Tom Sawyer's behavior reflected the interconnecting themes of separation anxiety and death anxiety in Mark Twain's fictional account of a preadolescent growth period. In the narrative, Tom's mischievousness greatly annoyed his Aunt Polly. When her patience gave out, she unjustly accused Tom of breaking a sugar bowl, and then slapped him out of anger. Her failure to apologize for this action hurt Tom deeply. The insensitivity triggered off in him the wish for revenge and fantasies about his own death. He particularly imagined the effect that its discovery would have on his aunt. Tom fantasized the recovery of his dead body in the river and her sorrow and guilt for having treated him so badly. Tom went to the nearby river in the midst of one of these depressions and almost consciously wished to drown. The drowning expressed the hope that Aunt Polly would then finally give him the love he had been denied. Later in the narrative, Tom took pleasure in his unrequited yearning for Becky Thatcher. The suffering gave rise to the exquisite fantasy that he might die under Becky's window just to have his beloved discover his dead body. This motherless boy's feelings of deprivation and need for nurturance combined with thoughts about death throughout his preadolescent period. He alternately feared death at the hands of Indian Joe or the river and wished for it as a means of rescue and emotional redemption. Tom and Huck Finn's plan to run away from home with their friend Joe Harper to live the life of river pirates represented the acting out of three elements: depression, conflicting feelings about separation from Aunt Polly, and the wish for reunion with an idealized mother. Tom persuaded Huck to join in his fantasies by running away to play-act the life of a river pirate. The lost boys were presumed to have drowned until they showed up at their own funeral service, where they were joyously embraced by their incredulous families. Tom's needs for nurturance, revenge, and for exploration and adventure all multidetermined the acting out of his suicidal fantasy and its undoing through the reunion with his loved ones. The preadolescent need for closeness with a best friend and the corresponding need for adventure and exploration of the environment became integrated here with the fear of death complex. Tom's fantasies typify the latency-age and preadolescent child's problems with psychological separation and its association with death. His fantasy about running away to be reunited with a good parent clearly illustrates the connections between separation anxiety, depression, and ambivalence about death.

In the character of Tom Sawyer, a lack of self-esteem and feelings of worthlessness were present in his attitudes about death to such an extent that death was fully equated with separation and the loss of love. Through Mark Twain's clearest prose Tom spoke of the conviction that he was a friendless, inadequate boy whom no one loved. Driven from his family by a perception of their callous indifference, Tom resigned himself to death only to become jubilant at his family's remorse and self-blame when they thought he had drowned. Tom initially experienced gloom and despair in terms of abandonment and rejection by his aunt. The soliloquies about his mistreatment and disappointment elucidated the contrasting wish for and fears of death. They illustrated the origins of death fears in the child's anxious anticipation of separation and the loss of love. Tom's fantasy about secretly attending his own funeral stemmed from a wish for revenge and a longing to observe his survivors confess their wrong doing. Moreover, it gratified the wish that at long last they would genuinely love him as he deserved.

The fantasy directly paralleled the suicidal child's unconscious wish for reunion with a truly loving, good parent through death. The risking of his life on the river and in caves documented the intensity of Tom's need for love and merger with a good, protecting parent. The fact that he would go to such lengths in trying to resolve his depression and injured narcissism reflects the potential for self-destructive behavior in depressed children and adolescents. The kind of fantasies Tom exhibited are commonplace in suicidal children who are trying to overcome their depression and separation fears. Even his innermost secret-fantasy identification of himself as a pirate—"The Black Avenger of the Spanish Main"—is typical of latency-age and slightly older children. Death was both a punishment for his mischievousness and wrongdoings and the unconscious solution to the dilemma of his depression and lost self-esteem.

Children's fears of death begin as a formless, undifferentiated anxiety and later take on specific dimensions as the fear of the dark, monsters, ghosts, and burglars. The descriptive studies of children's death fears have shed light on a variety of the contributing psychodynamic factors, which range from a fear of aggressive, hostile impulses to the aforementioned loss of love and narcissism. The child's understanding of death also varies with the developmental stage and the level of cognitive growth. The psychodynamic meanings of death attitudes in children differ with their developmental status. The ways in which death fears emerge in adjustment problems can present complex issues in treatment for the child clinician. Developmental researchers who have closely examined young children's attitudes toward death have reported two crucial steps in the early process of understanding death. First, the child attains the notion of the irreversibility of death; and second, the child equates death with separation and loss of love. Gesell found a consistent pattern of the child's struggle with these issues in coping with the death of pets, or animals, upon first seeing a dead body, and in learning of the death of someone familiar.[1] Schilder and Wexler, in one of the earliest studies in this area, reported that hospitalized children viewed death consistently as either a deprivation and loss or a sadistic attack that would be directed against them.[2]

Psychodynamic issues aside, the certainty of death arouses anxiety in children in different ways, depending upon the child's level of conceptual understanding. Nagy found that it is only at around age nine or ten that the child conceptualizes death as the final irreversible end to life, and as an actual experience that the body undergoes.[3] Death to the ten-year-old may, therefore, be no less frightening than to the younger child; it is just comprehended and symbolized differently. The idea of death is often equivalent to disappearance or departure in young children. Anthony stressed the close association in children between death, separation, and loneliness. After examining 117 normal children's Stanford Binet tests and other protocols, she concluded that punishment and death were readily seen by the children as the consequence of their aggression. In describing children's specific reactions to death, she found that death was often seen as both a sorrowful separation and as the feared consequence of the child's hostility.[4] Originally, researchers believed that children gradually came to an awareness of their own death by association to the death of older people. At that time, the child's understanding of death had not yet been assessed in terms of the Piagetian theory of mental development.

Age Changes and Death Anxiety

Parallels have been found between Nagy's stages of the child's understanding of death and Piaget's developmental studies of cognitive growth in animistic thinking. Parental explanations about death and attempts to assuage the child's anxiety may have little effect if the efforts do not reach the child's cognitive level. The child's intelligence, abstraction ability, and level of cognitive skills effects his death-related attitudes, bas does his personal experiences with death.

As far back as 1896, Scott observed a variability in death fears during childhood with a peak in the fears durirg early and middle adolescence.[5] The research findings on age differences in healthy children's death anxiety are inconsistent. Heightened emotional responsiveness to death attitudes after puberty has been shown to coincide with the adolescent's philosophical religious interests and altruistic concerns about reforming society. These heightened death fears mark the reemergence of the fear of death complex as a reflection of the adolescent "growth spurt" of ego functioning. The separation-individuation processes of childhood are reexperienced by the adolescent in the context of wider opportunities for interpersonal relationships. Identity formation coincides with further psychological separation from the parents. The anxiety and depression that accompanies the process of separation from the internalized parents catapults some adolescents into the Scylla and Charybdis of simultaneous fears of further separation and further fusion with the parents. The attempts at expanding the self and forming an autonomous identity may again bring forth the adolescent's fear of the loss of the self. The adolescent's heightened death fears could thus be interpreted as an age appropriate fear that accompanies individuation.

Young children's death concepts follow developmental stages that to some extent depend on the child's intelligence. It is particularly with the preadolescent and adolescent child that death anxiety intersects with the ego changes of the developmental stage. Peter Blor has described the ego changes and psychological growth as being at the center of the adolescent's emotional turmoil. The fear of death and its assoicated links with depression and separation anxiety complicate these growth processes. The adolescent's ability to conceptualize time and to foresee himself or herself as a continuous personality engaged in future experiences also influences the variability in death fears. Some of the inconsistency in the research literature arises from the inability of some adolescent subjects to structure remote future time and from the interplay of death anxiety with the adolescent's ego reorganizations.

In a retrospective investigation of death fears, Caprio interviewed a heterogeneous group of 100 adults with varying occupations, educations, religions, and socioeconomic status about their reaction to death during the prepubertal period.[6] He particularly asked for childhood impressions of funerals and reactions to the deaths of friends and relatives. For most of the subjects, death was associated with the fear of the dark, the blackness of mourning attire, and the darkness of night. Many of the people remembered the encounters with death as traumatic experiences contributing to a high level of anxiety about death that had persisted into adulthood. Some subjects had reported a fear of the dead mixed with such questions about what happens to the dead body as: "Where does it live?" and "What happens to the person in the body?" The fear of the possibility of the mother's death was a common experience that the subjects associated with the fear of their own death as children. The fear of death itself was directly or indirectly related to a great many neurotic symptoms in those children which stemmed from identification with the dead and their feelings of vulnerability and helplessness. The actual realization that one has to die comes as a serious blow to the omnipotence and narcissism of childhood. For those people in Caprio's study who had religious educations that emphasized hell and an afterlife, the fear of life after death compounded the already existing fear of death.

Death anxiety complements the infantile vision of the world as hostile and malevolent, according to Klein's formulation. The wish to kill the mother conflicts with the wish to be killed and eaten by her so as to be reincorporated with a more nurturing, better mother.[7] The projection onto the mother of the baby's own hateful feelings constitutes another part of the Kleinien view. By way of contrast, the fear of the loss of the child's self has been stressed in separation-individuation processes. The principal component of death anxiety comes from the equation of death with separation from the mother or surrender of the self to her.

Death in Children's Dreams and Fantasies

Louise Despert analyzed the dreams of two-to-five year-old children and found that the children's dreams contained frequent animal and human content in which the child was either pursued and chased or bitten and devoured.[8] Despert also found that the children identified the frightening attacking animal in the dreams with the otherwise benevolent parent. The content of such dreams presents sadistic and destructive attacks on the dreamer, who is often presented as a terrified helpless victim. When the young child experiences prolonged anxiety, the arousal of death anxiety is evident in fantasies or dreams, where it is experienced as the fear of the loss of the self. Its presence in even young children has been well documented, regardless of whether they have any clear notion of death. Extensive reports of investigations of preschool-age children's death attitudes, contributed by Lauretta Bender, confirmed the importance of oral fears and wishes in children's attitudes about death.[9] The child's oral wishes and fears can best be understood as object relational. Fantasies about being eaten express the child's feelings of helplessness and fear of loss of the self, which is equated with death. The sense of the mother's constancy develops only gradually, and this further reinforces the incidence of children's death fears. A sophisticated understanding of cause and effect relationships arises gradually in a child in a specific developmental sequence, and a child's death fantasies follow developmental patterns. From six-to-ten, the school-aged child dreams more frequently of personal activity, as Maruice Green has noted. The representation of the depicted self in the child's dream can be engaged in pleasant activity or psychological conflict. With the older child, dream language increasingly symbolizes the threats to the child's self and the family involvement in the child's insecurity. The loss of the child's grandiosity can account for a further affront to self-esteem when the concept of death does become recognized as permanent and inevitable. The child's need for protection from feelings of helplessness and vulnerability increases his need of the parents. The more developed the child's inner resources, the less his dreams may reflect absolute reliance on parental protection. Separation anxiety, and the fear of death loom again as greater threats in children's fantasies and dream language as these children's character defenses falter.

Analysis of pre-school and young school-age children's fantasies has consistently revealed contents of being torn apart and eaten, together with fears of witches, ghosts, and monsters. Latency-age children's anxiety dreams often contain Oedipal themes. Older children dream more about people and less about animals or fantasy characters. Children's dreams and fantasies provide the mechanisms for mastery of death fears as they unfold in a variety of developmental contexts. The child acquires the means to conquer fears of being destroyed and devoured through identification, and then later more independent defense operations. On an object relations level, the older child begins to overcome death anxiety by individuation and self-reliance.

The popularity of the story "Hansel and Gretel" has already been mentioned as an illustration of children's unconscious fears of being eaten by the bad witch-mother who puts small, helpless children into an oven and then cooks them. "Hansel and Gretel" solidifies the interconnected aspects of depression and separation anxiety as dimensions of children's fear of death. In this fairy tale, the story content contrasts the symbolism of being eaten with the fear of being eaten or dying. Throughout literature and mythology, the witch has symbolized the bad mother as often as the oven has symbolized the mother's womb. Thus, children of Hansel and Gretel's age use play and fantasy to come to grips with their own conflicting wishes to be eaten or reincorporated into the mother and to retain the self in autonomous actions. Fears of death arise at those points in development at which separation experiences become of central importance to the child. It seems to me that this is the case whether the child faces external social separations or internal psychic separations. Thus weaning, toilet training, absence from home, school attendance, the birth of siblings, and all of the major turning points in development reaffirm the child's separateness from his parents and bring with them the potential for death anxiety and depression.

For instance what might typically happen to a vulnerable toddler named Johnny in the preschool years is that longer periods of separation from mother might bring mixed feelings of pleasure over new-found independence and feelings of sadness or anxiety. The anxiety Johnny experiences then increases the need for mother's protection from further anxiety, and the conflict over separation from his mother intensifies. Given a modicum of "basic insecurity," Johnny might grow fearful and depressed as he experiences these conflicting feelings and needs toward his mother. While continuing to need the good, protective, nurturing mother, he may grow angry at his mother because of his anticipated discomfort or fear of abandonment. Unconsciously, he might fear that either he or his mother might be harmed, and his fear of death may come closer to consciousness. This disquieting state of affairs reawakens Johnny's fundamental fear of death, the origins of which were in infancy. A depressive reaction to the threat of separation may be further complicated by the corollary unconscious conflict stemming from the wish to kill this "bad" mother and the wish to be killed, eaten, and reincorporated by the "good" one. The anger of this child and his anticipation of his mother's negative reactions to him are both projected out onto the environment, where they may take the form of monsters, ghosts, robbers, or later the less specific form of anxiety attacks at school. Johnny's anxiety symptoms and pleading to be kept home might alternate with psychosomatic complaints of stomachaches and pains or generalized malaise when school time appraoches. If this anxiety reaction blossoms into a full-blown phobia, a psychic impasse is reached with a displacement of the conflicts onto the school as the new experience. School attendance, for example, signals not only the unconscious fear of abandonment by mother but also the prospect of death to either the mother or the child.

The reassurance of mother's presence at school may reduce the phobic child's anxiety over separation to some extent. However, the crux of the developmental task remains the child's disassociating daily separations at school from his death fears. The convergence of these factors in the school phobia does not represent the only possible course of death anxiety's appearance during early childhood. Each developmental milestone from toilet training to the birth of siblings presents opportunities for its occurrence.

As the fear of death does emerge in relation to separation and developmental tasks, it continues to be manifest in children's dreams and fantasies. As a two- or three-year-old who had just become acquainted with a newborn sibling, Johnny experienced nightmares about being chased and eaten by menacing lions and tigers as well as a regression in toilet training and an inability to be alone at night. Even if there is some symbolic connection between a child's fear of loss of identity and the loss of feces in toileting (or the fear of disappearing down the drain in the tub like the bath water), the larger meaning of the child's anxiety lies in the conflict about separation-individuation. For example, gaining control of the stool or playing with the bath water independent of mother's attention demands a certain amount of maturation, mastery, and autonomy. Such mastery presupposes some separation and break in the fusion with mother.

The three-year-old Johnny's anxiety dream about being eaten by a lion reflected the same developmental issues in his school phobia at age five. There doesn't seem to be a specific developmental stage at which the child formally overcomes these conflicts as much as there is a revitalization of the tripartite fear of death complex throughout all stages of development. The manifest dream content of the hungry lion typically disclosed three levels of meaning in the child's dreams: First, the child's own aggressive impulses; second, latent fears of being devoured by an angry parent; and third, a conflict between underlying fears of being eaten and wishes about being eaten that correlate with the wish for merger and fusion. Many of the anxiety dreams and nightmares of young children present these components simultaneously with the specific psychodynamic and affective data of the latent content. The central element at issue in the investigation of the above anxiety dream consisted of unraveling the psychodynamic pattern woven by the day's residue from the family events and the inner psychic stimuli for Johnny's dream. By no means am I suggesting that there is a universal interpretation for all children's dreams. I am suggesting that all three of the elements of death anxiety may be present simultaneously in dreams at the deepest level of meaning, supraordinate to the instinctual conflicts or age-appropriate types of anxiety and family data. In other words, children's dreams depict the struggle of the self for individuation and survival. Depression and death fears are as common in young children's dreams as in older children's in spite of the differences in the form of their symbolic expression.

Children's dreams disclose a magnitude of conflictual content that runs parallel to the fear of death complex as it touches on particular developmental problems. One might consider Johnny's dreams as reflections of the normal viscissitudes of young children's growth via increased mastery, psychomotor maturation, and more sophisticated adaptive ego functioning. It therefore becomes possible to pinpoint the emergence of death anxiety in his dreams when, at different ages, it manifested itself as separation anxiety. The dream about being attacked by the lion is a frequent type of anxiety dream among two-and-a-half- to three-and-a-half-year-olds. At age five, Johnny had a nightmare about being captured by a monster and forced to eat poison, after which he was chased by a Draculalike figure. At ages seven and eight, Oedipal material was increasingly superimposed upon the underlying death anxiety in Johnny's dreams. At eight, he had a series of dreams about ambiguous fierce-looking ghosts and robbers who invaded his room at night and threatened to harm and stab him. The ghosts then carried Johnny off to await rescue by heroic parent figures. Whereas classical theory might have accounted for such dreams as displaced castration anxiety, homosexual fears, or transformations of aggression and rage, the alternative point of view would pursue the less explicit, more elusive developmental meanings implicit in the child's imagery and experience.

It would not be likely that the bloodthirsty Dracula or ferocious burgler in Johnny's dreams simply stand for angry, devouring mother or punishing, castrating, seductive father. It would more likely symbolize both sides of the conflicting wishes and fears of being eaten and incorporated into the parent as a prelude to symbioticlike merger. Here again, death could be understood as the unconscious equivalent of either separation and abandonment or fusion and engulfment. At age eight, Johnny dreamed of drowning in a lake. He reported anxiety in the dream while struggling to get free of the twisted debris on the lake bottom before calling to a lifeguard for help. At age nine, Johnny dreamed of the invasion of his family home by werewolves that threatened to kill his mother, father, and siblings. A great deal of anxiety was experienced by him in trying to fight off these werewolves and to shoot them before they would kill his family. Upon waking from this dream, Johnny remembered feeling quite frightened that something might, in fact, happen to his family but not that they would be eaten by a werewolf. His associations to the dream were that they might get sick and die or "go away on a trip and never return." These associative links to the dream captured the essential relationships of death anxiety to the separation-individuation dilemma he faced at that particular time, the onset of his preadolescent period. At age eleven and a half, Johnny had a series of dreams about being lost in a haunted house. There, ghosts labored to trick him into an isolated part of the house where they could close all the doors and keep him captive. This dream occurred at a time when he was spending more and more time at the homes of his peers and engaging in a power struggle with his parents about how far they would let him travel from home.

The point I am making here concerns the conceptualization of the self of the dreamer and the conceptualization of death in separation-individuation processes. The development of the child's sense of self grows out of the infantile experience of self as helpless and totally dependent on mother. The growth of the self and associated self-directed feelings are fostered not simply by instinctual discharge and control but by the enhancing, nutritive attention and love of the mother. Whatever the specific dynamic meanings, the child's dreams depict statements about the self. The above dream fragments illustrate the child's vacillation between depressed helplessness and active struggling with separation anxiety and the fear of the loss of the self.

Death Anxiety, Defenses, and Fantasy

The typical course of death anxiety in childhood dreams and fantasies starts with the terror of animals and monsters and progresses to part-animal part-human monsters, to robbers, ghosts, and burglars. As the psychic changes occur, the dreaming child attempts a shift in the identification processes and abilities to conceptualize the self and represent it symbolically. The hungry lion that chased Johnny in the dream at age three disclosed anxiety about death and separation similar to that present in the later dreams about burglars. The werewolves that threatened to kill Johnny's family, and the ghosts who entrapped him in the haunted house, symbolized his anxiety about separation and death. The death anxiety he experienced arose from three sources: (1) conflicting wishes to destroy his family or be destroyed by them; (2) the fear of punishment for his instinctual life; (3) the fear of abandonment because of autonomous functioning. The reality dilemma he faced at the time of the later dream was whether to ride his bicycle further away from the parental home or to remain close by, safely within parental reach. Here again in the latent symbolism of Johnny's dream language, death anxiety was equated with separation and abandonment. The helpless childhood self was originally threatened with being destroyed by half-human avenging creatures. The subsequent ghosts that kept him captive emerged from his ambivalence about separation and from his attempts to master his own helplessness in relation to the introjected parents. The child in the dream who was stuck under water, fixed to the river-bed debris awaiting a lifeguard's rescue, assumes a markedly different view of the self from the one who attempts to foil robbers who invade his family home. The self of the dreamer represented in the context of this dream language achieves definition through activity and the struggle for individuation. The conceptualization of self in the above dreams varies from one of a helpless, troubled victim to an active combatant and militant adversary of the frightening devouring adult figures. The helplessness versus the resourcefulness and adaptability of the child does not vary in distinct reversible stages but in a rather circuitous route. The child's ego strength depends on his subjectively experienced strengths as a separate entity in relation to the influence of the powerful symbiotic partner. By the same token, the boy's differentiation and victory over death anxiety could not be defined simply as one of impulse mastery or drive regulation. It involved a much more active struggle of adaptation to the backward and forward juxtapositon of "embeddedness" in the parental image versus individuation and mastery. Passivity and terror alternated with active attempts at defense and conflict resolution through a new emergence of self. Death denotes defeat of the autonomous self and a regression to the symbiotic union in syncopation with the dreamer's fears and wishes about autonomy.

The construct of death anxiety, therefore, assumes a much greater priority of meaning than simply the fear of rage or the explosion of murderous rage at the parents. The developmental tasks Johnny grappled with differed at each of the ages when the dreams were reported. The motivational intent of the dreamer's symbolism was in part to conquer the fear of death throughout all the periods depicted in the dreams. The elements of depression in these dreams were provoked on two levels by the fears of abandonment and by the compelling helplessness of the dreamer in relation to the power of the internalized parent. The stark terror of destruction of the self in the dream symbolism was permeated by contrasting moments of resourceful adaptation and surrender to death. The inconsistency of denouement marked the vascillating power of the self as reflected in Johnny's variability of adaptive functioning. In collective longitudinal form, the dreams, therefore, assume a forceful, metaphoric strength. They also document the reality of death anxiety in children as a developmental phenomenon.

The appeal of witches, monsters, werewolves, and especially Dracula and Frankenstein continues to be enormous for children who need to identify with the aggressor. Their mixture of human and animal qualities, like the superhuman strength or powers of superheroes, elicits a strong fascination in children along with squeals of laughter that cover manageable terror. By means of identification with the aggressor and victim, the child can imagine being a powerful adult in fantasy. Even if it is only at the expense of being killed and eaten by a bad parent the child is less afraid of death. The fear of death becomes more manageable if resolution is sought through fantasy and play that the child controls. The equation of death fears with separation and depression would be expected to get more tenuous with the mere secure self that has a better developed sense of competency and a positive investment in autonomy. The appeal and fear of being killed by the evil Count Dracula or overpowered by the brute strength of Frankenstein would then lessen in fantasy. The permanence of the child's self-representation and healthy individuation should lessen the child's fear of the loss of the self in developmental problems. The self that is experienced with greater frequency as stable, separate, and competent is more resourceful in handling developmental tasks. A corollary point which has not been sufficiently emphasized in developmental research, concerns the mother's role in the formation and encouragement of specific patterns of defense in children. Projection, denial, reaction formation, and so on are not totally dependent on cognitive growth or a developmental timetable, as Anna Freud has said. The mother clearly monitors the child's adaptation to his own defenses. The mother consciously or unconsciously molds the precursors of the childs character. She accomplishes this by monitoring harmful stimuli, providing a feedback system, and by encouraging the child's autonomous use of defenses. (Bateson's research on the double bind with schizophrenogenic mothers and Sullivan's essays about parental influence on the childhood of schizophrenics and obsessionals especially typify this kind of approach.) The mother's influence on the patterning of the child's ego functioning is a culturally bound and normal development occurrence. The role of the maternal influence on early childhood defensive functioning has recently been granted greater attention. The mother's ambivalence about separation-individuation and conflicting attitudes about the borderline child's development of autonomous ego functioning have been observed by a number of authors. Erikson's famous study of the trait of generosity among Sioux indians, in his *Childhood and Society*, exemplified cultural influence on early characterological trends.

The extent of oral aggression and the fear of being devoured is considerable in normal and disturbed children's fantasy productions. Despert noted its frequency in two-year-old's dreams about being devoured, and Rosalind Gould reported its frequency in an extensive longitudinal study of children's fantasies.[10] It seemed particularly prevalent among four-year-olds in her sample of three- four- and five-year-old urban children attending nursery school. An observation of fantasy play and the thematic apperception test protocols of the sample's latency-age and young adolescent children showed the prevalence of these themes. Some science fiction and monster movies also employ threats of imminent death by having devourment as the central theme. There is unquestionably a developmental factor inherent in a child's ability to attach feelings to and clearly define thoughts about death. The research confirms the prevalence in fantasy of the child's death fears even if they are placed against a richer, detailed ground of imaginative products.

A certain characteristic style occurs in the unfolding of the child's ways of coping with death anxiety, aggression, and fantasy. Gould found that as early as age four, some children had a clear preferential pattern in the defensive identifications within the content of their fantasies. They varied from identification with the aggressor to identification with the victim to identification with the powerful adult rescuer. The children also varied in the complexity of their anxiety-aggression imagery and in the mode of expressing aggression within their fantasy. Anna Freud's great contribution to this area lies in her detailed study of the child's use of identification in fantasy. She observed its development as a principal mechanism in coping with fears and phobias. Adaptation to the fear of aggression, and to the child's own aggressive impulses through fantasy and play, by no means signals any pathological disturbance. The present evidence suggests, in fact, that the absence of these defensive identifications masks the onset of difficulty in the control of aggression, often because of the absence of appropriate parental modeling.[11]

The helplessness of a child in relation to the physical size and strength of the parent compounds the emergence of the young child's self as autonomous in both physical and emotional tasks. In light of the economy of the child's psychic resources, and the adhesion of death anxiety and depression to separation experiences, the task of individuation at various milestones in psychological development almost achieves the status of a heroic conquest. Ulysses' dogged persistence provides a telling metaphor for the child's eventual victory in accomplishing the necessary psychological tasks of individuation. The child grows in relation to significant others in spite of the emotional reliance on the parents and unconscious death fears.

Death Fears and Development

Children's conscious fantasies disclose the same three dimensions of death anxiety as manifested in the unconscious symbolism of their dream language. The adult's perception of the child's anxiety about death may be blurred by its appearance in developmental problems or diverted by the particular child's unique characteristic manner of coping with anxiety. The pediatrician, for example, might be able to observe stylistic and temperamental differences in accounting for the two-year-old's crying and temper tantrums: They might represent an explicit attempt at spite or retaliation against frustrating parents who withold some pleasure; or they might indicate characteristic moodiness arising from the earliest pattern of basic mood formation or from physical discomfort in organic distress; and they might also arise from the basis of underlying insecurity and anxiety in relation to the parents. Johnny's dreams illustrated that depression and "self"-reliance fluctuate as a function of the mutual fears of separation and death. When the fear of the loss of the self is uncovered in a child's anxiety, either by parents or a child therapist, its significance after lies in its relation to depression and separation-individuation. It is most clearly understood by a translation into the various developmental problems that evoke its appearance.

It has been suggested that the interaction of the three-dimensional fear of death complex with the particular demands of a developmental

stage influences the form of a child's symptoms. For example, Tom Sawyer's unresolved depression was complemented by his fantasies at a
point in the preadolescent period when individuation implied the need
for best friends to share in adventures. The acting out of his depression
and separation conflicts involved an attempted neurotic resolution of this
boy's problems. His behavior and fantasies concomitantly provided a
means for satisfying some of the specific psychological needs of that
stage of development. The specific content of the symbolism in Johnny's
dreams also varied at different ages while retaining the same formal elements of the implied struggle for individuation and intrapsychic relationship with the parents.

The adherence of the dimensions of death anxiety to particular developmental problems provides a framework for investigating adjustment
difficulties in childhood. Death anxiety encountered in mastering developmental tasks occurs in the context of family relationships. Temperamental differences among normal infants have been noted from the first
few weeks in life in terms of wake-sleep cycles, appetite and feeding, general responsiveness, and activity level. Difficult, cranky babies with inconsistent metabolic cycles create more difficult demands for parents.
They can initially be less of a joy if this discomfort engenders anxiety
and depression in the mother. The infant depends on the mother for the
establishment of the sleep cycle, feeding, comfort, and being changed.
Mahler has observed that part of the mother's psychological role in the
symbiotic union with the baby involves providing an emotional bond
and psychic mirror for the child. Developmental researchers have documented the mother's effect on development of the child's thinking, the
child's recognition of self, his awareness of bodily functions, and his impulse mastery. A key maternal function consists of monitoring and regulating the infant's biologic mood and the precursors of affective states.
Because of temperamental differences and psychological factors, the
mothering parent will be inconsistent in what is communicated to the
child about the control of bodily functions and the mastery of psychological tasks that evoke separation anxiety. Any developmental stage carries
with it psychological communications to the child about the biological
self, the interpersonal self, and the degree of dependence-independence
involved in the interaction with the parent. Judith Kestenberg has stated
that the toddler often gets mother to go to the bathroom more often than
necessary. The toddler uses feces as a means of undoing separation and
wooing the mother back after a period of independent exploration.[12] The
achievement of bladder and bowel control assumes an importance
greater than that of being the ego's first instance of control over id impulses. In the family atmosphere, subtle interpersonal communications
about the child may foster feelings about mastery and autonomy. Positive self-regard or feelings of contentment versus anxiety are connected
with the child's experience of bowel and bladder control. The child's experience of self reflects the mother's feedback and reinforcement in their
dialogue. Sullivan pointed out the disabling effect of anxiety in the self

and that the quality of the dialogue influences the course of all of the early phases of development.

Feelings emerge more fully in association with the baby's general growing sense of self-awareness. Affective experience or some anxiety, however gross or undifferentiated, exists as part of the psychological experience of impulse mastery in relation to the mother's attitude. As the child's self becomes even more fully differentiated from the mother during the second and third years, associative traces and "reflected appraisals" have already influenced the sense of self and attitude about the child's independent functioning. Toilet training and other landmarks are significant as statements about autonomy and object relations. It is not simply an associative learning utilized in the toddler's equating the self with lost feces. When this does occur, the one-and-a-half- to two-year-old might become fearful of the toilet or spiteful about bowel control and soils in opposition to parental wishes. Yet simple anality does not account for later death fears. The point here goes beyond the possible identification of particular defenses or the equation of the child's self with discarded feces. It rests on the emotional impact upon both mother and child of the youngster's exercise of self-control. Does the parent communicate anxiety, empathic concern or approval in relation to the child's acquisition of control over elimination and lapses into accidents? Even more important, what is the mother's emotional reaction to the child's exercise of autonomous control, independent of her influence? To the extent that negative emotions dominate the toilet-training experiences, the child learns to associate separation anxiety and depression with autonomous psychological functioning. The fear of the parents' disapproval and need for their support compounds the older child's developmental tasks. The early foundation of the interconnection between depression, separation anxiety, and death anxiety then becomes further reinforced by the emotional atmosphere of the parent-child interaction.

Death anxiety may intensify in preschool-age children when their anxiety about toilet-training experiences intersects with separation anxiety. An unconscious fantasy of merger with the parent serves to mitigate and deny the child's anxiety in the present moment. If mastery leads to withdrawal of mother's enthusiastic nurturing, then the childs' independence and psychological autonomy bring the unconscious threat of death via abandonment. The child's fear of death and the extinction of the self-representation becomes the unconscious stake in a situation where the bathroom and potty become a battleground. The child's experience of self in toilet training goes beyond the reduction of self-representations to feces and their equation with the body or penis. If the child's self-representations do become associated with the excreted feces, and then anxiety about toileting persists, death anxiety and separation fears may be reflected. The interplay of these psychodynamics in the interactional field between mother and child accounts for some of the anxiety of the child in toileting. The interpersonal communications in the childs' development of bowel and bladder control have two possible effects. They serve either to foster the child's psychological autonomy and maturation or to reinforce anxiety and the loss of the self. An interplay between the child's experience of self, his feelings, and self-representations can be hypothosized. The childs mastery of a task results in feelings about the self and the parents at all points of change in the biologically determined developmental timetable. The equation of death fears with dependency problems and depression has already been discussed in relation to phobias and school phobias in school-age children. The same three-part psychodynamic pattern of death anxiety can be ascertained in the context of children's feeding, sleeping problems, and anxiety about sexuality.

The interpretation of the legend of Prometheus provided a powerful metaphor for the child's conflicts about death and separation. It has been alleged that such fears intensify at points of resolution or mastery of developmental tasks. In the legend the vultures feeding on Prometheus' liver were interpreted as symbols for the child's fear of the loss of the self in the face of the persistent struggle for individuation. The Olympiad's celebration of the triumph of Promethean man therefore applauds an ebullient victory of life over death anxiety. It registers a dramatic purging of the child from the adult in all of us.

However, separation anxiety and ambivalence about autonomy in psychic functioning remain given in children's neurotic adjustment problems. Their symptomatic expression needs to be understood in terms of these possible links with the fear of death complex. This view contradicts the traditional psychoanalytic notion that neurotic character formation in children is earmarked by excessive reliance of a particular defense or by internalization of their conflicts over aggression and sexuality. Sexual and aggressive conflicts certainly constitute the dynamic content of neurotic symptom formation. The source of neurotic anxiety often arises from the developmental manifestations of separation problems and the fears of the loss of the self. The child's character structure is more flexible and subject to change than the adult's. Ego functions, such as the synthetic function of the ego, are molded by the parents' responses. The parents influence the child's characterological, stylistic tendencies. Take, for example, a six-year-old who develops severe obsessive-compulsive symptoms that far exceed the normal compulsive behavior of childhood. It makes little sense to understand this situation as simply the failure of repression and heightened sexual and aggressive drives. It makes more sense to be alert for underlying separation issues and unconscious death fears in the child's experience of trying to cope with the developmental problems of a six-year-old as they unfold in his interpersonal world.

The parents' responses to the child's anxiety in problem solving further reenforce the child's use of defenses and preferred styles for lowering anxiety. Faced with the phobic or severely obsessive-compulsive six-year-old, for example, the child clinician assesses several factors. The therapist looks for organic, developmental, and psychodynamic roots of the child's symptom, and the interpersonal implications in the family. An assessment also is made of the ways in which the psychodynamics of the family's interaction might elicit the child's anxiety or influence his style of responding to it. Only then does the uncovering of a particular unconscious sexual or aggressive conflict have a significant bearing on the child's experience of his neurotic symptom. At each juncture of the outbreak of severe anxiety there may be a need for the boy or girl to strike a delicate psychological balance. The child negotiates a course between using his own characteristic style of problem solving or adaptive ego functioning and reliance on the actual parents or the defensive modes learned from them.

Death Anxiety in Eating and Sleeping Problems

This dynamic relationship between the fear of death complex and developmental tasks holds true for toileting, sleeping, and eating problems. Sleep disturbances noted concurrently with neurotic suffering in children often indicate unconscious fears about death and separation. Once neurological problems and somatic distress have been ruled out as the basis for insufficient or restless sleep in children, psychological stress usually emerges as the primary factor. If sleeping problems exist as a part of a general picture of anxiety and insecurity, the child may be grappling with early neurotic fears. The unconscious equation of sleep with death may be even more pertinent in the young child's sleeping problems because young children do associate death with immobility and closed eyes. In my experience, the most commonly reported sleep problem in children is probably the young child's refusal to go to bed because "he can't sleep" or "he's afraid of the dark." The child who needs an additional bedtime story may also be expressing feelings about separation from parents. Waking up at night due to a nightmare and then needing to go to the parental bedroom for reassurance is another very common behavior in young children. Sleep disturbances frequently involve fears and dreams about death during the Oedipal period. Unconscious attitudes about death and separation mingle with the specific content of the child's anxiety dreams. Parental modes for dealing with the child's need for attention and reassurance affect the sleep problems. Although this is not the case with biological sleep disorders, the bedtime scene serves as a microcosim of the parent-child communication system and the effect of parental influences on the child's response to anxiety. Bedtime means not only the cessation of daily activities and withdrawal for rest but also separation from the parents. Fenickel cautioned that sleep means the loss of control over the conscious mind and susceptibility to the unconscious in which sleep can be equated with death. For the anxious, insecure, or depressed child, both of the above psychological contingencies bring with them the threat of anxiety. The overanxious defends against death anxiety by either actively fighting sleep or passively fearing its onset.

The wish for close contact with mother's protective embrace is an automatic response for young children to their experience of anxiety. For the anxious child, the demand for separation at bedtime triggers off the vicious cycle of separation anxiety, difficulty in falling asleep or early waking, the need for contact with mother, and then further anxiety when mother's physical presence is withdrawn. Although it is perfectly natural for a frightened child to want the comfort of the parents' presence, in the case of a child who has not resolved earlier separation problems, bedtime also becomes the battleground for control of the parents' responsiveness. Their continued presence serves three functions. It mitigates against the etiologic basis for death anxiety and sleeplessness by undoing separation. Second, it reinforces the connection between the child's overt or covert demands for attention and his or her ability to control the parents' availability. Third, it reassures the child against the anxiety inherent in relying on his own independent, psychic resources to cope with the nighttime stresses of the dark and the unconscious. At the same time that these factors have been operating, the dark becomes the depository of the ghosts, monsters, burglars, and ferocious animals. These unconscious demons populate the child's anxiety dreams and intensify the need for the parents' presence at night. What starts out as a completely normal developmental process of the gradual mastery of fears of the dark and nighttime separation becomes magnified by the parents' own anxiety or overreaction to the child. Very elaborate bedtime rituals evolve in this manner, and frustrated parents can easily become anxious, overprotective, or angry and punitive when attempts at logical explanations fail to assuage the child's fears. In any case, whether due to anxiety and unconscious fears of separation or manipulativeness and the struggle for power over the parents, or both, the approach of bedtime can signal the start of tempestuous battles and tearful pleas for additional time before sleep.

For the one- and two-year-old child, Spitz found that the bowel movement, and later solid foods, can constitute a means for reestablishing contact with the mother. Feeding problems due to emotional difficulty have long been understood as often arising from the mother-child interaction. To the extent that their dialogue is dominated by anxiety, the child's feeding at mealtime can take on an embattled air akin to the struggles embedded in the anxious child's bedtime and toileting rituals. Mahler's research confirmed her observation that the baby with nipple in mouth "reunites with the mother in a symbiotic bond." On an interpersonal and behavioral level, the common denominator in the feeding, toileting, and sleeping problem involved the parents' anxiety magnifying the child's into a situation of domestic warfare. The parents' frustration or anxious overconcern with the child's toileting problems, sleeping difficulties, and refusals for food or overeating intensifies the child's own anxiety. This reaction reinforces the child's unconscious fears of separation and death. The psychological world of the family and the child's mode of coping with anxiety are more important than individual differences in appetite or food preference, for both the fussy eater who refuses food and the compulsive overeating child.

From the earliest neonatal period, the mother helps to organize the child's experience as he attempts to make his needs and dislikes known through crying, movement, and various states of tension. The flow of communication from baby to mother depends on the mother's facility for understanding the behavioral cues of the infant. The mother needs to allow for the unfolding of emotional communication between them and to augment her skill as interpretor of the baby's crude biosocial communications. Under ideal circumstances, the mother first deciphers the meaning encoded in her baby's cries and movements. She then faces the task of responding to the demands for feeding, cuddling, changing, warmth, or physical closeness with a loving, accepting attitude more or less free from anxiety. Mahler beautifully described the unfolding of this communication during the oral phase as consisting of a mutual harmonizing that creates a dual symbiotic bond.[13] Through movement, crawling, and refined adjustments to tension, the baby alternates between states of fusion with mother and separation. Durign nuising, the symbiotic union is fully formed and the infant loses the sense of separateness and distinctness because of the complete harmony, feeling of total satisfaction, and shared body image. The mouth continues to be the primary organ for interacting with the world and the mother. Most things the baby encounters, once fingered, get put into the mouth. When apart from the mother, the hands, pacifier, or blanket in the mouth reaffirms the contact with her. The bottle, food, and much later on the teddy bear, security blanket, or Snoopy doll come to stand for the mother's presence and in themselves serve to increase the child's sense of security and well-being.

Death Anxiety in Obese and Anorexic Children

Spitz reported that after the introduction of solid foods to the infant, food and milk become the links between the child's and the mother's bodies.[14] As an outgrowth of the normal processes of separation-individuation, food can therefore continue to symbolize mother's presence and symbiotic love. This occurs naturally, but it is complicated by the child's idiosyncrasies and the mother's emotional response to the child's overeating or undereating. The child continues to rely on the mother to reduce separation anxiety as Spitz observed in the baby's eight-month stranger anxiety. Food becomes the heir apparent to the "royal symbiosis." Food's use as an anxiety reduction agent continues in lowering separation fears, depression, and death anxiety.

For some obese adolescents and children, the association between eating, symbiotic merger, and the lowering of depression and death anxiety remains constant. Dieting or weight-reduction programs are doomed to failure under such circumstances. Both the refusal to eat and habitual gorging with food can be understood in children in terms of the relationship of eating to the mother-child relationship, assuming that there are no significant metabolical or hormonal influences. In one of her first studies on eating problems thirty-five years ago, Bruch investigated the families of obese children and noted that they tended to have domineering mothers and passive, uninvolved fathers. Frequent quarreling and disharmony between these parents was apparent. A pattern of covert rejection of the children was covered up by overfeeding them.[15] Bruch wrote extensively about the close relationship between obesity and anorexia nervosa and has carefully documented the psychological function of food in providing security and compensating for disappointment. Food retains its capacity for achieving unconscious union with the mother. Carrying Spitz, Mahler, and Bruch's research to the next logical step, overeating or the refusal to eat in children serves the following multiple functions. It allays separation anxiety by maintaining symbiosis. It counters depression and allays anxiety about separate autonomous ego functioning and death. Anorexia is especially illuminated by its scrutiny in terms of the fear of death. The typical anorexic person is unconsciously interested in food. The anorexic either engages in self-starvation that starts out as an effort to diet or loses his/her appetite as part of a clinical depression. Anorexia has been given the clearest elucidation by Bruch and others as a profound emotional disturbance reflecting underlying separation problems and frequently borderline psychotic states. Some anorexics fantasize about food constantly but refuse to eat. Others go to pathologically obsessive extremes in establishing food rituals and criteria for their miniscule meals. Suicide can be a serious threat, as is severe malnutrition and death.

The much greater frequency of anorexia among female adolescents fits with the greater frequency of death fears and depression among females. Women's greater susceptibility to depression and death anxiety has been explained on the basis of cultural familial influences and conditioned characterological traits. When anorexics gross distortions about body image and food intake reach delusional proportions, their care may demand hospitalization and enforced feedings. Their progressive weight loss and apathetic disinterest frequently coincide with profound problems in sexual identification and unconscious fears of adult sexuality. Their suicidal contempt for food may endure beyond the efforts of parents and relatives to help them or feed them. There is a great deal of psychodynamic similarity between the older adolescent anorexic and the rebellious five- or six-year-old who pitches ferocious battle with mother at mealtime about how hungry he is and what he will or will not eat. On the one hand, the anorexic adolescent blithely refuses food while unconsciously retaliating against a "bad mother." On the other hand, it seems to me that the anorexic is clinging to a fusion with a "good mother." With neurotic parents, the mealtime becomes a subtle arena for battles over power and control with even the normal child. The child's tactics vary from sloppiness, procrastination, complaining, dawdling, and pleas for reprieves from eating to outright warfare, stomachaches, and tantrums. The parents, depending on their degree of patience and mental health, can lower the child's anxiety about new and different foods or get entangled in power struggles that reaffirm their position. Some parents will use guilt, threats, or punishment to modify the child's eating because of their own anxiety about their girl's or boy's health and appearance. In insidious family situations, the parents become desperate enough to confuse the child about how hungry he or she is or what foods the child actually likes and dislikes. In the latter case, the parent undermines the child's autonomy, then reinforces early symbiotic merger in a state in which mother and child share psychic apparatus, body image, and body ego. The anxious or depressed parent who routinely overfeeds the child also reinforces the connection between food, positive affect, and the early symbiotic union. In general, obese children tend to be a depressed, miserable lot who also have serious problems in self-image, socialization, and autonomy.

The defiant child who refuses food and the compliant overeater can use the intake of food as the focus of the struggle for separation-individuation. Magnified, persistent problems may endure because of the parent's interaction with the child at mealtime and the unconscious messages that are exchanged about the significance of food. If the mother and child are deficient in the mutual harmony and synchronization of the symbiosis or are later unable to tolerate separation, it is not uncommon for the difficulties of their relationship to be translated into prolonged feeding and weight problems. To oversimplify matters greatly for the obese child, separation may be tolerable only because food is the link to the mother. Hunger sensations signify abandonment and death. To equally oversimplify the situation of the anorexic adolescent who refuses food, individuation is fraught with anxiety. Feeding for the anorexic child may signify either engulfment by the mother or abandonment and death. The normal child who refuses to eat at mealtime may be attempting to cope with a psychological issue similar to the anorexic who falls at the other extreme end of the continuum of eating disorders. In true anorexic cases, Bruch states that the refusal to eat is a way of maintaining autonomy and control over the body. The fight against hunger and the body's expansion following food intake represents a fight with the intrapsychic mother for survival of the self, or autonomy.[16] The body is identified with the mother, and starvation becomes the anorexic's sole means for controlling this process. Because of the pathological parenting, the child who later develops anorexia feels both overwhelmed and disregarded in the parents' presence.[17A] The anorexic's later movements toward autonomy may be discounted and criticized. The takeover of his or her independent ego functioning by the parents contributes to the anorexic's cognitive distortions and profound disturbance in body image. If both separation and individuation have come to be equated with death for the child, it is no wonder that depression and ambivalence about death result from anxiety associated with food and feeding. Food for the anorexic and the obese person continues to serve as the principal mechanism for restoring the greater safety of the early symbiosis. Eating or starvation became the unconscious strategy for dealing with the psychodynamic and family based problems that threaten the individual with the loss of the self.

These studies on anorexic adolescents point to a communality of features with borderline psychotic children whose symptoms can also be best understood as evolving from disturbances in the normal separation-individuation process.[17B] To the extent that the interpersonal atmosphere of the family has interfered with the emotional development of the child, depression and anxiety occur at the points of conflict with the parents. Food often remains a major medium for conflict resolution and protection from the fear of the loss of the self. This same interrelationship between separation fears, depression, and death anxiety inherent in feeding, neurotic problems, and developmental phenomena stands out in bold relief in borderline and psychotic children. Their fear of death can be an almost constant preoccupation because of its equation with the terrors of abandonment and engulfment.

Death anxiety partially accounts for borderline children's conscious concerns about violence, their aggressive fantasies, and their occasional outbursts of aggresive behavior. On an intrapsychic level they fear fragmentation of the self as well as its loss in symbiotic union. The chaotic nature of their clinical presentation and the variability in their reality testing and ego functioning betray their struggle for psychic survival. Unconscious fears of physical and psychological annihilation routinely appear in their projective test protocols and daydreams as projections of their violent, threatening internal world. In some, tenuous ties to reality may be threatened by fantasies of fires, bombings, explosions, and mutilations. For others, these fantasies can be used as a means of resolving an underlying terror of the anticipation of death via abandonment or symbiotic merger or disintegration of the self. The borderline and psychotic children need a barrier of defense against disintergration of the self, which is also equated with death.[18] The source of the threat is externalized, but the fear of the loss of the self persists.

These psychodynamic contingencies exist more or less apart from the progression of gradually more realistic and accurate attitudes about death in children. The sophistication of the child's knowledge about death follows a maturational pattern from vague and diffuse to personalized conceptions of death, but the unconscious meaning of death can continue to remain the same. Even though it seems illogical at first blush, for these reasons the depressed child, the anorexic child, or the borderline child who attempts suicide may not be responding simply to depression per se but rather to unconscious threats of abandonment or disintegration of the self. In fact, under some situations the suicidal child may be much less depressed than anxious and unconsciously conflicted about death and separation.

Parental Influence on Death Anxiety

As was suggested above in regard to feeding, sleeping, and toileting difficulties, the child's discovery of his own sexuality and adult sexual relations may cause anxiety. The parents' reaction to the child's death fears has great bearing on the child's way of coping with related feeling of sadness, helplessness, and separation anxiety. Fenichel hypothesized a close relationship between death anxiety and sleeping problems because he posited an interrelationship between a fear of sleep, a fear of dreaming, sexual pleasure, and the witnessing of the primal scene.[19] According to his formulations, children fear death and sleep because of the unconscious expectation of punishment for masturbation. Curiosity about their parents' sexual relations and the pleasure of genital sensations in infantile masturbation produce guilt and the fantasy of death as a punishment. Fenichel was extending Freud's theory of infantile sexuality in arriving at these notions about sleep anxiety and the fear of death. They were based closely on Freud's own work on infantile sexuality, which he restated in his "Analysis of a Phobia in a Five-Year-Old Boy," published in 1909.

This charming case of little Hans documented the first attempt at the psychoanalysis of a child, albeit a circuitous one conducted by post with the father serving as analyst under Freud's supervision. Through the correspondence with Hans' father, Freud was very much interested both in curing the child and in finding ample evidence to support his clinical theories. Freud used this case of little Hans as an example of his second anxiety theory of the formation of neurosis and as tangible proof of the reality of the Oedipal complex and castration anxiety.

Children's anxiety about masturbation and sexual knowledge can also be understood in terms of its relation to separation anxiety and death anxiety. The case of little Hans illustrated the impact of parental behavior on such death anxiety. A summary of some aspects of the case will clarify the connection between death anxiety and separation anxiety that underlies the child's guilt and Oedipal conflicts. Freud was first contacted by Hans' parents in 1906 because the boy had been afraid of going into the street and afraid that horses would bite him.[20] The fear of being bitten had been associated with having been frightened by the large penises of the horses in the street. The father theorized that his wife's motherly tenderness had somehow caused sexual excitation in the boy. His father speculated that Hans had given a significant clue to his own disorder by announcing his inference that his mother must have a "widdler as large as that of a horse." When Hans was about age three-and-a-half, his mother gave birth to his little sister, Anna, and at age four he was confined to bed because of a tonsillectomy. For all appearances, Hans' fears had grown worse. Eventually, he developed a severe phobia of being hurt, fell into extremely low spirits at night, and grew anxious of the prospect of venturing out into the street. Freud interpreted these symptoms as Hans' disguised sexual wishes for his mother and fear of his father's punishment for aggressive feelings toward him. Freud analyzed the child's play fantasies to demonstrate Hans' concern about anatomical differences between the sexes. The mysteries of sex and his growing affection and preoccupation with female playmates compounded Hans' anxieties. The horses symbolized the father, according to Freud, so he could argue that Hans' wishes to have his sister and his father out of the way contributed to his fear of being hurt. Hans' phobia was the expectation of the punishment for his incestuous wishes.

Three- , four- , and five-year-old children commonly have animal fears and unless they are extreme, as was the case with Hans' fears of animals, they constitute one of the "normal phobias" of childhood. My purpose here is to draw attention to some of the parent-child communications that expressed, the psychological atmosphere of Hans' family. The importance of separation anxiety, was emphasized in the communication in addition to Oedipal themes, in the formation of the boy's fears. Hans identified with both his father and mother as he unconsciously sought their protection and approval with each of the sexual discoveries he made. At precisely those points when he unconsciously wished to be independent of them, Hans needed his parents' emotional availability. Freud reported at the onset of the case presentation that, upon discovering him with his hand on his penis, Hans' mother threatened him with being sent to "Dr. A to have his "widdler" cut off." She knew that the little boy equated the "widdler" with his penis, but she told Hans that she also had a "widdler" when he became curious about seeing her undress. Both parents told Hans that the stork was bringing the baby when his sister Anna was born. They then noted with amusement his suspiciousness about the appearance of the stork. At age three-and-a-half Hans had reported a dream of being in "Grumdem with Mariedl" following the birth of his sister.[21] Freud interpreted the dream as a wish to return to a summer residence where he had enjoyed the company of his landlord's children as playmates. Hans was really seeking reassurance that he was loved and had not been abandoned by his distracted parents. He was emotionally vulnerable at the birth of the sister and struggling with his sexual curiosity.

Hans' fear of separation from his mother was intertwined with the unconscious fear of death. The separation anxiety arose only because of Hans' castration anxiety but also because of conflicting wishes to kill the parents and to be killed or reunited with them. The fear of the loss of the self might underlie Han's need for empathy and wish to be reincorporated into the symbiotic union with his mother. Han's mother's comments consistently aggravated his separation and castration anxiety. They did nothing to reassure him of the normality of his developing intellectual curiosity and sexual interest. The remarks did little to reduce his death anxiety and ambivalence about separating from his mother. Furthermore, Hans seemed really anxious about separating from both his parents. His love and need for his father also conflicted with his budding development and wishes for independence. The unconscious fear of his own helplessness and his separation anxiety were reinforced by the parents' misreading of some of Han's communication to them. On one level, Hans became terrified of venturing outdoors because of the castrating horse-father in the street. Not leaving his home also maintained a symbiotic bond with his mother and insured greater availability of his loved father's protective presence. Hans' anxiety about playing in the street and exploring the world to make new discoveries, like his nighttime depression, stemmed as much from the fear of separating from his parents as from castration anxiety or simple hatred for his father. Could it be that the horse represents not only the castrating father but also the terror of death and the loss of the self? If this speculation is correct, then Hans' symptoms highlighted a family drama about separation individuation.

Hans' hostile wishes toward his father and sexual feelings toward his mother certainly emerged in the development of his sexual curiosity. However, Hans seemed equally concerned with testing his parents' emotional availability and tolerance for his sexual curiosity and autonomy. In line with his self-perception and body image of a tiny, powerless creature with an inadequate "widdler," Hans would venture only so far in expressing his need for independence. It was natural that he would relate these processes to his parents in the hope that they would then protect him from his fears. At one point, Hans put all of this quite directly to his father: "When you are away, I am afraid you are not coming back home." Although Freud would have stressed here the meaning that Hans wished that his father *would* leave or die, Hans may also have been pleading: "If you leave, I will be abandoned. What will become of me?" When Hans' little game of going into the wood storeroom and pretending to urinate while calling the closet his "w.c." was discovered by his father, Hans proudly explained that he was "widdling." This autoerotic activity may have been less exhibitionism than Hans' attempt to get his father to calm his fears. At one point, Hans wandered into his parents' bedroom with the vague thought of shooting people on his mind. Hans' father then angrily sent him out of the room with the threat that his fear of horses would not get better. Hans was clearly experimenting with being like the father and supplanting him in the bedroom. Yet his ambivalence about an Oedipal victory persisted in light of his profound need for his father. Freud stated at another point in the narrative that Hans' parents were in fact in the habit of taking him into bed with them, but makes little further mention of it in elucidating Hans' behavior. Aside from the erotic feelings this might have stimulated, it helps to explain the naturalness of Hans' wandering into the parental bedroom at night. If he was afraid of the dark, separation, or his aggressive feelings, being in bed between his parents would provide a tremendous sense of security for Hans, like it does for many children. By recreating the illusion of a symbioticlike state during sleep, Hans was safe from the threat of death anxiety. On the simple level of overt interaction in the family, what was Hans to do? It apparently pleased his mother when he got into bed with her, but this angered his father. His mother's response to his father was then on the order of: "It will only be for a minute" or, "What is all this fuss about anyway?" Doing the very thing that unconsciously satisfied his needs and pleased his mother meant displeasing and angering his father. Their inconsistency and lack of agreement on how to handle the nightly visits to the bedroom certainly reinforced Hans' behavior. It did nothing to quell his nighttime fears about aggression, separation, and death.

At another point, upon being put to bed, Hans said that he wished to sleep with Mariedl (the landlord's daughter). When he was told that he could not, he announced that he would then sleep with Mommy and Daddy. After first questioning Hans if he really wanted to go downstairs with Mariedl, and go away from his parents, Hans' mother told him, "Well, if you really want to go away from mother and daddy then take your coat and knickers and goodbye."[22] When Hans started to do just that, his mother quickly fetched him back. It is no wonder that Hans was confused and ambivalent about separation. His parents may have misinterpreted his behavior and were rather unaware of their own unconscious ambivalence about his sexual development. Hans' parents were close followers of Freud. Hans' father interpreted to the boy that Oedipal wishes were really the basis for his anxiety over the shattering knowledge that his mother does not have a "widdler," i.e., was a castrated man, and for his fear of horses. The father's interpretation worked in alleviating the child's symptoms, either because it was correct or because to a five-year-old boy having one's father make such interpretations provides limits and protection from the more deeply unconscious fears of abandonment and death. Freud intended the case of little Hans to provide the clearest evidence for the reality of the Oedipus complex and the role of castration anxiety in infantile sexuality. It also documented the role of separation anxiety and death fears in children's emerging interest in sexuality.

Children's Reactions to Death

Studies of children's actual encounters with death, whether the death of their parents, friends, or their own terminal illnesses, register the impact of age-specific developmental tasks on death anxiety. It is generally agreed by psychoanalysts that the ability to undergo genuine mourning requires a certain state of psychic maturity that is lacking in very young children. Their imaginative prelogical views of death might associate death with sexual intercourse, the arrival of siblings, or the intermingling of sexual impulses with aggression and violence. Full acceptance of death and the genuine process of mourning can be impossible for a young child. Their lack of mature cognitive attitudes about death and the intrusion of the underlying fear of death complex into their logical ideas about death and dying compounds the task. Accepting the death of a parent, for example, remains an impossible task far an early-school-age child. A young child has not fully separated from the parent and is therefore, conflicted about autonomous ego functioning.[23] The fear of the child's own helplessness without the dead parent increases feelings of guilt and aggression such that the prospect of separation becomes a terrifying punishment. Guilt, depression and ambivalence therefore, play a major dynamic role in the child's anticipation of the death of a loved one. In one fascinating study, Wolfenstein, Kliman, et al. assessed children's reactions to the death of President Kennedy, and reported that general widespread feelings of shock, disbelief, and outrage among adults at that time did not explain individual differences in the children's reactions.[24] There seemed to be a two-part response to J.F.K.'s death in their sample of school-age children that consisted of acceptance and grief on one level with denial and inhibition of affect about the death on another level.

Content analysis of their fantasies and comments about J.F.K.'s death revealed that the boys tended to see the young president as an ego ideal, while the girls saw him more as a perfect father or future husband. The younger subjects in the study, and those who seemed most in touch with Oedipal conflicts, spoke of his death in terms of themes of murder, revenge, punishment, and identification with a slain hero. Others showed concern about the president's children and his replacement as a husband and father. The latency-age children focused more on themes of power, succession to the presidency, and the trustworthiness of the president's cabinet and assistants. The death of the president, in other words, provided a blank screen. The children projected into this blank screen their age-specific developmental concerns, which they connected with their own anxieties about death and separation.

In an exhaustive study of fifty children who died from cancer over a two-year period, Morrisey interviewed hospital staff and families of dying children to index their degree of anxiety about death and its source. The degree of the children's awareness was a significant factor in their adjustment, as was the degree of the parents' participation in their care.[25] Almost all of the children had some type of severe anxiety about their condition and 60 percent were most troubled by separation anxiety as the single most prominent feature. The lack of sensitive parental involvement combined with a high degree of anxiety in some children resulted in the poorest cases of emotional adjustment in the children. The quality of the parents' interaction with the child was the most important variable in the hospitalization experience. For that matter, recent experiments with having the child who is dying from cancer remain home have been reported to be successful. Being in familiar surroundings in the midst of family lowers these children's anxiety level. It also seems to have beneficial effects on the later mourning period for parents and siblings.

Summary

Developmental factors help to account for the wide range of differences and incongruities in the expression of depression and separation anxiety as they are interwoven with death anxiety. Characterological differences and organic factors help to determine whether a given child experiences depression associated with death anxiety by withdrawal, impoverishment of affect, hypochondraisis, fighting, assaultiveness, or hyperactivity. Heightened self-condemnation or antisocial acting out may both be expressions of attempts at resolving depression and separation anxiety. The child's level of cognitive operations also influences the conscious attitudes about death and separation. Even when children attribute irreversibility to the concept of death, it may remain reversible in their unconscious attitudes. The fear of death may conflict with the wish for death in the depressed child's need to seek a reunion and a reestablishing of the early symbiotic bond. Separation anxiety and depression are also two prominent features in children who are actually facing death.

Content analysis of preschool children's fantasies and longitudinal research studies revealed early stylistic differences in the handling of aggression and death anxiety. Research findings by Despert and Bender were cited as evidence of the oral language of infantile fears and wishes for death. Mahler and Spitz's research emphasized the relationship between symbiosis and the child's affective experience in separation-individuation. The contrast between the fear of the loss of the self and wish for surrender of the self was noted in merger fantasies. These crucial psychodynamic patterns were mentioned in the dreams of depressed children. Reunion fantasies were described as being widespread among suicidally depressed children. A summary of this research led to the hypothesis of the emergence of death anxiety, depression, and separation anxiety in the normal, commonplace developmental tasks of childhood. In keeping with developmental and interpersonal psychoanalytic theory, the connection between death anxiety and object relations was traced in the young child's sleeping, feeding, and toilet-training problems. Sleep disturbances, battles for elimination control, anorexia, and obesity were all examined in relation to the emergence of the self in the interpersonal atmosphere of the family. Analysis of the ancient Greek legend of Prometheus yielded a metaphor for the child's vacillation between helplessness and resourcefulness in coping with death anxiety. Prometheus' fate at the hands of Jupiter recounted the symbolism of the childhood self in its struggle with death, depression, and separation-individuation.

Tom Sawyer's exploits and fantasies in Mark Twain's *Adventures of Tom Sawyer* illustrated depression and ambivalence about death in the preadolescent growth period. The psychodynamic linkage between his efforts at individuation and death anxiety typified the interaction of the fear of death complex with the demands of particular developmental epochs. The extreme to which Tom Sawyer carried his death fantasies and their acting out were accounted for on the basis of unconscious needs for symbiotic merger. My experience suggested that these needs and fantasies are widespread in the suicidal child. Overlapping areas of psychological conflict were asserted for dying children and neurotic or merely disturbed youngsters who show death anxiety. Some experiments with terminally ill children suggested that home care, when possible, outweighs the disadvantages and complications involved in hospital medical care and pain control. One finding noted in several studies is that when such children have a choice about where they would like to die, many choose a living room couch or some other location central to family activity. Anxiety and depression seem to be lowered by the family right up to the moment of death. The maintenance of the close, emotional, symbioticlike bond with the family members accomplishes this task by reducing separation anxiety.

The promise of the reestablishemnt of the close emotional bond lowers the dying child's anxiety in the same way that it reduces the healthy child's depression and death anxiety. The related death terrors of abandonment and destruction of the self require the maintenance of a psychic level of defense, for which the child turns to the parents. The young child's need for parental support and resources then conflicts with the drive for autonomy. From the myth of Prometheus' exploits to the mischievous adventures of Tom Sawyer it was shown that death anxiety is manifest in childhood depression and separation anxiety. The human child attempts growth and autonomy from within the intersecting vector forces of the three-part fear of death complex. A biologically determined bonding evolves into a psychological symbiosis, which later has bearing on the child's maturation and adjustment problems. Because of the emotional messages expressed in the nuances of the parent-child communication, the family either inhibits or fosters the child's autonomous defensive operations for dealing with death anxiety. The fear of the loss of the self is either curbed or intensified to the extent that the family atmosphere complicates the child's ambivalence and anxiety about individuation. Depression and death anxiety then adhere strongly to the adjustment problems characteristic of a child's developmental stage.

CHAPTER SEVEN

Purpose in Life and the Fear of Death

Purpose in Life

The affirmation of a personal meaning of existence lies rooted in the certain knowledge of death. After integrating the fear of the loss of the self in neurosis with the research on death, it can be readily seen that the adult's continued lack of purpose is synonymous with depression and death anxiety. To some existentialists, meaning and purpose in life fall into the realm of illusion since immortality remains unproven and unknowable. For Sartre life seems absurd and purposefulness is a groundless flight of fancy. Ralph Waldo Emerson stated that the concept of immortality was the cornerstone of human optimism and hope.[1] Without it, morality, ethical conduct, happiness, and passionate feeling became feeble, ephemeral matters that fleet away as men grow older and more aware of their death. Emerson, therefore, held that men and women over the age of thirty would wake up feeling sad every morning because of that certainty. He believed further that everyone over thirty would continue feeling sad every morning until the day of his or her death. Patients beginning psychotherapy currently complain about emptiness in their lives in such existential terms. Sophisticated patients who intellectualize cope with meaninglessness and a lack of purpose at the center of their emotional experience by deflecting their pain into philosophical discourse. Existential frustration and a lack of purpose in life can be readily attributed to neurotic suffering and death anxiety. Their persistence derives from a high degree of death fears, depression, and separation anxiety in a combination that is unique to the individual's defensiveness. Existential complaints can be contingent upon a poorly integrated sense of identity, and they seem to be the indications of psychological conflict.

Existential despair reflects neurotic death anxiety or ego deficits more than necessary components of the human condition. Beginning with Victor Frankl's writings and Erich Fromm's contributions, attempts have been made to define lack of purpose as a relative lack of responsibility for coming to terms with life.

Fromm argued that unresolved emotional conflict, self-hatred, and disgust lie at the root of war and international competitiveness. He belives that self-deception and dishonesty underlie much neurotic misery. Frankl's "logotherapy" also emphasized "choosing" suffering and coming to grips with death as essential to human freedom. My research study on the fear of death, detailed in Chapter Five, provided empirical data for an inherent relationship between a lack of purpose in life and the fear of death. The study did not directly support Fromm's ideas or Frankl's notion that religion plays the crucial role in finding a "will to meaning" or a purpose in life. Victor Frankl developed this concept of spiritual freedom as a result of his confinement in a concentration camp. He knew on the basis of his own experience that it is the spiritual freedom to decide what one can become that renders life meaningful [2] This inference places his position within the neo-Freudian existentialist view of mental health. Much of the research that dealt with the relationship between death anxiety and the sense of purpose in life has been based on these theoretical positions. According to Frankl, the primary motivation in man consists of a "will to meaning," which is more basic than the drive for pleasure or power. This meaning is unique and specific to each person. Its achievement brings satisfaction in spite of human suffering, guilt, and death. Frankl, like Fromm and several existentialists, has maintained that it is the transitoriness of life that gives it meaning. An appreciation of the full meaning of human life has as its foundation the certainty of death. Death no longer looms as a threat in the future when it provides the context for meaningful actions in the present. Recognition of the value of suffering and the genuine possibility of decency under the worst of circumstances enabled Frankl to survive the concentration camp. His sense of purpose allowed him to embrace living under the most horrible conditions.

Existential purpose in life was related in his theory and research to the development of the spiritual side of one's personality. Fromm and Frankl have both stressed the relinquishment of neurotic over-involvement in sexual activities, aquisitiveness, and power needs as crucial to growth. Frankl examined religion's psychological role in conventional religious worship and the personal belief in God. He believes that religion defines one's purpose in life, even if it just consists of some metaphysical concept of a divine providence. Frankl claimed, quite correctly, that existential conflicts don't necessarily indicate psychological disturbance. A man's concern over the worthwhileness of his life may be appropriately manifested in spiritual distress without any indication of a mental illness. When that self-analysis evolves into existential despair, under ordinary circumstances, it covers neurotic helplessness and the fear of the loss of the self. Despair results from the encroachment of the fear of death and depression into what may be very legitimate self-scrutiny and appropriate self-criticism.

The concept of the "will to meaning" represents the striving to construct meaningful wholes from the discrete elements of experience, and the translation of that striving into a unified philosophy of life. Personality questionnaires have been devised for use in empirical studies of the "will to meaning" that assess such interrelated humanistic notions as: uniqueness, responsibility, courage, and transcendence. Administration of these questionnaires in research studies have been typically done with hospitalized mental patients, outpatients, hospitalized medical patients, and undergraduate students. These research subjects were thought to be representative of the population at large, and higher scores on "will to meaning" were consistently reported for the undergraduates and the non-mentally ill people. A Purpose in Life Test was devised in 1964 and standardized on a variety of objective psychological personality tests.[3] Research was done in the late 1960s to substantiate purpose in life as a viable concept and to distinguish different groups of people according to their degree of purpose in life. Purpose in life was not related in the research to the presence or absence of conventionally designated forms of mental illness. A variety of validity and reliability investigations of this test were carried out during the 1960s and early 1970s.

The basic function of this Purpose in Life Test was to detect an "existential vacuum" that was equivalent, in Frankl's theory, to the failure to find meaning or purpose in life. The test assessed "existential vacuum" as a dimension of human personality rather than as an indication of neurosis or abnormality per se. It was used widely for counseling purposes and in group administration for research purposes. Businessmen and professional people, active Protestant parishoners generally, tended to have higher purpose in life scores than undergraduate students, hospitalized medical patients, outpatient neurotics, alcoholics, and hospitalized psychotic people, in descending order. According to the investigators, no consistent relationships were ever found between purpose in life and age, sex, education, intelligence, or values in the usual sense of personal values. A variety of psychological research studies were conducted that related high purpose in life to a sense of well-being, psychological mindedness, and achievement. A number of investigators in the late 1960s found negative correlations between purpose in life and depression on such standard psychological tests as the Minnesota Multiphasic Personality Inventory (MMPI). The implication of these findings was that people with a high sense of purpose in life were less depressed than people with a low sense of purpose in life. These research findings confirmed Frankl's observation that finding meaning and value in suffering was a key factor in successfully facing the brutality and inhumanity of the concentration camp. Edith Jacobson has written similar, but much more technical, descriptions of the strength of character of concentration camp survivors.

Frankl noted that to the degree with which concentration camp inmates found purpose—whether in the Judeo-Christian ethic, a specific vocational context, or in the love of one's family and fellow prisoners— relief from depression was made possible. With a purpose in life, it was feasible to enjoy, even if only in memory, the beauty of nature, the arts, and science, or to appreciate the generosity in small acts of kindness. A sense of purpose in life allowed some prisoners the chance to find humor in the concentration camp, together with the courage to survive. Even with the knowledge of the death of part or all of their family, these inmates could overcome depression in spite of the tragedy and degradation. With this sense of purpose, the concentration camp prisoner could avoid despair and make good use of his/her will to survive in the presence of death. A commitment to their purpose held in check the tendency toward despair from the knowledge of the gas chambers.

Based on the impression that purpose in life might be a cornerstone of psychological attitudes toward death, The research design detailed in Chapter Five, was constructed to assess death anxiety, religion, and purpose in life. The intent of the study was to determine whether a high fear of death in a physically healthy person, living in safe surroundings, would be correlated with a low sense of purpose in life. Since Frankl had maintained that a highly developed purpose in life makes death meaningful, it was expected that subjects with a high purpose in life would have lower death anxiety. Religious variables were included in the study for two reasons. First, one of my preliminary studies had indicated a relationship between death anxiety and the intensity of religious participation. Second, Gordon Allport and other humanistic psychologists had speculated that the fear of death might not be intense among people who have a strong internalized "intrinsic" commitment to religion.[4] Intrinsic religiosity had been experimentally defined, whereas Fromm's notion of humanistic religion had not. This variable of the type of religious commitment had not been coordinated with the research on the meaning of anxiety about death. Several investigators had argued that a spiritual life of religious devotion constituted one of the most important ways of maintaining an existential sense of purpose in life. On a broader level, it would have been interesting to find out if religious faith reflected existential mental health. It seemed logical that freedom from death anxiety— the neurotic fear of the loss of the self—would be more characteristic of people with humanistic or intrinsic religion.

Death Anxiety and Purpose in Life

Death anxiety as a construct in the psychological research literature referred to measured anxiety reactions at the thought of one's own death. It implied the affective component of experienced anxiety. Fears of death may be either vague and general or specific, whereas death anxiety so defined signified some intense measurable feeling of anxiety. Anxiety about death had been measured in the research studies by many of the psysiological and psychological tests that assess anxiety and emotional reactions. The Death Anxiety Scale (DAS) was originally devised in 1970 because of the inadequacies of the previous methods of assessing death anxiety: questionnaires, psychiatric interviews, and projective tests.[5] The selection of the DAS items was based on a variety of validation procedures and correlations with other psychological tests of anxiety. A number of types of studies using the Death Anxiety Scale were done with adolescents, college students, middle- , and upper-middle-class urban groups of people. No meaningful or consistent relationship was found between death anxiety and age, type of religious affiliation, and general personality variables.

The researchers who had studied religion in depth, from Freud in the 1900s to Herman Feifel in the 1960's, had suggested that religious people often use their religion as a defense against death. The above findings were therefore surprising. A summary of the death anxiety research up to the 1970's could be encapsulated in two statements. The consensus among the investigators was that religious people were personally more afraid of death than non-religious people, just as they were thought to be concerned about salvation and the possibility of life after death. It was also generally believed until the early 1970s that the fear of death increases as religious people get older, so that old age is the time when it was feared most.[6] In younger religious people, the fear of death was found to be closer to consciousness than in non-religious youths who make greater use of repression. When college-aged youths were studied at that time, according to self-reported concerns about death and physiological levels of arousal to death-related stimuli (psycho-galvanic skin response readings), and then were divided into high, medium, or low religious groups, the intermediate group was the most fearful of death.

In another large study of undergraduate students, no significant relationship was found between death anxiety and specific religious belief systems, attachment to belief systems, frequency of church attendance, strength of religious convictions, belief in the Bible, or belief in an afterlife. In a number of these studies on the Death Anxiety Scale women had significantly higher death anxiety than men, which agreed with the generally reported greater fear of death in women. High religious involvement was correlated with a high fear of death, in other death anxiety studies, so that these findings were inconclusive and the results contradictory. As a consequence, the interrelationship between purpose in life, the fear of death, and religion remained speculative and open to question.

Reaserch Findings: Purpose in Life, Death Anxiety, and Religious Orientation

The purpose in Life Test scores were affected very little by differences in sex, age, intelligence, education, or socioeconomic factors. It was expected in the study that Frankl's notion of "existential vacuum," the failure to find a purpose or meaning in one's life would coincide with the fear of death. I had speculated that death fears were manifest in depression and separation anxiety, but the general concept of death anxiety was the variable that could be most reliably measured. Except for simple correlational studies, Frankl's concept of purpose in life had remained basically untested. The purpose of the study described in Chapter Five was to assess the above relationship between death anxiety, purpose in life, and intrinsicness versus extrinsicness of religious orientation. The study suggested that Frankl was correct about the importance of having a purpose in life, only if the variable of type of religious orientation is taken into account. People who have a high purpose in life do have a more positive or accepting attitude toward death and they fear it less. Hypothesis 5 of the study had stated that Roman Catholic sisters who have an intrinsic religious orientation would not differ from intrinsic lay religious Roman Catholic women in either death anxiety or purpose in life. In fact, there was no difference on death anxiety between intrinsically religious nuns and lay subjects. The nuns initially had higher purpose in life scores than intrinsically religious lay subjects but not after adjustments were made for the age differences between these groups. Purpose in life differences between the religious and lay groups were therefore not significant. There was no substantial support for Frankl's claim that personal religious involvement provides the groundwork for an existential commitment to purpose in life. Instrinsic or humanistic religious faith could not be fully identified with existential mental health. Expected differences between intrinsically religious and extrisincally religious subjects were not found on purpose in life. However, some hypotheses drawn on the basis of Frankl's point of view were verified, particularly the supposition that high purpose in life subjects had less death anxiety than low purpose in life subjects. This was true for intrinsically religious nuns, intrinsically religious lay subjects, and extrinsically religious nuns. For the group of extrinsically religious lay subjects, death anxiety differences were insignificant.

The commonplace notion that death anxiety will increase with age was also not supported by the study. The significant positive relationship between the subjects' age and purpose in life was simply due to the older ages of the religious groups of subjects. The absence of a direct relationship between death anxiety and age was expected in the study because most of the other investigators had reported that death anxiety was unrelated to age. A large number of subject protocols had to be disregarded for failure to pass the scale's cut-off scores necessary for inclusion into the high and low purpose in life and intrinsic or extrinsic religious groups. It seemed unlikely that such select groups could be obtained who were also matched for age. Future research on purpose in life might involve the assessment of death anxiety and depression in different religious groups who have been matched for age. Since differences in death anxiety were found according to the degree of purpose in life, it could be argued that the intermediating variable would be depression (and separation anxiety). One-dimensional religious differrnces per se do not account for differences in death anxiety.

Significant negative relationships were reported between death anxiety and depression among elderly people in the literature, but no such results had been obtained for any other age groups of people. The experimental studies had suggested the need for more research to be conducted on a variety of personality variables related to death anxiety and purpose in life. The framework and focus of this research study was limited to the area of existential psychology. By design, it did not assess a wider range of personality variables pertinent to purpose in life or the fear of death. More research on religion might focus on the unanticipated finding of the relationship between increasing age, length of membership in a religious order, and an extrinsic religious orientation.

Purpose in Life and Depression

The use of subjects of the same sex and religious denomination was considered both an advantage and a disadvantage of the above study, since uniformity of subjects in research restricts the generalization of results. The matched experimental approach was essential because of the sex differences reported on death anxiety. Women's higher levels of death fears and the negative relationship between death anxiety and purpose in life can be best understood in the light of the three dimensions of death anxiety: the fear of death, depression, and separation anxiety. More heightened death fears among women was explained on the basis of their susceptibility to more prevalent depressions and culturally conditioned problems with separation anxiety. A serious difficulty with this kind of quantitative research format lies in the gap between research and directly unobservable internal psychic events.

The fear of death exerts a powerful influence on personality functioning as an outer reflection of an inner psychological process involving the fear of the loss of the self. The fear of death reflects the end product and the expressions of either a poorly integrated self or an intact self that is not well differentiated from the internalized parents. A lack of purpose in life has been described previously as a general indication of depression. The concpet of death anxiety also implied the helplessness and lack of resource of the self in the face of such processes. The concept of the lack of purpose in life involved more of a displacement and projection of such inner mental states onto the world. Furthermore, the rich complexity of attitudes about death and purpose in life arises from the individual's unique experience of self. The self evolves in the family atmosphere and sociocultural milieu, which both influence the individual's depression and death anxiety. The resourcefulness of the self was described in the previous chapter in terms of the degree of activity versus flight from attempts at mastery of psychological developmental tasks. Research designs have not yet fully or adequately assessed such phenomena. The greater value of the aforementioned study lies in the implications for an individual psychology of the loss of the self.

Quantitative research designs have failed to account for cultural influences on the interaction of depression with death anxiety. Cultural conditions unquestionably influence the psychology of the loss of the self. The self structure of Western man may not be vastly different from that of Eastern man. However, a society's prevailing attitudes about selflessness and collective versus individual identity have great bearing on the individual's propensity for death anxiety and purposelessness. For example, the Japanese respect for *harakiri* and *junshi* highlights the association of death with beauty and reunion fantasies. This thematic mixture was often present in the work of the English and American romantic poets. The helplessness and captivity depicted in the Japanese film *Woman in the Dunes* partially symbolized the depression of the subservient self. The suicides and violent deaths in the work of the late Yukio Mishima point to a continuum of positive attitudes about death as the loss of the self. The meaning of the suicides ranged from the comfort of an honored tradition to an expiation of guilt and disgrace through a romanticized reunion with dead parents and ancestors.

For the traditional Japanese, the disgrace of dishonor carried with it the threat of the worst possible humiliation: incurring the displeasure of ancestors and peers. Their experience of depression evolved with the pain of such anticipated humiliations. Japanese psychiatrists have reported that such depression rendered death by suicide a welcome and culturally sanctioned means of resolution. The suicide of Yukio Mishima, like the death missions of the World War II kamikaze pilots, may have signified in part a punishment and murder of the psychological self. It seems likely that these suicides also were carried out with the subconscious hope of merger with the collective self of the ancestors and the community. The prospect of reunion and psychological merger through death accounts for a willingness to die. As Mark Twain's Tom Sawyer illustrated, a powerful wish for death can be the means for renewed symbiotic merger with good parental figures. Perhaps the psychological mechanisms underlying the Japanese manifestations of depression resemble the Occidental's psychodynamics of depression. Nevertheless, the cultural attitudes toward the death of the self and the purpose of life remain very different. The traditional Japanese culture would encourage selflessness; it would also condone the honorable suicide, which avoids disgrace, while blending both of these attitudes with the overall eastern religious ascetic sensibility. The absence of striving, desire, and power needs corresponds with the highest degree of religious experience. The Eastern surrender of the self is compatible with the suspension of willing and purposeful consciousness. In other words, the purposelessness of Eastern aesthetics suggests a specific attitude about the loss of the self. It retains a cultural clarity that differs greatly from the lack of purpose of the Westerner's depressions. The former, to some extent, constitutes a cultural attitude about social dependence. The Japanese veiw of the loss of the self has its extreme manifestation in the blurring of boundaries between self and other in the unconscious fusion sought in the ritual suicide.

The vacuousness and despair of the Westerner's severe depressions and death anxiety betray neurotic failures of a different type. It has been the central thesis of this work that the depressed American's purposelessness betrays a neurotic inner emptiness that marks separation anxiety and ambivalence about death. The prototypical American frontiersman found happiness and material success in the West through independent exploration and industriousness. For him, the Eastern striving for the loss of the self and the submersion of the individual psyche in the group might seem mysterious. A delight in selflessness or a willingness to totally submerge oneself in nature or the teachings of gurus struck a sympathetic note in the American youth revolution of the late 1960s. It signified a requiem from ambition, greed, and moral corruption in the Vietnam and Watergate eras. The oriental Buddhist seeks fulfillment through an integration of the self with family, countrymen, and the beauty of nature. The Japanese who suffers from severe depressions may experience profound feelings of guilt and worthlessness. He or she may even seek refuge from painful suffering through death. Perhaps the traditional Japanese would not find the prospect of personal death as frightening as his or her Occidental counterpart. The nuances of these cultural influences on personality traits related to death anxiety are lost in the typical research methodology of experimental design.

The lack of purpose due to entanglement in the fear of death and depression accounts for a major aspect of neurotic conflict. It is not simply that the fear of death causes neuroses any more than, as Schopenhauer said, it is the cause of all religion. The notion of a neurotic symptom becomes more meaningful when understood in light of its interpersonal implications, characterological or psychodynamic source, and associated type of defensiveness. Confusion about purpose in life and unconscious problems with death anxiety can be expressed in conflicts of the adolescent or young adult in psychic rites of passages and the older adult in the midlife crisis. Attitudes about time in which time is conceptualized as an enemy denote a penchant for purposelessness and death anxiety. When people use slang expressions such as "killing time," "filling in time," "letting time slip by," "having no time to waste," or "time to kill," their speech may not simply reflect the shorthand of semantic convenience. The expressions capture the depression and purposelessness of an attitude in which present time is experienced as the enemy of the "self." The full conscious experience of oneself in the present implies a continuum of self-awareness. Self-awareness includes a sense of one's wholeness in the past, present, and anticipated future. People who lack purpose in life and greatly fear death have not synchronized past time with present realities. They retreat from the experience of 'I' to avoid the fear of the loss of the self.

The psychological research of the last fifteen years has proven that people with strong death fears view the future with vaguely anxious anticipation. When depression and death anxiety play a strong role in neurotic symptoms, their interaction contributes to the fear experiencing time in the present. Like death, time does not "fade gently into the night." When the fear of death reaches truly neurotic proportions, time becomes a series of discrete fragments. To the neurotic, the passage of time may feel like an obstacle to be overcome. Time then assumes the posture of segmented steps that one perceives as threatening. The passage of time can bring with it a neurotic anxiety that masks depression or purposelessness. English expressions such as "capturing time," "stopping time," and "making time stand still" imply this unconscious process of battling with oneself in relation to time. People who constantly complain of having "no time" to pursue social activities or other interests may be touching on this process. No matter how harried their schedules or legitimate their complaints may be, time is never the real enemy. The extent to which unstructured leisure time feels awkward or even anxiety-provoking for others also corresponds to the experience of time as an enemy. The rigid neurotic fights depression or death anxiety in its abrasive disruption of a carefully structured pattern of living. Leisure time that is not filled with travel or with the constant repetition of recreational or social activities suggests the passage of time. The continuous ebb and flow of time, in turn, suggests death. When freedom from activity or work pressures provides an opportunity for introspection, death anxiety and the associated uneasiness about the lack of an authentic purpose in life can spring into consciousness. A hectic pace of daily activities allows for the more defensive use of a "manic defense" or the denial of purposelessness and death anxiety. Leisure activity can therefore be pursued either out of interest and enjoyment or because it "fills" time" and helps to hide depression and anxiety.

Karen Horney wrote about this theme extensively under the heading of the drive for neurotic goals. Neurotic goals augment the neurotic's more basic need for finding a substitute for his lack of security and for representing his neurotic character solution with the trappings of virtue.[7] Thus, the obsessional applauds organizational ability and orderliness. The paranoid personality delights in the latest public revelation of the FBI or CIA's counterespionage and illegal invasions of privacy. From the neo-Freudian psychoanalytic perspective, the lack of purpose in life evolves into characteristic lifestyles that have as part of their unconscious focus an intense struggle with death anxiety. The principal patterns for expression of these conflicts entail avoidance of death fears, confrontation of death fears, and withdrawal from life. The neurotic styles for dealing with death anxiety and purposelessness go beyond the ordinary day-to-day denial of death to the point of blindness to one's fear. The neurotic remains unaware of the impact of death anxiety and purposelessness on living and character traits. Some people assume a pose of nonchalance or studied disinterest in death that masks an effort to avoid strong fears of death. The impact of death fears on such a person's life pattern and modes of interacting with other people will be discussed in a later chapter. "Lifestyles" in this sense refer to the pattern of feelings, character traits, thoughts about the world, and manner of dealing with other people in interpersonal relationships. The three types of lifestyles mentioned above are frequent adaptations to depression, a lack of purpose, and the fear of death. They are by no means mutually exclusive or idiosyncratic diagnostic entities. Lifestyles based on the use of avoidance, withdrawal, and defensive confrontations can be found in people regardless of the presence or absence of mental illness. Horney stated that the extent to which they dominate one's life and characteristic way of relating marks the extent to which they are neurotic. As general patterns of defense these three tendencies are universal. They are organized similarly to defensive styles for coping with more diffuse anxiety states and they allow the individual to pursue what Horney called neurotic goals, such as power, meaningless sexual conquest, and so on.

People who have a high fear of death often report a lack of purpose in the present. They are also troubled by a disquieting sense of anticipated future time and anxiety about present time. It has been shown that men and women fear death to the extent that they lack purpose in life. The demonstration of this inverse relationship removes one of Frankl's suppositions and Fromm's theories from the plane of speculation. It raises their views of health as freedom and purpose in life to more of a homologous concordance. The safe, healthy person brings a primarily neurotic anguish to his or her anxiety about death. Death anxiety corresponds with a resurgence of purposelessness and depression. Furthermore, the lack of purpose in life can be blatantly obvious or subtly oblique in its emergence in separation anxiety and neurotic problems in living.

Purpose in Life and "Identity Confusion"

One of the implications of the above reaserch study lies in the bearing of the fear of death on the dimensions of what Erikson called identity crises. During the college years or a midlife crisis, people will often contemplate psychotherapy because of the sudden recognition of the emptiness, or purposelessness, of their lives. For fifty-year old men or women who begin to recognize the reality of their own death as friends begin to die and mature children move away, depression is frequent. It is often an end product of introspection that life has become senseless and meaningless. For the college-age person who feels tormented in facing the need to find satisfying work or successful love relationships, anxiety over purposelessness and depression can be a dominant mood. For the young adult and middle-aged adult in a midlife crisis, anxiety and frustration over a lack of purpose may easily mask depression, death anxiety, and separation problems. The concepts of the "search" for personal identity, the "existential crisis," or the "midlife crisis" all reflect the presence of an attempted resolution of these areas of conflict. Their continuance in a given personality persists with the uncertainties of self-definition during the developmntal tasks of adulthood. Healthy, safe politically free people who live in despair about the absurdity of life and the certainty of death really communicate their neurotic suffering. Depression and difficulty in separation are psychodynamically related to death anxiety at all of these crisis points in development. These three interrelated dimensions of the fear of death can be ascertained in prolonged dissatisfaction with life. The term *separation* is again used here in the sense of the internal psychic representation of one's parents. At the completion of college or the point in middle age when goals have been accomplished and the possibilities of life seem limited a choice point is met. The person again needs to struggle with independence versus dependence on the internalized parents in defining choices about significant aspects of living. The problems of "identity formation" go hand in hand with the personal struggle to find a purpose in life and overcome depression.

The period of puberty entails a stage of maturation that integrates psychological physical growth and sexual development. One of the chief results of the "growth spurt" of the ego lies in the adolescent's increased capacity for independence from the parents and the associated potential for ambivalence about separation. This process of renewed separation-individuation continues throughout adolescence. It provides fertile soil for the growth of the adolescent's conflicted thoughts about the future and death. The need to separate from the influence of mother and father in favor of autonomy and independence conflicts with the need for the parents' availability. When separation anxiety and purposelessness surface in young adulthood, character traits or defenses may be inadequate. Part of the appeal of authoritarian youth movements and cult religions is based on a defense against the depression that arises from these conflicts. Cults bring the means to lower depression and purposelessness by projecting and externalizing meaninglessness onto the world. The more difficult it is for the young adult to achieve independence and the attainment of an autonomous identity, the more vulnerable the person becomes to depressions. Threats to self-esteem stand out in the midst of such crises of self-definition. Part of the significance of youth cults lies in the substitution of a group culture and identity for internalized parental attitudes. The cult religion, like the Nazi party thereby yields a sense of security by reducing anxiety and depression during the struggle for independence and autonomy. Since victory is rarely complete in the face of the demands of adulthood, maintenance of an identity and purpose in life is sought by even some people well into their twenties or thirties.

The adoption of a unique sense of purpose in life, on the other hand, coincides with a better, more continuous sense of one's "self." The emotionally successful adult achieves a sense of identity with a sense of purpose. The view of the world described by Kafka, Beckett, and some of the existentialists presupposed a contrasting veiw of man as formless, fragmented, and lacking in such substance or direction. The film anti-hero of the sixties and early seventies also exemplified the neurosis of purposelessness. A shaky sense of self and identity increases one's difficulty in the demands of social exchange. This kind of helpless or at times nameless violent character suffers from a lack of an inner central core of the self-experience. The fictional, alienated anti-hero lacks an ego and a self that can transcend fleeting impressions and moments of feeling. In spite of self-absorption, the person without purpose and identity flounders in both relatedness and the quest for satisfaction. Real self-awareness and a recognition of the "self" as a continuous whole person is missing in this neurotic state of affairs. There is little substance that holds together the ambiguities of personal experience. Self-awareness then remains limited at the level of "How do I feel?" "What do I want?" "What is my perception of the other's experience in this situation?" or "What is the mutual effect of our interaction?" However, it is even more constrained in grappling with the questions existentialists pose about purpose in life. "Who is the 'me' that is thinking, feeling, and relating in this way?" "Of what kind of stuff am I made that I experience myself as being myself?" "Where do I exist in space and time in relation to others?" and "Of what relevance is my life?" Without some facility for this kind of self-awareness, life can certainly seem absurd and lacking in purpose. When the young adult lacks the ego strength to form an identity and chose a purpose in life, the world will seem depressing and quite frightening.

In contemporary American society, the equation of lack of purpose with a poorly established sense of identity emerges clearly in the cult popularity of youth movements. As the sense of "self" develops during middle and late adolescence, depression and the fear of death are normal occurrences, a part of the ambivalence and disillusionment about the parents of childhood. Attachment to any dogmatic ideology brings rigid lifestyles that provide a built-in sense of identity and purpose. A cultist lifestyle combats depression, separation anxiety, and the fear of the loss of the self. Moreover the cult gives the adolescent self-esteem by allowing him or her to share in the group identity and sanctioned modes of thinking, feeling, and relating.

For example, the popularity of the Unification Church in my opinion points to the process by which the identity of the group provides security for the anxious young adult. The cultist is promised love in exchange for obedience in spite of any deficiencies in the self. Total identification with a group, adoption of its philosophy, and worshiplike devotion to its leader all give the individual member a false sense of self through a shared identity. Death anxiety and purposelessness vanish as the self is surrendered to the cult. The members' rejection of the parental culture and their susceptibility to the group's influence appear to represent adolescent rebellion. Perhaps it is more of a pseudo-salvation, or transformation of the self into one that appears glorious, loving, and no longer troubled by uncertainty and anxiety. The grandiosity of the cult leader reduces feelings of inadequacy in the follower. The illusion of fusion and shared identity temporarily rescues the worshipper from the pain of purposelessness and death anxiety. Belief in the church or the head of the church supplants the need for self-affirmation. Choices about relationships values and ways of thinking about the complicated and confusing world are neglected for sharing in the collective ego of the cult. Early adult and late adolescent conflicts about leaving home, finding work, choosing partners or lifestyles usually entail anxiety over making decisions. The cultist never has to make a personal decision, since uncertainty can be avoided by submersion of the self in the observances of the group. A cult leader's charm helps to demonstrate his principal position as replacement for good parents of early childhood. In exchange for obedience, the young adult members of the cult are able to fend off the fright and fatigue of personal responsibility. They center their emotional dependence on a new substitute parent and no longer feel overwhelmed by the task of identity formation. The mystique of the cult leader promises emotional salvation to prospective members, together with protection from negative feelings of shame and inadequacy. The implication or fantasy of a profound transforming love counteracts the disillusionment felt with their parents. It precludes future disappointments and the anxiety of finding a purpose in life. The cult leader becomes the idealized transferential father or mother in the unconscious of his followers. The illusion of perpetual security and happiness is granted in exchange for the abandonment of the follower's self. The leader's charisma and omnipotent power relieves the young follower's depression and lack of purpose. His positive attributes are seen from the vantage point of a young child who needs constant parental protection from the fear of death. His power or goodness seem infinite to his followers in relation to their failure to achieve autonomy. The cultist's fusion with the group identity reduces the pain of separation-individuation and the purposelessness of death anxiety. It provides them with a false idealized self defined by the group. This kind of transferential distortion of the religious or political leader has been described by a number of authors as being akin to the zeal of the Hitler Youth Corps. It explains the enigmatic allure of the Reverend Jim Jones in Guyana before his followers' mass suicide. The love for the Fuhrer transformed the ordinary Nazi into a glorified superman who no longer had to deal with feelings of inadequacy and self-doubt. The young cultists present the facade of a psuedo-identity and purpose in life. They disguise their lack of genuine purpose in life by a neurotic surrender of the self that prevents individuation.

Summary

The concept of purpose in life has been extended beyond its original existentialist origins. Fromm and Frankl's contributions touched on meaninglessness and lack of purpose in life as fundamentally neurotic problems. An experimental attempt to document an existentialist notion of health related the lack of a sense of purpose in life to death anxiety.

The ability to handle suffering and a positive genuine religious outlook were hypothesized as dimensions of this existential concept of mental health. Fromm and Frankl both implied the possibility of positive attitudes about the certainty of death. The recognition of non-being could be regarded by the healthy individual if not with acceptance, then with a determination to form a unique purpose in life. As part of the outlined experimental study, purpose in life and death anxiety were compared and contrasted in different types of religious groups. It seemed that people who have Allport's intrinsic religious orientation and Fromm's humanistic religion would be the most likely religious groups to have low death anxiety and a high purpose in life. I had argued earlier in the research study that a high purpose in life would be congruent with low death anxiety. It was a small logical jump to infer that people with a genuine intrinsic or humanistic religion would be less troubled by either a low purpose in life or death anxiety.

Differences on purpose in life tests appeared to reflect more than just depression, since the Purpose in Life Test included the assessment of depression in its standardization and validation procedures. The obtained relationship between a low purpose in life and death anxiety could not fully substantiate Allport and Fromm's ideas on the basis of this study. The research study did not unequivocally prove the importance of depression as an intermediating variable in religion and death anxiety. However, the results did point to one general trend. Intrinsic or humanistic religious groups do not always fear death less than the authoritarian or extrinsic groups. Intrinsically religious people who have less purpose in life consistently showed a high fear of death. That high degree of death anxiety could be explained on the basis of depression.

Speculation about the interplay between depression and the lack of purpose in life was supported by brief accounts of cultural influences, attitudes toward time, and the purposelessness of identity problems. Woman's higher death anxiety was also explained on the basis of depression and the inherent relationship between these two factors and separation anxiety. It was hypothesized that when time is experienced as the enemy of the self, the individual struggles with depression and difficulty in forging a purpose in life. The Japanese ritual suicides were mentioned in passing as evidence of the wide divergence of possible attitudes about purpose in life and the loss of the self. Erikson's concept of "identity confusion" was included to explain pathological extremes of the young adult's lack of purpose in life.

Blind devotion to a religious or political cult leader becomes a source of emotional salvation for the young adult who gives up the struggle for individuation and identity formation. The cult obviates the need for the member's finding a purpose in life or dealing with the certainty of death. The cult followers thus avoid separation anxiety, depression, and death anxiety that would accompany their growth. Young people's susceptibility to the appeal of cult movements has been correlated with the degree of their own difficulty in maintaining the continuity of the self and the identity. When their lives are attuned to the goals of their leader, the individual's purpose in life becomes one of compliance.

The uncertainties and stress of finding meaning in life have been described as fundamentally normal experiences that need not cause overwhelming depression. The neurotic's strategies for coping with purposelessness and death anxiety follow the path of the individual's characteristic defensiveness. According to existentialist theory, these outgrowths of the deficiencies of the self obscure the neurotic's failure at finding authenticity. The elevation of love, success, power, or subservience to the level of a primary purpose in life constitutes the secondary neurotic line of defense against "identity confusion" and death anxiety. The overlap between death anxiety, depression, and lack of purpose is apparent whether viewed from Frankl's existential stance or from Horney, Sullivan, and Fromm's neo-Freudian psychoanalytic position. The zeal of the Nazi party member and the subservience and fanaticism of the religious cultist were said to hide their lack of purpose. Neurotic fears of death and difficulty in finding an autonomous identity thus go hand in hand. The neurotic's death anxiety and lack of purpose make him resemble Victor Hugo's Quasimodo in *The Hunchback of Notre Dame*. It was only after his death that Quasimodo's body embraced that of the dead gypsy girl, but their embrace disintegrated into dust at the close of the novel. His blind love for the gypsy girl became a central purpose and guiding passion in life. The neurotic often finds out too late that defensive goals are not worth the efforts of the struggle. Quasimodo's purpose remained steadfast against the eccentricities of fate and the inevitability of death. Even after death, love was denied him. Neurotic avoidance of commitment to a purpose in life insures similar disappointment.

CHAPTER EIGHT

Existential Psychology and the Fear of Death

Existentialism

The early plays of Harold Pinter and the prose of Samuel Beckett, Fyodor Dostoevski, and particularly Franz Kafka consistently dramatized modern man's alienation and difficulty in honest communication. A sense of despair was keenly felt by their characters in the face of death and the prospect of nothingness. Given the certainty of death, they succumbed to a psychic impotence. They were defeated by the meaninglessness of life, the terror of freedom, and the uncertainty of knowledge. Their spiritual malaise and emotional suffering brought to life three essential problems addressed by the existential philosophers of the late nineteenth and early twentieth centuries. From Nietzche and Kierkegaard to Sartre, the existentialists shaped a phenomenological inquiry into the nature of knowledge, the implications of death, and the meaning of freedom. Dissatisfied with political and religious philosophies, they called for the end of ideology. The existential movement focused on man as an existing being, who can only attain authenticity and truth inside his own experience. From the existential psychoanalytic view, health involves experiencing onself fully in the present. Mental health is antithetical to the preoccupation with death anxiety. The experiencing active self that is fully known need not be very fearful of death or overwhelmed by the depression and separation anxiety of neurotic defensiveness. An introduction to the existentialist studies of knowledge, death, and freedom will underscore their description of existential awareness and its relation to death anxiety.

For Dostoevski, the central aspect of life was freedom.[1] This human condition compels man toward insecurity and anxiety in light of the limitless possibilities of freedom of choice. The exercise of freedom and the pursuit of meaning in life both characterize the existential man who is unwilling to achieve self-definition through material comfort or conventional conformity. Dostoevski's concern with God and the problem of good and evil differentiated him from other existential writers who concentrated more fully on the suffering of man's plight in a world where God was unknowable. To the existentialist, if the challenge of freedom was not adequately met, then life became death, a never-ending dialogue with nothingness. The neurotic self abhors freedom, or at the very least is threatened by the possibilities of autonomous active living.

The existentialists consistently addressed the question: "Of what use and certainty is knowledge, if man does not know in his heart, senses, and body?" Traditional epistemology, religious dogma, the scientific method, and political ideology have led man away from the necessity of finding the meaning of life and truth as rooted in experience. Ionesco's *The Lesson* represented the height of danger in seeking knowledge through a non-existential framework. The Professor, who is charged with the tutoring of a young girl trying to pass her examinations, escalates the lesson into an authoritarian, totalitarian attack. He humiliates her and berates her ignorance, finally murdering her in a rage impassioned by the quest for order and perfect factual knowledge. The innocent eager student was victimized by the absurdity of her need for a nonexistential knowledge more than by the fury of her demanding demented tutor. The rigidity of their artificially defined roles obviated any legitimate existential dialogue between them. In *The Chairs* and *The Bald Soprano*, Ionesco documented the loss of identity and the shallowness of such relationships. The emptiness of life for the ordinary man and woman lies rooted in the failure to find a meaning in life and a solution to the problem of freedom. The conversation of Ionesco's protagonists evolved into a meaningless babble of cliches and nonsense words. The authentic existence of another person's thoughts and feelings becomes unreal and impossible in the discourse such communication symbolizes. To these existentialists, fully confronting the possibility of one's death did not serve as much of an aperitif to life. It resulted in an endless encounter with despair, psuedo-knowledge, and a lack of personal freedom. The emptiness, boredom, and unrelatedness in modern life rose in cacophony in the late 1960s films of the New Wave of cinema. In Jean-Luc Godard's film *Weekend*, for example, death took on the form of a mindless accident hardly noted by the principal characters. The so-called existential suicide also rested on a similarly fashionable assumption. Since life has little meaning, ending it out of boredom, or frustration over lack of purpose, took on the aspect of a glamorous victory over the human condition. When life is seen as having absolutely no meaning, death seems both a logical alternative to suffering and a welcome relief. The lack of genuine feelings and the absence of empathic concern for others in the light of despair preside in a number of existentialist works. Since death and life overlap, death, therefore, does not result in mourning. Under such circumstances, the loss of the self is experienced as well as feared. There may be no true mourning or real experience of loss in actual death, as, for example, James Agee portrayed in *A Death in the Family*. Once death is accepted as being the inevitable consequence of man's helplessness in the universe, then death, like life, comes to have little or no meaning. It is experienced by the neurotic as a reflection of passivity, depression, and separation anxiety inherent in their failures at living. The depression and fear of individuation in neurotic death anxiety further contributes to the alienation from the self and the fear of the loss of the self.

I mentioned in discussing Franz Kafka's dream of Josef K. that his work epitomized the neurotic passivity in death anxiety. The despair of the characters in Kafka's stories mirrored the cripping depression and suffering he felt during his short lifetime. They faced the neurotic fear of the loss of the self in grappling with the problem of freedom and the problem of knowledge. Kafka's stories repeatedly document depression's dual role as a defense against and an expression of death anxiety. Throughout his prose accounts, man was consistently thwarted in attaining goals and in attempting to govern life and chart a personal course of direction.

Kafka's characters typically feel helpless in the face of freedom and unable to have much impact on the world. Whether unjustly accused of a crime and put in jail, or transformed into an insect, their free will is lost in neurotic defensiveness. The bureaucracy of society and the uncertainty of freedom frustrate inner-goal-directed behavior. The land surveyor mysteriously dies among strangers in *The Castle* before reaching his assigned work. In *The Trial*, K's confusion about the nature of his crime and the identity of his accusers renders him helpless to come to grips with his predicament. It is only as K approaches death that he begins to realize the nature of his crime—namely that he is on trial for having destroyed himself. Erich Fromm concluded that K's crime consisted of passivity, complacency, and the failure to live an authentic, meaningful life.[2] K responded to freedom by shrinking from inner-directed existential life. *The Trial* symbolized Kafka's pessimistic position that only meek hope becomes possible in the face of despair through transcendence of the existential dilemma. K was punished in the trial just as Gregor died of starvation in *The Metamorphosis* after having been transformed into a loathsome insect. Freudian theoreticians might interpret Gregor's change into a hideous human-sized beetlelike bug as a punishment for Oedipal strivings such as hostility toward his father and incestuous sexual wishes toward his mother and sister.[3] The existential analysts would see his metamorphosis into a slop-eating bug as a clear metaphor for the psychic wages of Gregor's failure to live an autonomous authentic existence dictated by free choice and his unique purpose in life. Capitulation to family pressure, jealousy, possessiveness, competition, and self-deception all contributed to an inner psychological neurotic transformation that was symbolized by the change of his body. The ugly human-sized insect provided graphic description of the impotence and self-loathing of his inner psychic state. The existentialists argued that the neurotic failure to transcend the existential dilemma leads to a life of anguish and emotional suffering, like the physical suffering of the twisted bodies in George Grosz' paintings.

Existential anxiety that arises from the contemplation of death or non-being in my opinion comes quite close to a more experiential description of some of the phenomenon of depression. The fear of death or the fear of lifelessness consisting of boredom, meaninglessness and lack of purpose reflect a projection outward onto the world of inner emptiness and a lack of psychological strength. Sociocultural repression, political oppression, or bureaucratic obstacles to human needs represent genuine aspects of the evolution of so-called existential anxiety. Yet psychotherapists treating people with existential complaints often do not have to look too far to uncover the primacy of conflicts and depression underlying fears of death. Despair that arises from sensitivity to the existential complaints can be seen to have a unique menning for each individual that stems from his or her psychological functioning, personal history and way of being.

The philosophy of existentialism concerned itself with the aspects of man's existence. Facing death and the potential of nothingness constitutes the "existential challenge" of honest, authentic human experience. The contention that anxiety, approaching terror, and despair constitute the natural outgrowth of the existential dilemma remains open to question. Despair and depression that arise in the act of contemplating the prospect of death can just as easily derive from a non-philosophical source of anguish, namely the psychological conflicts of the neurotic character. Existentialist philosophers and writers on the whole make little mention of the positive aspects of the joys of living and short shifts of the beauty of the world. In a laudable effort to achieve honesty in describing the human condition, they tend to depict despair and anxiety as the most likely consequences of the knowledge of death.

Existentialism and Psychology

Existential psychology is the accrual of the attempts made by psychologists and psychiatrists to combine the tenets of existential philosophy and the method of phenomenology with the clinical study of mental functioning. This attempt provided a fresh viewpoint for clinical work and a conception of health that seems congurent with Fromm and the neo-Freudians' positions. Questions concerning the meaning of life and death, the nature of time and space, man's helplessness in the universe, and the place of values or religious questions in psychotherapy have led psychotherapists to an appreciation of the existentialist movement. The esistentialists' concern for twentieth-century man's complaints of isolation, loneliness, and lack of meaning have not fallen on deaf ears among practitioners. The early existentialists felt dissatisfaction with both behaviorism and traditional Freudian psychoanalysis. They therefore emphasized that man's most crucial characteristic is his awareness of his own existence, together with his changing strivings and goals. From a historical perspective, much of the origin of this existentialist position lies in the writings of Kierkegaard and Heidegger. Jaspers, Sartre, Nietzsche, and to some extent Miguel de Unamuno also influenced existential psychology by their appeal to a reality that assumes "both objectivity and subjectivity." As an outgrowth of the existentialist tradition in philosophy, existential psychotherapists have come to view the "patient" as constantly emerging and becoming. The patient is presently seen as struggling to define himself in space and time, and in relation to other people through the choices he makes. Existentialism can be partially defined as a psychology of knowledge. It attempts to understand modern man by deemphasizing subject-object distinctions and focusing on self-awareness in experience.

Ludwig Binswanger, a Swiss contemporary of Freud, found direct applications for existentialism in clinical psychiatry. Binswanger criticized psychotherapy for its subject-object orientation in theory which he rejected in favor of an "existential analysis." Rollo May, Viktor Frankl, Medard Boss, Roland Kuhn, R. D. Laing, Enri Ellenberger, and others have also contributed to psychotherapy via the existentialist view of man as a creature who is aware of himself as continually coming into being, changing, and evolving. The adoption of an existential approach by these authors led to significant and original contributions to psychotherapy. A brief sampling of the historical development of existential philosophy will serve to clarify existential approaches to psychotherapy and psychopathology. These approaches have dwelled largely on a neurotic meaninglessness and helplessness that have been designated here as death anxiety. The existentialist works are filled with experiential and theoretical descriptions of the fear of the loss of the self. Sören Kierkegaard first described the anxiety of dread, or *angst*, in several insightful essays touched with psychological acumen. Kierkegaard maintained that when sexuality and materialistic strivings take over and dominate man's freedom, then dread and guilt are the results.[4] Dread is a phenomenological indication of the terror in freedom. When life is lived on a purely sensory level, despair results.

Much of Kierkegaard's work involved a reaction to and a refutation of Hegel's dialectical systematization of existence. Kierkegaard condemned the dialectic by maintaining that any such system of existence is impossible since existence is constantly changing. Abstract truth cannot be reality, as Hegel had maintained, because truth exists only as a person experiences it in action. There is no objective knowledge according to Kierkegaard but, "subjectivity is truth." He abandoned the traditional philosophical speculations about the meaning of existence in favor of the position that all theories must be realized "in existence." Knowledge should attempt to bridge the gulf between what is abstract truth and what is essentially real for a given person. As the foremost early exist-

entialist thinker, Kierkegaard insisted upon applying the whole personality to the problems of existence. The theoretical understanding of truth
had as its essence the need to reflect on the subjective relationship between the knower and the object that is known. Whether the mode of
this relationship is objectively valid or invalid, it defines the truth for a
given person as he experiences it.[5] Although the position skirts the issues of the possibility of absolute truth, absolute morality, and the certainty of knowledge, its implication cannot be escaped by any psychotherapist who works within the psychoanalytic or interpersonal
mode. The patient's present experience, his conflicts, genuine feelings,
thoughts, fantasies, attitudes, prejudices, needs, wishes, and distortions
in interpersonal relationships all constitute the given of therapeutic interchange. The patient's subjectively reported knowledge about himself,
other people, and the world must be listened to, at least at first, for its experiential validity.

Truth was not obtainable by distance or objectivity in this framework
because man as subject could not be separated from what he observed as
object. Thus, the existential man is one who understands himself in his
own existence as he acts and experiences himself in time, space, and in
relation to other people. Thinking existentially, therefore, demands intelligence, feeling, imagination, and commitment to living in the present.
In *The Concept of Dread*, Kierkegaard anticipated Freud's position on the
importance of repression in psychoanalytic theory. Kierkegaard stated
that when truth is known and accepted as part of one's being, it makes
one free.[6] True knowledge involves commitment, since the knower must
produce the knowledge in action and in his consciousness. When one
knows truth by living it, then existence is characterized by the consummation of freedom. Kierkegaard's psychological description of the
importance of anxiety constituted the first important serious treatment
given the subject aside from Freud's. His idea that freedom creates anxiety and that anxiety is the potential reality of freedom to some extent
parallels Fromm's view of neurosis.

Most contemporary psychotherapists hold the concepts of freedom
of choice and responsibility as central to work with patients' character-
ologiclal problems. Freud's later description of the goal of psychoanalysis, as the replacement of id processes with ego activity, may have implied just such an assumption. Removing repression, unconscious
conflicts, and symptoms served to enable the patient to become more responsible and better able to choose one course of action over another.
Modern, humanistic psychotherapies decry the primacy of concepts such
as cure, symptom reduction while simultaneously emphasizing freedom
of choice, individuality, and responsibility for being oneself. Even
though there is considerable variance between the classical Freudian
theoretical understanding of the ego and anxiety as drive or impulse related and current neo-Freudian or existential humanistic views, they
have in common the respect for the patient's freedom of choice and responsibility for behavior that evolved from the existentialist orientation.

The existential notion that neurosis includes an inability to think, feel or act responsibly in the present also is shared by both psychoanalytic traditions.

Martin Heidegger placed the existential dilemma in a broader context in *Sein and Zeit*. The fundamental existential dilemma grasps the inevitability of anxiety, since man's anxiety comes from the threat of realizing the possibility of his non-being. Extreme concern for the reality a person is immediately experiencing followed from Heidegger's concept of *Dasein*, the mode of human existence. This concept was adopted by the phenomenologists and it stimulated the development of an existential psychotherapy, particularly Ludwig Binswanger's approach to existential analysis, or *Daseinanalyse*.[7] *Dasein*, or existence, is the essential experiential life, which is composed of "being (*sein*) and there (*da*)." Since man alone can know himself as a being who is present in time and space, he can be conscious of his own existence in experience. Another related influence on the later existential psychologists was Nietzche's description of Western man's sickness of the soul. Friedrich Nietzsche criticized his society for its loss of self-consciousness and its ignorance for not seeing that truth must be grasped in experience. Nietzsche observed the disintegration of society, the lack of relevance of the Hebraic-Christian tradition, and the increasing intellectual dishonesty of organized religion. His claim that "God is Dead" was accompanied by a call for "will to power" and individual self-fulfillment. Nietzsche illustrated existential thinking only insofar as he described the will to power in an ontological sense as man's affirming his own being or existence as an individual. According to Nietzsche, man "seeks power not pleasure."[8]

With the realization that one's own choices can lead either to personal fulfillment or the loss of being, authentic living takes on a new aspect. Authenticity may be defined in part as openness to the challenge to avoid letting existence be a series of chance accidents. Although Nietzsche saw the implication of that position as the quest for a "superman," this inborn need for fulfillment does have interesting parallels in the writings of the existential psychologists. The concept of self-actualization has been stressed by the humanistic psychologists as much as authenticity has been stressed by the existential writers. Although Nietzsche reportedly never read Kierkegaard, there is a striking similarity between their views on subjectivity and passion. Nietzsche mirrored Kierkegaard's conception of knowledge through experience, particularly in his insistence that he could write and speak only of those things that "he had experienced," not simply of thought processes in his head.

Another forerunner of existential psychology, Miguel de Unamuno, incorporated much of the tradition of Nietzsche and Kierkegaard into his poetry, plays, and novels. Unamuno viewed man existentially as a being of flesh and bone, an individual existing in space and time. Using Descartes' famous principle as a springboard, Unamuno affirmed existence over thought. In his philosophical novels and plays, Unamuno rejected the Cartesian formula "*Cogito, ergo, sum* (I think, therefore, I am)" in favor of the notion "I feel or I love, therefore, I am,"[9] or, even more clearly stated in *The Tragic Sense of Life*, "I am, therefore, I think."[10] This concept was quite similar to Heidegger's later statement that "cognition is simply a mode of existence" that can only be understood as an activity. Knowing is therefore not a passive reflection. It is an active process of interchange with the world similar to what existentialists identify as other forms of being in the world.

According to Unamuno, to act is to exist and to exist is to act. Objectivity of knowledge represented an insoluble problem for which the only reasonable approach could be keeping perceptions rooted in experience. Much of Unamuno's work dealt with spiritual crises in the course of a search for personal immortality. His religious faith became a matter "of the heart," since he could not accept any rational basis for religious beliefs. In fact, in *The Tragic Sense of Life*, he added that his reason "laughed at his faith" but that he was content to find God in his heart.[11] Unamuno's answer to the seeking of meaning in existence was to wish that God exists and thereby impose an order on the chaos of human freedom and potentiality. This affirmation of a faith driven yet passionate and spiritual life enabled Unamuno to accept pain and suffering as the highest forms of consciousness. His immediate reality was one of suffering, the inevitable consequence of the disharmony between flesh and spirit. Emotional and physical pain were equated with the substance of life. This existential attitude toward suffering was paralleled in the writings of later existential psychologists. It is related to another major tenet of both psychoanalytic and existential psychotherapy: that human growth derives from and necessarily depends on some measure of suffering and anxiety. The giving up of neurotic, immature, non-productive behavior patterns and modes of inauthentic living is often accompanied by the experience of anxiety. These existentialist contributions provided an alternate framework for understanding death anxiety which has been defined as synonymous with depression and the fear of the loss of the self.

Sartre commented directly on these issues by attacking psychoanalysis for reducing man to a passive object of conditioning who is seemingly enslaved by unconscious forces.[12] Sartre rejected the unconscious and the analyzability of man as an absurd reduction in favor of the existentialist view that each man "is his choices." His position posed that human nature is "reduced" through deterministic analysis. The pronouncement that existence is freedom might be considered a philosophical principal in Rogerian, client-entered therapies even though Sartre's criticism of pyschoanalysis bears little relevance to modern existential psychotherapy and psychology. However, Sartre's definition of freedom comes close to providing a philosophical groundwork for the importance of the concepts of self-actualization and maximization of human potential. Both constructs underlie humanistic psychotherapy and the popular human potential movement. Even without adopting an avowed existentialist postition, psychoanalytic therapists can accept the phenomneological orientation. Beginning with the immediate experience of the patient provides this aspect to the dialogue as it unfolds in the presence of the therapist.

Heidegger and Unamuno's work do not seem inconsistent with the view that intense death anxiety combines depression, separation anxiety and helplessness in the face of psychological death. Fear and defensiveness account for the person's failure of the spirit in simultaneously fearing life and death. A richly endowed mixture of personality traits assemble in the individual's idiosyncratic defense against the fear of death.

However, Sartre's attacks on psychoanalysis as a theory of the mind reflect a rather shallow understanding of the development of psychoanalytic theory, which in no way reduces man to a spineless composite of drive tendencies. The image Sartre painted of the well-psychoanalyzed man as a kind of amorphous indeterminate clay mixture, passive to experience and compartmentalized into drive tendencies, comes from a picture of the early psychoanalytic model without the ego. It predated current Freudian theory and the post-Freudian contributions on the ego, the self, and the growth of character.

Existential Psychotherapy

Ludwig Binswanger first applied the philosophy of existentialism directly to the study of mental illness and psychotherapy. As was the case with most of the advances in existential psychology and psychiatry, Binswanger could point to specific existential philosophers who had influenced him. He insisted on understanding a patient's life history as a structure that constituted his or her unique "being in the world." In Binswanger's most famous paper, *The Case of Ellen West*, he readily credited Kierkegaard's influence on his thinking. Ellen West's schizophrenia was fully illuminated as a kind of "sickness unto death" that Kierkegaard had described.[13]

This relationship between schizophrenia and the unbearable anxiety of death has been developed by several modern existentialist psychoanalysts. The whole existential orientation to psychiatry, psychotherapy, and psychology has commanded a lasting effect on theory and the practice of psychotherapy. As an outgrowth of Heidegger's philosophical principle of *Dasein*, Binswanger's approach to psychotherapy promoted conscious awareness and the patient's responsibility for his own life and behavior. The healthy individual or the successful patient creates solutions by realizing his own existence, or being as becoming. Current third force humanistic psychotherapies have expanded this position. They include in defining health, a patina of self-actualization, creativity, love, peak experiences, and transcendental or transpersonal experiences. Rollo May, the American existentialist, pointed to the influence of both Binswanger and Kierkegaard on his personal psychological history and on the theoretical development of his existential psychology.

Kierkegaard's elucidation of *Angst*, or anxiety, deeply affected May's acceptance of his own suffering during his confinement in a tuberculosis sanitarium.[14] Kierkegaard's major works, in fact, formed the basic premises for some of May's contributions to theories of psychopathology. May defined anxiety as a basic human reaction to a danger to existence or to some value that could be identified with existence. Death, the ultimate threat of non-being, constitutes one segment of the source of such danger.[15] The mode of behavior concerned with "being in itself" was identified by May as the developing changing self. Since a consciousness of self implies the possibility of denying the self, existential anxiety was consequently seen as a necessary part of life. May affirmed Kierkegaard's idea of anxiety, or *Angst*, as the realization of the struggle between being and non-being. He added that existential anxiety arises at the realization of the possibility of non-being. The principal crisis faced by the self remains the handling of such existential anxiety. May further claimed that neurosis was an attempted denial of the full range of one's responsibility and sense of being to hold onto a central part of the self.

This elaboration of the existential position is congruent with the view that death anxiety is the intense fear of the loss of the self. The neurotic develops defenses and a lifestyle that seek to preserve part of the self. His behavior implies attempts to cope with immediate situations and his symptoms are therefore methods for affirming or denying one's potentialities. May and Erich Fromm have both stressed the role of distorted values in psychopathological states. Behavior disorders and neurotic symptoms thus result from unsuccessful resolution of problems in living. Neurosis has been viewed by both as the result of the struggle for autonomy and responsibility in light of defensive egocentric processes.[18] For example, according to May, a realtively complete victory of existential anxiety results in schizophrenia. This process is one of "existential impoverishment," in which an increasing rigidity of the self occurs and potential choices in living are given up. The schizophrenic has a disordered sense of space and time, whereas the "healthy" person can be aware of time subjectively as it unfolds in a continuous stream of experiences. One who successfully meets the crisis of existential anxiety was said to have "ontological security". May believed that the schizophrenic lacks onotological security and is without a continuous sense of presence in the world. A number of other existential analysts have also stated that the schizophrenic has given up freedom, wheareas the neurotic individual is so incapacitated by anxiety as to be unable to live fully in the present.

It is clear that an ontologically secure person would grasp his or her own autonomous identity in relation to the identity of others. Primary "ontological insecurity" was defined by May as a lack of confidence and corresponding need to defend one's identity rather than expand it through meaningful intimate relationships. What remains unclear in May's development of existential anxiety is how it differs from the ordinary experience of neurotic insecurity and anxious or agitated depression. Aside from the intellectual content of thoughts about non-being, is not the inner emotional experience of the person who undergoes existential anxiety one of anxiety and depression per se? In May's works, existential anxiety adds the "dimension of existence" to the psychoanalytic conception of neurosis. Anxiety about death does not simply stem from the contemplation of non-being. Death anxiety intensifies with the psychic interplay between depression, separation anxiety, and the fear of death. Existential anxiety in my view constitutes a phenomenological description of the fear of death. It is both stimulated by and expressed in neurotic problems in daily living.

Victor Frankl, the Austrian existentialist, developed a theory of "logotherapy," somewhat parallel to Mays ideas, which he called the Third Viennese School of Psychotherapy. Frankl's theory of personality and views on psychotherapy are within the existentialist tradition, even though their specific philosophical roots cannot be easily uncovered. *Logos* can be translated as "meaning" and logotherapy's basic premise holds that striving to find a meaning in one's life is man's primary motivational force. This "will to meaning" is supposed to replace the pleasure principle as a future-oriented motivational system. Frankl believed that man does not seek a homeostasis, or an equilibrium, as in the original analytic economic model of tension reduction.[19] If the will to meaning was frustrated, Frankl describes an "existential frustration" that resulted in neurosis. Since tension, and struggling to achieve goals, was thought to be an essential part of life, existential frustration was not considered pathological in itself. The purpose of Frankl's logotherapy was to help the neurotic by demanding that he assume responsibility for his own life, find meaningful values, and act on them. The existential philosophy portrayed in the characters of Unamuno's work was based on an acceptance of pain and suffering as growth-promoting experiences. Frankl developed a view similar to Unamuno's position that pain and suffering can be the highest forms of consciousness that need to be experienced. Just as Freud hinted at some physiological basis for neurosis, Frankl also speculated that there must be a physiological basis for both neuroses and psychoses. Nevertheless, Frankl stressed a phenomenological view of neurosis in which the psychodynamics involve spiritual or existential conflicts. Neurotic symptoms were depicted by him as condensations of existential anxiety. In agreement with Fromm, he considered that the neurotic's symptoms sustain a fear of death and a simultaneous fear of life.

Although some existential conflicts certainly have legitimacy of their own, the existential anxiety depicted by Frankl, like that defined by the other existentialists, seems indistinguishable from depression and despair. The experience of depression and defensiveness comes much closer to an accurate description of the neurotic's anxious state than a disordered will to meaning. The arousal of some degree of anxiety at the prospect of death is in fact a universal experience. That such fears of death can lead to an "existential neurosis," which in itself constitutes a neurosis, in my opinion seems doubtful. The description offered by the existential theorists of the neurotic who experiences existential anxiety clearly involves anxiety, depression, and the simultaneous fear of death and life. However the phenomena of existential anxiety could be accounted for as a variant manifestation of depression rather than a distinct entity. The existentialist techniques obscure this point.

Frankl described the schizophrenic as one who experiences himself as an object, very often the object of the persecutory intentions of other men. There is insufficient psychic activity in schizophrenics, according to Frankl. He developed techniques for their therapy on this existential model. Frankl saw the schizophrenic's ego as limited in awareness and also that he experiences psychic activity passively. Paradoxical Intention is his technique for treating all symptoms as a condensation of existential anxiety, and its goal is to transform the neurotic's ego by giving the person a new attitude toward his neurosis. The neurotic in Frankl's model must eventually do what he fears and become conscious of his own responsibility for growth. Neurotics then reduce their fear by divorcing themselves from their symptoms and by learning not to identify themselves with their own anxiety. It seems to this author that Frankl's assertions are only partially true. The inner experience of despair and anxiety about the possibility of non-being, which Kierkegaard described as "the sickness unto death," needs to be understood in its uniquely personal meaning and origins for a given individual. Simply addressing such complaints at the level of "existential anxiety" obscures the importance of the therapist and patient's mutual exploration of the underlying significance and development of the existential complaints. It also covers up the interplay between depression and the patient's unique style for coping with the fear of the loss of the self.

Existential Psychotherapy and Neurosis

Throughout the 1960s and early 1970s, a number of existential writers extended these theoretical contributions to psychotherapeutic work with neurotics and schizophrenics. Salvitore Maddi supported Frankl's idea of an existential neurosis. He distinguished this "true" neurosis as the belief that one's life is meaningless, accompanied by an affective tone of apathy and boredom.[20] Meaninglessness and a lack of values was the cognitive component of the existential neurosis for Maddi. Affective blandness and boredom was accompanied by a chronically low activity level in the existential neurotic. Maddi differentiated existential neurosis from neurasthenia and depression by claiming that in "existential neurosis," depression was found to be the exception and apathy the normal affective state. The existential neurotic was described as alienated from himself and society as one who defines himself as nothing more than a player of social roles and an embodiment of biological needs. Severe social stresses and the threat of imminent death could cause severe anxiety in the neurotic because of his false sense of identity.

Maddi characterized the pre-morbid personality of the neurotic as so limited that it did not grasp the uniqueness and potentiality inherent in his own human nature. When this pre-morbid disposition was combined with stressful life situations, there was an outbreak of symptoms of existential neurosis. In spite of the clarity provided by this notion of existential neurosis, the argument that it differs from depression because of affective states of boredom or meaninglessness remains unconvincing. Vague reports of boredom, a lack of interest in life, or complaints of anhedoni and meaninglessness can often, in themselves, be symptoms of an underlying depression. Even when such an affective state is deeply rooted in cultural conditions, it can reflect adjustment conflicts in refining one's sense of identity at a given stage in life. When a patient complains of boredom and apathy, it often serves as a sure sign of depression or some other underlying psychic reality. The feelings of boredom can relate to underlying depression about unsatisfying work, relationships, or personal neurotically based limitations in living. Although they may have surface validity, these existential symptoms can reflect general insecurity, faltering personality defense, and psychic conflicts. The fear of death needs to be understood in this context not simply as an existential complaint but as an expression of the struggle for personal growth. Death anxiety is not a general symbol for anxiety as much as it is a powerful psychodynamic influence on personality functioning. The process of adult maturation and psychological change often leads to an encounter with depression and problems in separation. Growth for the neo-Freudian culturalists is more a struggle of differentiation and autonomy. Health represents independence from internalized parental images and neurotic needs and character traits.

Further support for the existential view of psychopathology was provided by the distinction between reactive and process schizophrenia and by the body of R. D. Laing's work.[21] A number of authors have held that reactive schizophrenia is existential in form, and that its primary characteristic is a loss of the will to meaning. The schizophrenic, in this definition, was one who has lost freedom and purpose in life, after having developed as a non-entity or a non-person due to the absence of love.[22] The schizophrenic is thus as limited in the ability to love as in the capacity to give freely. He is unable to freely choose a course of future behavior because the psychosis involves a distorted primitive self-image.[23] Once the onset of the psychosis has begun, the schizophrenic does not enter into growth-promoting social relationships and remains glued to the past. The entire reactive process is renewed by repeated failure in attempts to find meaning in life. Kantor and Herron believed that reactive schizophrenia is fully an existential disorder. They are in essential agreement with Frankl, Ernest Becker, and to a lesser extent Harold Searles' conception of schizophrenia as the simultaneous denial and anticipation of death.[24]

In spite of the value of these existentialist contributions, there is little clinical or experimental evidence for the existence of an existential neurosis per se.[25] Few well-constructed studies or clinical investigations have tested the existential model of psychosis and schizophrenia. The three basic concepts of personal responsibility, free choice and the relationship of freedom to anxiety have undeniable value for psychotherapy, even if there is insufficient evidence to construct a purely existential model of psychopathology. The realization of the possibility of non-being and the fear of death are to an extent universal and characteristic of human life. However, to portray this existential dilemma as the etiology of all psychopathology seems unwarranted. To isolate it as a specific neurosis distinct from depression and neurotic defensive character movements seems an over-generalization.

On the extreme end of the continuum of existential psychotherapies stands Laing's conceptualization of illness and psychotherapy. Laing feels that the mode of insanity itself must be appreciated by the therapist rather than cured.[26] For Laing, the therapist-patient relationship attempts to externalize and share experientially the patient's inner world of experience. This world constitites a highly valued mode of being which cannot be validly viewed as "mad." Laing's approach comes quite close to Karl Jaspers' efforts at phenomenological description and empathic understanding of the subjective experience of psychotic patients. Laing suggests that the therapist's chief concern lies in tuning into the psychotic patient's "unreal" world, and drawing him out of it by relating to it, not by curing it. The patient's mode of being could also be scrutinized in its relation to the family structure and the mode of being of family members. Laing's view of therapy therefore involves "being with" the patient in his or her unique disordered experience and conflicts. Perhaps more than other existentialists, he makes a concentrated effort to define mental health through the concept of ontological security. He readily credited the concept's origin in existential philosophy and admitted that his explanations were quite similar to the interpersonal psychoanalytic formulations of Harry Sullivan and Freida Fromm Reichman.

Laing's "ontological security" derives from self-validating experiences that have the effect of making a person feel real, whole, and autonomous. The "ontologically secure" (or unneurotic) person possesses a sense of identity, rooted in the body and the self, that is felt to have inner substance and worth. For Laing and Sullivan, the interpersonal experiences that result in self-validation help a person experience himself as being real, alive, and as having worth. Laing's concept of ontological insecurity appears to be quite similar to Horney's "basic insecurity." The ontologically insecure person experiences himself as unreal, lacking in continuity, and as being split off from his body. Interpersonal relationships are threatening rather than potentially satisfying in the midst of ontological insecurity, because the person's energy needs to be directed toward preserving the self. Laing, like the neo-Freudians, says that until the sense of ontological security becomes firmly established, even the ordinary occurrences of life threaten the person. The neurotic has to be consistently engaged in a process of self-defense. Psychosis becomes the ultimate expression of this insecurity, and it lingers as an empty, despairing existence of "death in life."[27]

Specific therapeutic techniques are difficult to pinpoint in the works of many existentialists, and few other than Frankl touch directly on the fear of death.[28] Their greatest contribution might be described in the careful approach to really listening to the patient in all types of depth psychotherapy. Seeing therapy as a mutual interactive process of becoming provides the therapist with a new, deeply felt responsibility for personal growth in the therapeutic experience. The phenomenological existentialist position overlaps humanistic traditions in providing a view of mental health and a consequent orientation to psychotherapy. In the humanistic psychotherapy of Fromm, Maslow, Rogers, and others, the existential dilemma is seen as a central issue in establishing a psychology of health. Maslow arranged man's basic needs into a hierarchy according to their priority, and subsumed them under the needs for freedom, authenticity, and self-actualization. Self-fulfillment encompasses freedom for the development of one's future capacities and responsibility for behavior in the present. In the humanistic psychotherapies as well as in the existentialist, the mentally healthy individual is one who is continually aware of himself or herself. They define healthy growth as a series of free-choice situations in which one chooses to abandon safety and to experience the delights and anxieties of inner-directed choices, responsible conduct, and genuine relatedness. The healthy individual thus continues to be responsible for behavior and opens up to experience through choices. Self-responsibility and existential presence serve as important goals for all the existential humanistic psychotherapies. Striving toward these goals requires a courage that the therapist and the patient must share. The theologian Paul Tillich, summarized the existentialists' contributions to psychotherapy by stating that the goal of therapy is to assist the patient in developing the "courage to be."

Summary

The eighteenth- and nineteenth-century existentialist writers attacked the underpinnings of traditional philosophical discourse by insisting that true knowledge must be rooted "in experience." Kierkegaard, Jaspers, Heidegger, and to some extent Nietzche and Sartre shared a phenomenological approach with their inquiries into the nature of knowledge, the meaning of freedom, and the fear of death. The inauthenticity of knowledge, the uncertainty of freedom, and the terror of non-being were described by them as essential aspects of the human condition. It was particularly the terror of the prospect of nothingness that was reported to compel man to a life of anxiety. Capitulation and flight from terror constituted a failure of the existential dilemma. On the basis of later psychological personality theory, an "existential neurosis" was hypothesized as a natural outgrowth of the existential dilemma. In an effort to find the heart of experimental knowledge, the existentialist philosophers and psychologists have contended that despair and anxiety are likely consequences of the knowledge about death. I have conjectured that "existential neurosis" and "existential anxiety" are not essentially different from anxious depression and the failure of defensive character movements in the neurotic fear of death. Kafka's dramatizations of the terror of his victims actually depicted such death anxiety: the depression and separation anxiety inherent in the neurotic fear of the loss of the self.

The existential psychotherapists contributions have been summarized with respect to existential philosophy's carryover in clinical work. Binswanger, May, Frankl, and Laing credited their assumptions for psychotherapy on the above philosophical systems. "Existential anxiety," "the disordered will to meaning," and "ontological insecurity" have been compared and contrasted as descriptions of the neurotic's depression and death anxiety. Attempts at constructing a purely existential model of psychopathology have been described as under emphasizing the importance of depression and neurotic characterological problems in existential complaints. The fear of death has been depicted in this context as much more than an existential complaint or as a symbol for anxiety. Death anxiety can be understood as a powerful psychodynamic influence on emotional functioning, manifest as the person's fear of the loss of the self. What May has called the "existential dimension" of psychotherapy has been put in the perspective of its partial agreement with the humanistic neo-Freudian view.

As an outgrowth of the existential philosophical position, the existential psychoanalyst is concerned with the patient's mode of being and mode of knowing. The existential-humanistic emphasis on the goal of authenticity directs the psychoanalyst to also examine his or her own anxiety, personal style of defensiveness, countertransference problems, and tendencies toward dishonesty and self-deception. Tillich's statement about the goal of existential therapy came close to Fromm's criticism of American society for its reluctance to abandon the "need to have" or "to possess" in favor of the "need to be" and "to be real." The lack of courage in the face of the knowledge of death coincides with depression and the neurotic's lack of psychological resourcefulness. Given relatively good health, despair at the knowledge of death, like intense fears about living, constitutes the outer layer of some conflicts about emotional growth. The neurotic's "ontological" or "existential anxiety" puts into more phenomenological terms the felt experience of neurotic depression, separation problems, and death anxiety.

CHAPTER NINE

Neurosis and the Fear of Death

Neurotic Defensiveness

Throughout childhood the patterns of defense mechanisms become more organized and gradually more integrated. They later emerge as a characterological style that is shaped by the child's temperament, the parents, and the psychodynamic world of the family. According to Anna Freud, the young infant initially organized defensive responses to anxiety by variations in motoric posturing. The infant's patterns of defense eventually take shape through the repeated use of either withdrawal or undifferentiated aggression in response to anxiety-producing stimuli. Karen Horney's theory of the adult's defensive neurotic movements accounts for fully formed characterological trends in which the movement is directed primarily "toward people, away from people, or against people."[1] These stylistic tendencies provide the organization for the interchange of the neurotic's needs and preferred defenses in search of an elusive security. In Horney's theory, they corresponded roughly to compliance or dependency, withdrawal and aggression as the individual's dominant character styles. Their rigid use in defense against basic insecurity robs the neurotic of self-awareness and relatedness. The neo-Freudian culturalist view of neurotic suffering, as it was developed in the psychoanalytic writings of Horney, Fromm, and Sullivan, has emphasized the centrality of underlying power needs, alienation from self, and impaired relatedness in neurosis. They describe these difficulties as "impairments in living" rather than instinctual conflicts. Heightened awareness of these character flaws and their psychological manifestations assumes the greatest significance in working through neurotic conflicts in psychoanalysis. The patient's symptoms or surface complaints become clarified in therapeutic work not only in terms of unconscious psychodynamics but more importantly in relation to the self and to persistent neurotic styles. The form of the neurotic's defensiveness broadcasts the fun-

damental insecurity, distorted self, and problems in relating to self and
to others. The manifest symptom picture of the patient by no means de-
pletes the field of therapeutic investigation. In contrast to the classical
psychoanalytic formulations of neurotic symptoms, as converted libido
or derivatives of unconscious drives, post-Freudian psychoanalysts attend more to the patient's hidden distortions, interpersonal communications, and the nuances of unconscious meanings in their distress. The
characterological implications of the neurotic-symptom picture play a
crucial role in treatment. For example, the obsessive compulsive or dis-
associative neurotic symptom benefits more from exploration when examined in terms of the way it exemplifies the whole person with his underlying personality style and neurotic problems. The neurotic's basic
defensive style and associated neurotic needs are regarded in theory as
an unconscious guiding principle for avoiding basic insecurity and anxiety. Even though it cannot be fully successful in accomplishing this goal,
the neurotic character style curbs enjoyment and genuine self-respect,
and it inhibits intimacy in interpersonal relationships. It protects the depressed, resourceful neurotic self and disguises the spontaneous resourceful adult self. Horney and Sullivan beautifully described the way
in which the neurotic maintains a superficial self-satisfaction by organizing perceptions and feelings according to this guiding principle. At the
same time, the neurotic's lack of awareness permits him to endow the
particular character style itself with the trappings of virtue.[2]

The neurotic character process thus involves the avoidance of anxiety
and self-knowledge as well as the individual's execution of the guiding
stylistic tendency in neurotic traits and interpersonal distortions. These
aspects of neurotic defensiveness are mutually reinforcing, as David Sha-
piro has observed in his work *Neurotic Styles.* In interpersonal psychoanalytic theory, the impact of the neurotic process is felt most keenly at
the outbreak of anxiety, which signals threats to the self and security
system. It has been argued here that unconscious defenses against death
anxiety constitute one of the major influences on components of neurotic
conflict throughout life. The fear of death complex and the person's
characterological means of avoiding death anxiety spring forth from the
earliest overtures at personality defense. One could reason, based very
loosely on Horney's delineation, that three typically neurotic personality
styles eventually evolve in the adult as characteristic defensive maneuvers against death anxiety. The three styles endure through a consistent
reliance on avoidance, confrontation, and withdrawal, which minimizes
threats to the self. Expressed in the form of depression, death anxiety
guides and shapes problems in living and relating to these three directions of stylistic attitudinizing. It has been argued further that death anxiety deeply affects the sense of identity and purpose in life. Death anxiety by no means exhausts the psychodynamic origins of all neurotic
conflicts. On the other hand, its components of death fears, separation
anxiety, and depression seem to play a tangible part in all neurotic conflicts. The mutual fear of living and dying lies at the heart of the neurotic's struggle for security.

An actual death anxiety attack exemplifies only one of the varieties of surface expression on the three neurotic personality styles that counter death anxiety. As an illustration of neurotic functioning, the phobic death anxiety attack demonstrates the more visible conscious presence of the fear of death component. The possibility of the unobtrusive, less visible presence of the two remaining depression and separation anxiety components can be accounted for in the death anxiety attack. Death anxiety need not be altogether localized or specific. It might, instead, take the form of vague terror and anxiety about thoughts of death. The death anxiety attack confers its frightening effect as a stimulus that reverberates with the person's neurotic style. An obsessional person will, for example, make use of obsessive-compulsive defenses against a death anxiety attack. She or he would typically employ obsessional defenses whatever the unconscious source of the symptom or percieved threat to security. The use of obsessive-compulsive defenses in a death anxiety attack can thus be said to stem from the more basic personality style that recalls the characterological organization. On a superficial level of meaning death anxiety can be formulated as a troubling symptom. The organized characterological defenses lower death anxiety but render the person habitually using them as more or less neurotic.

For instance Freud claimed that religion was one such primary line of neurotic defense against thoughts about death. Franz Kafka admitted in his letters that, for him, writing was the means of legitimizing a fantasy about his own death and objectifying his terror of it. Kafka's neurotic misery certainly captured the helplessness and horror of bureaucratic annoyance turned into totalitarian dehumanization. Kafka's depression and intense fear of death were symbolized in the inspired hallucinations in his prose, and the grotesque ironies of his work attempted to exorcise neurotic death anxiety. In Freud's description of religion as a defense against death anxiety, and in Kafka's self-revalatory letters about his writing, it was implicit that a defensive character style could be developed to combat death anxiety. Both statements identify possible ways in which a conscious activity is made use of to cope with death anxiety and unconscious demons. The driven writer and religious zealot may thus mold their deepest yearnings for security to the form of their interest and talent. The synthesis creates a blend of worthwhile activity, artistic product, and unconscious defense. The zeal of religious fanaticism and the artist's drive for creative self-expression can be used to conquer the neurotic fear of death. Both retain their capacity as media for the unfolding of character styles that can be either creative or neurotic. Based very roughly on the above delineation of character defense, the combination of withdrawal, aggression, and avoidance denote the three most frequent neurotic mechanisms of defense against death anxiety. The dominant character trend unfolds in its organization as the person experiences neurotic conflicts, particularly those present with the threats of intimacy, responsibility, and self-awareness. The related fear of death and life described by Fromm becomes more entrenched the greater the degree of entrapment in the particular neurotic character style. The stylistic maneuvering, therefore, represents dominant trends of the personality in relation to death anxiety. This current model of neurotic death anxiety, with its emphasis on depression, helplessness and threats to the self, stands in contrast to much of the pertinent research literature. Psychological research on death anxiety and neurosis has traditionally concentrated on tracing specific dynamics in neurotic symptoms. A typical study, that represents the methodology of this approach was that of Brumberg and Schilder, mentioned in Chapter Four. Bromberg and Schilder interviewed neurotic patients and saw separation and the loss of loved ones through death as the essential dynamic in the attitudes of hysterics and anxiety neurotics. In depression, they found that the relation of death to guilt and to time was crucial. In depressed people, underlying feelings of guilt continued to be projected onto the future and eternity. Death, then, was unconsciously defined as eternal blame for transgressions and aggression. In obsessive compulsive neurotics, death fears were reported by these authors to be the expression of sadomasochistic attitudes. As aggressive feelings increased in these obsessionals, the fear of death became overwhelming and death was again velwed as eternal punishment. Because of a strict superego in the obsessive compulsive personality, aggressive feelings were directed against the "self" of the person. The inability to accept the expression of destructive, hostile feelings toward a loved person intensified their expression against the self. Bromberg and Schilder argued that death became the ultimate punishment for the obsessional. These investigators also noted the presence of such attitudes toward death in a variety of normal people as well as in neurotic and psychotic people. It has been my observation that these attitudes are indeed widespread as are fears of death in many types of individuals. They are simply more intense and multidetermined in neurotic character types who experience depression and death anxiety at the prospect of psychological individuation.

Neurotic Symptoms and Death Anxiety

In the defense against death anxiety, the implicit fear of life provides a model for the individual's character problems that is in full concordance with the person's overall neurotic symptomatology. Freud's case of the "Rat Man" provided documentation of such an interplay between neurotic symptoms and death anxiety. Kafka's writing revealed his own attempted resolution of morbid depression and his fascination with and fear of death. In fact, his short stories make ample reference to the neurotic's projection of helplessness as well as the depressive's belief in the inevitability of the death of the spirit. The short stories elevated Kafka's own neurotic pain to the level of truth and provided an outlet for his perpetual mourning of himself. Rather than describe the neurotic process inherent in death anxiety solely through clinical material, its operation will be traced more fully through literary works. Defensive movements of neurotic character traits underlie the symptom picture in coping with death anxiety. The purpose here is to touch on these movements in relation to death anxiety rather than define specific neurotic symptoms in relation to death.

One episode in Freud's famous case of the "Rat Man" exemplifies the "Rat Man's" use of a typically obsessive-compulsive defense against death anxiety. This episode was not reported in terms of the "Rat Man's" fear of death per se.[3] As he and his girlfriend were suddenly caught in a thunderstorm during a stroll in the countryside, the "Rat Man" became paralyzed with a fear of being killed. As thunder roared, the "Rat Man" counted aloud to the number forty or fifty to control his terror. This compulsive counting served the same psychic function as did his earlier prayers and pious declarations. Prayers, religious rituals, and their counterpart in counting performed the unconscious function of protecting the "Rat Man" from the fear of death. His obsessive doubting about the prospect of his marriage was well documented in the case study. The "Rat Man's" uncertainty enabled him to remain psychically attached to his parents. His anxiety about death obscured his lack of differentiation and fear of separation from them. The three components of death anxiety could be interpreted as the basis for his neurotic ambivalence as much as Oedipal guilt or anticipated reprisals for his hostile fantasies. The very dilemma the "Rat Man" feared—whether to marry for love or choose a wife who would be more in keeping with his parents' wishes— betrayed his rootedness in the fabric of his parents' personalities. His terror of death during the thunderstorm involved a projection onto the thunderstorm of the inner anxiety he felt at the prospect of separation. Anxiety about individuation seemed to signal death in the unconscious. The "Rat Man" himself had dated the onset of his illness at age six, when he had first thought that his parents could read his mind. He remembered childhood wishes to "see girls naked," but was afraid that some evil would befall him if he continued to think of such things. The obsessive thoughts and compulsive actions enabled him to prevent any such evil from occurring. Freud interpreted his fear of rats and the anxiety-laden fantasy of a rat boring into someone's anus as a symbolic displacement of the Oedipal complex. Freud felt that the rat symbolized the penis and that the fantasy represented the "Rat Man's" own repulsion at the thought of his father having sexual intercourse with his girlfriend. Religion had provided the "Rat Man" with a strong line of defense against death anxiety. It also secured protection from his horrifying thoughts about rats through its involvement with magical thinking and denial of separation.

By filling his mind with thoughts about immortality and life after death, the "Rat Man" unconsciously reinforced the fantasy of union with his father and mother and pushed his depression and fear of separation even further from his awareness. In this way, his piety and prayers served as a means of denial and defense against death anxiety. They relieved him momentarily of the depression associated with his separation anxiety and failure in growth. By a resolute, obsessional determination to think only of the afterlife, his soul, or his father's welfare in heaven, the "Rat Man's" obsessive defenses acquired a new point of reference for further obsessing, uncertainty, and doubt. Separation, death, and his failure at adaptation to adult life could thus be more thoroughly repressed and minimized for him as a source of future anxiety and depression.

The central context of the "Rat Man's" obsessive thoughts unconsciously linked him to his father and the prospect of eternal psychological union with him. The front of a devoutly religious life provided him with eternal protection from the specter of death. Although the particular stylistic approach used was clearly an obsessional one, the vignette points to his more basic problems. His obsessional style not only protected the "Rat Man" from death anxiety and separation anxiety but also simultaneously reinforced his ambivalence about individuation from his parents. He feared risking their displeasure by marrying for love. On one level, the death anxiety attack stimulated this obsessional defenses. On another level, it brought to the surface the "Rat Man's" fear of separation and submersion in the protection of his parents' views and prohibitions. In a microcosm of a neurotic obsessional world, the death anxiety attack itself illuminated the "Rat Man's" character style as he had tried to cope with a more basic underlying fear of the loss of the self.

The need for autonomy clashed with his need for security and protection. The latter may well have been represented to the conscious self as loyalty and filial obedience. His personality makeup combined obsessional defenses with a compliant character organization. These defensiveness and character style overlapped at the onset of the death anxiety attack. Like Kafka's depression and preoccupation with death, the "Rat Man's" fear of individuation provides a focus for understanding neurotic character style. The "Rat Man's" conflict about his decision exposed an ambivalence about individuation that lay at the root of his anxiety and fear. His simultaneous fear of living and dying could not be fully countered by the obsessional defenses. The more serious underlying character problems were exposed by the death anxiety attack and dealt with in the "Rat Man's" characteristic way. His depressions, like those of many neurotic depressions, accompanied the persistence of unconscious dependency and separation anxiety. This thumbnail sketch of the "Rat Man" illustrates the powerful symbolism of death anxiety in neurotic character traits. Neurotic death anxiety, expressed as depression, brings an anxious suffering that either tortures the sophisticated, sensitive person, or becomes an object of enduring sentiment to the masochistic one.

Neurotic Avoidance

In the first of the character styles, defined as defensive maneuvers countering death anxiety, avoidance is the chief tactic that is superimposed on the defensive patterning. There is a clear paradox in the avoidance type of personality style. The more intensely one tries to avoid the fear of death or to cover up an associated lack of purpose in life, the more fully one becomes entangled in the whole fear of death complex. A most striking illustration of this neurotic process of attempted avoidance and entanglement with the fear of death is embodied in the persona of Ivan Ilych in Leo Tolstoy's *The Death of Ivan Ilych*.[4] This short novel portrays depression as death anxiety in a minutely detailed account of the fear of death and the fear of life in both mundane daily events and significant moments of missed intimacy.

The plot opens with the announcement of Ivan's death and its initial impact on his friends and fellow workers. Their first thoughts concerned who would get the deceased man's position as a judge. How would Ivan's death affect their own chances for advancement? Their immediate feelings consisted of anger that he had died and a relief that they were still alive. Their anger at Ivan for dying and feelings of loss were combined with the wish that he would have died sooner, with less obvious suffering. Their next reaction was to displace the anger by blaming the doctors who treated Ivan. The doctors having misdiagnosed a series of non-fatal illnesses bred an annoyance that served to disguise feelings of guilt and helplessness at having to watch Ivan die. They could do nothing to alleviate the pain from either Ivan's sores or his emotional anguish. His pain and depression had made Ivan an embarrassemnt to his friends. He reminded them of both the certainty of their own deaths and of the futility of their attempts to reassure him. Reading the announcement of his death in the newspaper struck all of Ivan's friends with the thought that at that moment they were alive. They needed to find some means for coming to terms with their own perplexing feelings about death. Visiting the dead man's family, while managing to remain detached from all of the associated "unpleasantries," became the next focus of thought. The courtesy call on the widow was complicated by the need to look like they were officially in mourning. Propriety demanded that they look good in the eyes of the family in spite of the complexities of their genuine feelings about his death.

The widow, Praskovya Fedorovna, had vacillated "between bouts of tears and demonstrations of strength." She also denied honest genuine emotional responses to Ivan's death. She had isolated herself from real experiences of feeling by compulsively organizing first the details of the funeral and then the intricacies of the government pension that she had been allotted. Ivanovich, Ivan's friend, pondered the horror of Ivan's suffering and screaming in the last days of his life. However, he too found this unbearable and retreated to the more secure ground of inane conversation with the widow about pension allowances. All of Ivan Ilych's friends and family divorced themselves from intense feelings about his death and remained relatively aloof and unable to begin the work of mourning. The characters colluded to ignore Ivan's suffering in life so as to obscure their own suffering and death anxiety. A preoccupation with intellectual exercise and attention to detail helped the mourners to avoid the impact of the death. Ivan himself had covered up his superficiality and lack of existential purpose in life by embracing the ceremony of his office and position. This had enabled him to avoid thoughts about death until the cancer stripped away his defensive use of denial and avoidance. Finally his depression and fear of death became obvious and intolerable. Ivan's wife and friends shared this avoidance type of neurotic style, and they grew anxious at the possibility of exposure in their unrelatedness.

Ivan Ilych's code of living concerned itself with doing one's duty and conforming one's behavior to what was expected by those in authority. He, therefore, had no real interests, enthusiasms, passionate or intense feelings for anyone, including his family and friends. The status of being a magistrate and a certain dignity of bearing were the only ideals close to his heart. Ivan lived walled within a contained emotional isolation that seemed impermeable. Little penetrated this wall of isolation in Ivan's life. He never allowed himself the experience of caring very deeply or feeling too intensely about anything or anyone until the last weeks before his death. One of three sons, Ivan became determined to become "success-ful," and he had chosen law and the hope of an appointment to the bench because of an attraction to the precision and power in the cautious exercise of legal judgment. His only real pleasure in life lay in playing bridge. From his early days as a student and prosecutor to the period of middle age, his central concerns were doing the "right thing" and re-fraining from displeasing superiors or highly placed associates.

There was no enjoyment of life in Ivan Ilych's relationship with people or any real involvement in his marriage to Praskovya Fedorovna. Theirs had been a marriage of convenience that he had entered with an eye to her social connections and family income. Ivan initially gained some satisfaction in Praskovya's interest in their home furnishings and in the entertainment of their friends. Gradually, however, he began to experience her needs as intrusive demands and he then withdrew further into probity and self-containment. Although Ivan could derive great pleasure from the choice of wall covering decorating his house or the ele-gance of a carefully written legal brief, his life lacked purpose and sub-stance. Even the birth of his three children and the death of one of them did not ruffle his uninvolvement with life. He secured this self-righteous detachment from his wife and family by burying himself in work and modest bureaucratic ambition. Praskovya attempted to disrupt their do-mestic status quo, but aside from some occasional quarrels, their rela-tionship consisted of a mutually alienated truce. Ivan's pity for himself and contempt for his doctor's indifference masked rage, depression and a fear of death. His initial reaction to his symptoms and pain was to be-come obsessed with health regimens and scrupulously following his doc-tor's orders. When the long dominant fear of death at last edged close to consciousness, Ivan was able to dispel it by a faith in the doctor's vaguely worded innuendos. As he had done at other crisis points in his life, he reasoned: If I carefully follow the recommendations of these authorities, then surely I will be protected from the horror of death. His denial and avoidance at this stage of his illness was typical of terminally ill people, but with Ivan these traits punctuated a lifelong neurotic fear of death expressed as depression. As his health failed, the pain grew worse and death at last seemed a real possibility. Ivan then finally experienced despair. Previously manic buoyant spirits and the false hope of a miraculous recovery had alternated with rage and depression. Unacknowledged depression had always accompanied Ivan's fear of life and death. He defended himself from the profound despair that could no longer be hidden by retreating to the study of his house in order to search for "peace." What Ivan thought of as peace of mind really amounted to the familiar, comfortable isolation from others and a certain distance from his anxiety-arousing feelings and newly gained self-awareness. Enclosed in his study in the last weeks of his life, Ivan could protect his family and friends from the sight of his decay. He continued to make truly neurotic use of avoidance in isolating himself from the certainty of death and his own feelings of depression and helplessness. His wife and relatives progressed from at first being astonished and horrified at the quickness of Ivan's wasting and decay to later feeling annoyed at his depression and unacknowledged, smoldering resentment of them.

Ivan's despair at this stage of his terminal cancer brought Praskovya in contact with her own lack of purpose in life. It mobilized the dissatisfaction she felt with her own life and purposelessness. His despair touched off her fear of death and depression. Praskovya's defensive avoidance then escalated to such an extent that at times she treated Ivan's illness as a bothersome inconvenience that was totally his fault. His despair was too painful for her to experience or respond to openly. Praskovya needed to perceive it as another of Ivan's awkward bits of misbehavior that had been a constant source of minor annoyance to her. It is not unreasonable to assume that Ivan's· despair grew not only from the cancer but also from the desolation of his emotional life. The failure of hope mirrored his failure in living and finding purpose in life. The deadness of feelings that were rooted in his body recalled the emptiness of his long-standing neurotic fear of death. The intolerable pain in his side became the last straw that was superimposed on the emotional pain of his combined fear of dying and living. The depression manifest in his fear of death became as unbearable as the physical agony. As a result, Ivan finally wished for death to become free of the emotional and physical suffering. After a review of his life revealed only fleeting moments of joy in childhood, Ivan began to die emotionally. Two hours before his death, however, Ivan began to be tormented with the thought, "What if I have not lived correctly?" Suppose those parts of life he had suppressed were really those that led to true happiness? Was it too late to find genuine purpose in life? That recognition freed Ivan from his lifelong depression and fear of death. At last he could give up the need for convenience and begin to feel sympathy and concern for his wife and son. By sparing them more pain, he concluded, he could live meaningfully the last hour of his life. He no longer feared death when he ceased being threatened by the loss of his neurotic self. At the moment of death his doubts about the value and purpose of life remained unresolved, but death was experienced more as a relief than as a punishment for not having lived.

Neurotic Aggression

The character of Ivan Ilych seemed to have suffered a continuous mild depression and fear of death throughout his life that was defended against by his avoidance character style and superficiality. He failed to be honest in relating to others and avoided living by reducing life to matters of comfort and convenient ritual. His lack of purpose in living finally emerged into awareness at the precipice of death. The acknowledgment of its meaningfulness resulted in his finally finding a more genuine purpose in dying. Nuances of his neurotic defensiveness remained consistently within his stylistic tendency to use avoidance or denial to cover up the fear of death complex. The second related neurotic lifestyle that is based on unresolved death fears and depression becomes evident in a continuous need for confrontation with death. Toying with death, whether through stunts of dangerous behavior or tests of the will that confront death, often involves a strong unconscious death fear as well.

It seems to me that depression and separation anxiety accompany aggressive confrontations with death anxiety. Because of the implicit role of the defense mechanisms of reaction formation and identification with the aggressor, this kind of counterphobic behavior actually covers up unconscious death fears. In reaction formation, the denial of an unacceptable unconscious impulse or feeling is accomplished by the conscious adoption of its opposite. The person who needs to confront death because of the so-called thrill, enjoyment, or need to prove strength actually unconsciously tries to fight death anxiety and depression. The fearless, untrained daredevil who takes reckless unnecessary chances in driving an automobile, in dangerous sports, or in mountain climbing may be either acting out self destructive wishes and unconscious depression or a related fear of death and lack of purpose in life. Camus needed to find existential meaning in life by risking his life driving carelessly at high speeds. Ernest Hemingway's fascination with hunting, killing, and bullfighting cannot simply be understood as attempts to support the fantasy image of himself as a super-virile man, or as compensations for underlying doubts about his masculinity. His need to understand death in combat, the hunt, and the bullfight emerged dramatically in his life and fiction. He demonstrated this both in the need to maintain power over death and in a consistent image of the masculine man as fearless, omnipotent, and unbothered by the prospect of death. Whether or not Hemingway feared death consciously, these recurrent themes reflected in his prose clearly illustrate the use of defensive confrontation with death anxiety. The bullfight particularly affirms man's struggle to overcome these primitive conflicts via the graceful ballet with the bull. The bull represents both the unleashed aggressive power of man and the force of death. As the matador reaches the moment of truth in conquering death, the audience triumphantly celebrates their identification with him as the aggressor and their mutual defeat of death. Continuous aggressive confrontation with death anxiety betrays a character style that may be no less neurotic than one that makes extensive use of avoidance or withdrawal.

Neurotic aggression points to a different stylistic trend, a preferred mode of defensiveness and way of organizing experience that is just as mired in the fear of death complex. The aggressive daredevil may be no more free from death anxiety, depression, and separation anxiety than the passive bureaucrat who uses avoidance and denial. They differ in characterological style but may suffer equally with depression and separation anxiety as key underlying character problems. In both, the fear of living and the fear of death evoke characteristic styles of defenses that fit with their character organization. Their defenses become apparent in the two divergent directions: both imply the same fear of the loss of the self. The daredevil racing driver who crosses over the edge between skillful maneuvering and inviting death or injury likewise gratifies his or her audience by defeating their unconscious death fears. The unconscious motivation for this kind of behavior can easily be understood as the need to counteract or resolve depression and the lack of purpose that accompanies the fear of death. The dangerous sport or risky feats have to be repeated over and over again not simply out of thrill but because the underlying depression and death anxiety persists until they reach some resolution. In some people with this personality type, the neurotic aggression persists throughout life until death or suicide. The successfully completed suicide under those circumstances is the ultimate neurotic solution to the lack of purpose and fear of death. Death may no longer seem as frightening or life as depressing when one feels able to end it whenever it is emotionally necessary. The puberty rituals of male children in primitive cultures emphasize these themes in their tests of masculinity. Masculinity was traditionally defined as bravery in the hunter or warrior and fearlessness in the face of death. The successful youth who completed the rite of passage reassured his tribe of their power over death while providing them with an opportunity to feel less vulnerable and frightened.

Essential purposelessness and death anxiety also drive modern man and woman to repeatedly confront death. Excessive speeding while driving a car and testing oneself continuously in some physically dangerous situation need not be tests of ability or strength as much as powerfully driven attempts to overcome the fear of death by actively confronting it. A striking example of the acting out-confrontational style of defensiveness that is enmeshed in the fear of death complex can be found in the character of Captain Ahab in Herman Melville's *Moby Dick*.[5] This classic American novel touches each dimension of the three-part death anxiety complex with imaginative stroies from its beginning to its final paragraph. *Moby Dick* has usually been portrayed by critics as the great American novel of good and evil, in which Ahab's duel with the white whale represents the interplay of these forces in a battle to the death.

From another perspective, the character of Ahab could be interpreted as one of a depressed, disfigured man whose obsession with the whale arose from the context of a lack of purpose in life, revenge and a fear of death. The voyage of the *Pequod* romanticized the resolution of Ahab's self-torture as he consistently confronted the evil part of himself and death in the form of his nemesis, Moby Dick. In the plot development, Ahab was drawn beyond the point of reasonable revenge to destroy the whale. Perhaps he needed psychologically to do battle with his own fear of death, meaninglessness, and depression. The pleas of the common seamen and ship's officers to give up his obsession with Moby Dick fell on deaf ears. There was no relief from the narcissistic rage and the turbulent fury that tormented Ahab. The narrator, Ishmael, established the emotional tone of the work at the onset by connecting his emotional state with that of the whaling town of New Bedford. Whenever he experienced a "November" of the soul, Ishmael would return to the sea. His depression became manifest in seeking out coffin warehouses and involuntarily following every funeral procession that he met by chance. To Ishmael, New Bedford seemed to be nothing but "blocks of darkness" in which one could move about like in a "tomb." Ishmael's depression and difficulty in separation from the sea and seafaring life correlated with Ahab's fascination wih death and fear of death. Ishmael remained depressed while on land and felt driven to return to the sea. Life aboard ship provided him with hope and a new life. The sea and the whale both served as symbols of the life-giving mother throughout the novel, just as the *Pequod* continued to be symbolic of death.

At several points in the narrative the seamen described Ahab's descent into his cabin as "going into the tomb." Melville contrasted references to the whales as either serpentlike destructive demons or maternal and protective, innocent victims of greedy whalers. Interwoven with the chapters on whale anatomy and the stripping and boiling of whale blubber, Melville painted these two alternate images of whales as death—the evil monstrous demon—and life—the nurturing mother. In passages on the composition of the hunt scene, Melville described the richness of whale's milk as it was mixed with blood in the turbulence of the sea. Furthermore, he labeled the harpooned whale attached to the pursuing long boat as being attached by the "umbilical cord" to "Madam Leviathan." When whales were alluded to as ferocious and evil, they were usually referred to in masculine terms. When they were referred to as being majestic or warm-bodied, they were depicted in feminine terms.

Part of the impetus for writing *Moby Dick* may have come from Melville's 1842 whaling voyage to the Marquesas Islands. One of the features of the native poeple that must have had some impact on Melville was the fact that they sanctioned canibalism. Not only was Ahab partially devoured by Moby Dick in the novel, but in addition, the crewmen of the *Pequod* and the ship itself were devoured by the sea in the book's final scene. Through these elements Melville dramatized rage and aggressive confrontation with death anxiety and linked them thematically with the wish for separation from the parent and the fear of separation. This ambivalence about separation-individuation and the presence of reunion fantasies common to depression has been highlighted as fully congruent with different types of neurotic defensiveness. Did part of Ahab's obsession give concrete form to unconscious conflict between the angry wish to be devoured and reunited with the mother versus the fear of being devoured or psychologically reintegrated into the mother? Support for the separation anxiety aspect of the plot could be found in the character's inability to change, give up, or even modify his rage and obsession with the whale. Ahab had just taken a young bride before the start of the *Pequod's* final voyage, knowing full well that the great white whale would keep him away from her. The more successful Ahab became in killing whales, the more unsatisfied he felt, and the greater was his need for Moby Dick. The little we know about Ahab's life outside the *Pequod* suggests the sketch of an aimless man who was lacking in enthusiasm except for whaling. The death of Moby Dick symbolized for Ahab the attainment of a goal that he needed to pursue at all costs. It seemed that the whale's death and pursuit were needed to keep Arab alive. In the three-day pursuit of Moby Dick that led to the destruction of the *Pequod*, Ahab pushed his men to the limits of their endurance. In order to triumph over his own deadness, emptiness, and fearful living, Ahab could not stop himself from confronting death in the form of Moby Dick. Moby Dick's death somehow seemed essential for the survival of his damaged self. Ahab was able to feel glorious and see himself in heroic proportions as an omnipotent avenger only in frenzied pursuit of the white whale. One assumes that his self-image compensated for the other side of Ahab's personality, the depressed, morose, half-dead wanderer who was no longer young and who feared death. The fury of the whale hunt seemed the only means for coping with Ahab's narcissistic wounds.

Other characters in the book play supporting roles in establishing the recurring themes of depression, fear of death, and separation anxiety in the shadow of Ahab's neurotic quest for Moby Dick. During his illness, Quequeg also became depressed and convinced that he would die. The thought of his dead body being wrapped in a hammock and tossed overboard was intolerable for the Indian harpooner. Quequeq needed to be protected from becoming "a drowning shroud." He asked for and obtained an elaborately decorated thick wooden coffin with a specially designed cover. Until his recovery, Quequeq slept daily in this coffin so as to prepare himself for the journey into the savage afterlife. The womb symbolism of the coffin was again portrayed as the unconscious wish for reunion and resignation to death. Here also Melville juxtaposed in the character of Quequeq the fear of death via the fear of being devoured, with descriptions of depression and separation anxiety. It could be spec-

ulated that in the safety of his coffin womb, Quequeq felt less frightened
of being devoured by the sea (or reintegrated as a helpless child into the
powerful parent on whom he depended for life or death). The resulting
depression and fear of death drove him unconsciously toward reunion
with the coffin-womb. This transformation of Quequeq's personality
during the illness provides a metaphor for the fear and rigidity of the
avoidance type of character style. Lacking the resources and character
strengths of a robust, noble savage, this type of neurotic person becomes
more inhibited and constricted in the face of death anxiety.

In the final pursuit of Mofy Dick, the ship became a hearse that
awaited the frightened crew. In these passages, the crewmen remain conflicted about Ahab's mad desire for revenge but they were caught up in
the chase to such an extent that they were fully taken over by Ahab's
will and vengeful fury. Fused together as an integrated hunting force,
they were bent on taking the white whale. They blindly followed Ahab's
orders even at the point when their ship was being wrecked. When
Ahab's obsession finally destroyed him, a harpoon line pulled him into
the sea and symbolically attached him to the whale. Out of the whirlpool
formed by the sinking Pequod, Quequeq's coffin sprang forth as a life
buoy for Ishmael. The coffin symbol again served as a protective womb
for Ishmael and it provided him with a second birth and a new life. This
wooden coffin-womb provided Ishmael's salvation, just as earlier in the
book it had consistently served as a symbol for depression and death.

Ahab's overwhelming need to do battle with Moby Dick exemplified
aggressive confrontation against death anxiety and depression as a defensive character style. Ahab's air of invincibility swayed his crew's
judgment and lent them an air of invulnerability. He pursued Moby
Dick beyond the point of reason to protect the intact part of his psychological self. Ahab protested his fearlessness in a counterphobic way by
claiming only that "kings" were capable of killing him. On the verge of
death, he continued to act out death anxiety by bragging to his men that
there was no coffin or hearse that could hold him! This illustrates the
grandiosity of the neurotic's defensiveness and his elevation of distorted
purpose in life to heroic heights. Ahab's fear of death and purposelessness found expression in his grandiose hunt in the same way that the
character Lord Jim's depression found expression in a grandiose delusional psychosis. Ahab's obsession with Moby Dick also implied an intense
neurotic drive for an activity that would seemingly render him less anxious about death. His obsession with revenge expressed a compensatory
drive for the relief from his depression. His persona thus typified the
neurotic's singular intensity in achieving goals that promise to lower
death anxiety. One wonders whether an Ahab who had been more successful in killing Moby Dick would have been any less troubled by neurotic living or any less fearful about the loss of the self. The need for revenge—the need to be paid back for the unkindness of parents and the
suffering of childhood—can be an integral part of the depressive's anxious intensity and the narcissistic deficits of the violent person's aggres-

sion. Getting even with one's parents or indirectly forcing one's loved ones and contemporaries to give what seems one's due also smack of the neurotic's dependency, manipulativeness, and fixation in childhood experience. Ahab's countering death anxiety via relentless aggressive confrontation confirmed the extent of his emotional limitations. This confrontational type of neurotic character is no less free from death anxiety, depression, and separation anxiety than the avoidance or withdrawal types.

Neurotic Withdrawal

The third typically neurotic style for overcoming lack of purpose in life and associated fears of death involves persistent withdrawal from life. Withdrawal from relationships in response to depression and death anxiety is a defensive process that can be repeated over and over again. Withdrawal and detachment from affect limit the possibility of threats to the self and can serve to reinforce depression. When the fear of death, depression, and separation anxiety conflicts reach a painful intensity, withdrawal can become a customary, defensive operation that dominates the person's character style. The work and life of the poetess Emily Dickinson provided striking illustrations of these personality mechanisms. One could easily interpret her prolonged withdrawal as syntonic surrender of the self to death anxiety. The sensitivity and genius of her poetry and the depth of her contributions should not be confused with the character problems that apparently plagued her. Her period of productivity as a writer coincided with a complete withdrawal from the world and self-imposed isolation in her home. Other than writing, doing household chores, and caring for her parents, her life as she recorded it consisted of little more than introspection and thought. Out of her own choice, she isolated herself from friends, acquaintances, and especially those whom she most wanted to see. Both her conflicts about relating to women and men and her withdrawal from life found consistent expression in her poetry. Her depression and extreme self-absorption tapped a simultaneous fear of life and death that lay at the opposite extreme from the aggression and bluster of the confrontational neurotic type. Emily Dickinson was apparently inhibited by psychological conflict from exposing herself to substantial human encounters. Simply to think and to write became her purposes in life. A life of thought devoid of decisive action or meaningful relating typifies the obsessional, the withdrawn personality, and other types of neurotic character problems. Her writing attempted not only to record human experience but also to resolve her own death anxiety and terrible unhappiness. She seemingly abandoned the hope of any meaningful relationships or productive interpersonal living in the face of her intense fear. Because of her enormous talent, however, she was able to translate her suffering and fear of death into poetry, which posthumously accorded her a powerful voice.

When I hoped, I feared,
Since I hoped, I dared,
Everywhere alone
As a church remained
Spectre cannot harm
Serpent cannot charm
He deposes doom
Who hath suffered him.[6]

In these few lines, Emily Dickinson depicted capitulation to withdrawal and fear; the fear of vulnerability, of being alone, of being independent yet intimate, and ultimately the fear of death. The wily "serpents" of intimacy, responsibility, and emotional entanglement with the disappointments and uncertainties of relationships could not charm her from her self-imposed isolation. No one can know with certainty whether withdrawal and self-absorption limited her talent or more fully fanned the sparks of her creativity. The message of her autobiographical poetry was quite clear, however: death was not to be feared in the present since withdrawal protected the self. Living had become synonymous with fearing death, so that life had been reduced to the least threatening alternatives. Harley Shands has pointed out that Emily Dickinson's poems demonstrated her inability to love and the development of her infatuation with her own reflection as documented in the written word.[7] He put forth the formulation that the period of her greatest productivity, from ages twenty-eight to thirty-five, seemed to coincide with a self-analysis through poetry that enabled her to fully adapt to her lonely, isolated life. Following this period, the productivity dropped off, perhaps because she was no longer troubled by symptoms or her isolation. In this sense, her creative output may have served the dual functions of adapting herself to a neurotic character style and exorcising the suffering that comes with choosing withdrawal and death anxiety as modes of living. Whether or not her primary character flaw was narcissism, as Shands suggests, or the choice of withdrawal and isolation as a neurotic style congruent with death anxiety, her lifestyle documented both points of view. I believe that her poetry and her lifestyle exemplified detachment and withdrawal as a defense against the death anxiety that accompanies individuation. Her depression and fear of death were more obvious in the body of her work than the separation anxiety component of the fear of death complex. Yet most of her adult life seemed to have involved a well-armored defense against separation from her parents and individuation from them. She chose safety within the confinement of her parental home and was unwilling or unable to venture out of it.

By her own account, Emily Dickinson reduced living to a combination of thought, reading, and writing. These activities may have fully exhausted all of the avenues in which she felt relatively safe from anxiety. At the prospect of meeting a new person or leaving her parents' house for any reason, she became quite anxious. At one point after having written a male friend repeated invitations to visit her, she felt compelled to

dismiss him from her home without seeing him.[8] Her obsessing and ago-
nizing over the invitations were bearable in thought and fantasy, but we
may suppose that the anticipation of the real experience of a shared exchange or even intimacy brought with it too much anxiety. Her phobic
reactions to strangers and new experiences shrunk the perimeter of her
opportunities to a narrow spectrum of intellectual activities. Their merit
and allure reduced the ambivalence she must have felt about withdrawal
from relating and living. Here again, as with the other neurotic character
styles dominated by death anxiety, it can be hypothesized that these
symptoms served multiple defensive purposes. Intense anxiety about
separation from her parents and individuation from them could easily be
countered by a phobic reaction to new people and experiences. A terror
of experiences became glorified in the name of artistic expression and religious faith, obscuring the likelihood that introspection and writing
were simply safe activities that did not threaten her emotional ties to her
parents. All of the real experiences of life were lived vicariously through
fantasies to eliminate threats to the self. The fantasies may have been
satisfying enough not to more fully disturb the status quo of her encasement in her family. Emily Dickinson's reliance on withdrawal and isolation affirmed the inherent relationship between death anxiety, depression, and separation anxiety in this type of neurotic character defense.

Her withdrawal assured the neurotic self of an inner psychic safety
akin to that sought after by the avoidance type neurotic and the aggressive acting-out type. Her unconscious defensive maneuverings implied
the same use of psychological mechanisms in little Hans' fear of horses,
the school-phobic child's fear of school, the "Rat Man's" fear of light-
ning, and the toddler's anxiety in eating, sleeping, and mastering elimination control. Internal psychic fusion with the parents and clinging to
the protection of the parental home appeared to be major unconscious
goals sought after in her characterological organization and use of withdrawal. Her detachment from affective experience reflected that end, insured its permanence, and obviated her need for close intimate contact
with others. Her experiences as a young child and adolescent somehow
predisposed this woman toward a particular neurotic style that limited
her emotional living. She reported in her letters that publishing her poetry or meeting friends were fraught with as much anxiety and ambivalence for her as the hope of developing any new relationships or venturing out of her house. Because of Emily Dickinson's strong Christian
faith and identification with Christ, her neurotic character solution may
have seemed to her somewhat of a virtuous marvel. Her suffering could
assume the appearance of a spiritual union with Christ, which further reduced the possibility of any conscious outbreaks of separation anxiety.
The niceties of modest restraint can thus show a grandiose air typical of
unconscious neurotic defense. This was Horney's point about the self-
importance of neurotic character traits as they accrue in assembling a
distorted, idealized self. Miss Dickinson seemed aware of her suffering
and ambivalence but was unable to extricate herself from the smooth-

ness of her character solution. Writing became her purpose in life and means for avoiding death anxiety, just as the character of Ivan Ilych had chosen bureaucratic conventionality.

If these speculations are correct, then Emily Dickinson's depression and misery were an inevitable outgrowth of her failure in separation-individuation and her mutual fear of life and death. Her fearful living, via withdrawal expressed and exacerbated the constant depression she faced. The depression, however, could be rationalized into religious suffering, like that of Christ, which guaranteed her future happiness in heaven.

> I can wade Grief—
> Whole Pools of it
> I'm used to that—
> But the least push of Joy
> Breaks up my feet—
> And I tip—frunken—
> Let no Pebble—smile—
> Twas the New Liquor—
> That was All!...[9]

Here Miss Dickinson recounted the neurotic's fascination with his or her own misery and depression. Happiness and real joy in living cannot be trusted or fully embraced without cautious restraint. The self cannot let go of the neurotic misery long enough or fully enough for any joy to be experienced and apprehended. There is a threat experienced at the prospect of too much happiness that may cause the neurotic to falter and stumble. Letting go of "oneself" sufficiently enough in positive, pleasurable experiences implies some degree of responsibility and individuation. The "new liquor" of happiness has to be minimized, denied, or otherwise defended against. If it is not, then the neurotic cannot ignore the changes in feeling and altered perceptions of self that accompany autonomous living. This presents the individual with the threat of the loss of the self—the neurotic self. The irony of Miss Dickinson's alienation and withdrawal lay in her sensitive talent for describing this state of affairs to others. She beautifully and euphoriously depicted the neurotic's perpetual "wading" in "grief" and anxiety. The symbolic content of her poetry divulges many of the chief components of neurotic character organization in its defense against death anxiety.

> The Soul unto itself
> Is an imperial friend—
> Or the most agonizing Spy
> An enemy could send—
>   Secure against its own—
> No treason it can hear—
> Itself—its Sovereign—of itself
> The Soul should stand in Awe—
> Adventure most unto itself
> The Soul condemned to be;

Attended by a Single Hound—
Its own Identity.[10]

Total withdrawal from living marks the neurotic adoption of a distorted purpose in life. The latter is synonymous with the failed identity crisis or identity diffusion. The glory of neurotic suffering aggrandizes alienation from self and others. Self-contained in the alienation and depression inherent in severe death anxiety, the neurotic need not fear the encroachment or demands of relatedness. New experiences and the uncertainty of relationships can be avoided and the avoidance perhaps glorified as self-reliance, independence, or religious faith. "The soul unto itself" conveys the alienated self's agony of perpetual ambivalence and fear of exposure. It brands suffering with the label of self-righteousness and elevates it to a purpose in life. The agony of this kind of suffering and fearful living does not obscure its origins in neurotic torment. It is synonymous with fearful living and death anxiety. The "enemy" Miss Dickinson worried about is the same one that the neurotic engages in battle. It is the self that is torn apart by the fear of life and death. The neurotic character in its defensive adaptation is the "imperial friend" of the "soul" that lends the person's unique type of defensiveness, royal privileges and impunity. "Secure" in the defenses of his or her own personality style, the withdrawn type of character has no more insight into his or her unconscious death anxiety and depression than the avoidance or acting-out type. The three types of personality styles imply different modes of defense, but the three convey related characterological adjustments to death anxiety and the common denominator of fearful living.

Summary

The fear of death in neurosis cannot simply be reduced to the wish for the return to the womb, nor can neurosis simply be defined as the fear of death per se. Death anxiety first arises in infancy and continues its influence on the formation of psychic defenses and the organization of characterological trends. The early psychoanalytic formulations of death anxiety in neurosis looked for a specific psychodynamic root in each particular neurotic symptom, they thus fell short of an appreciation of the relationship of death anxiety to overall defensive character movements. Brumber and Schilder, for example, pointed out that some neurotics fear death as being an annihilation and an eternal punishment for their aggression.[11]

In classical analytic theory, the neurotic's fear of death was the intensification of the aggressive drive. Brumber and Schilder traced the origin of death anxiety to separation anxiety or the fear of sudden object loss only in hysterics and anxiety neurotics. In neurotic children, its origin was seen as their own aggressive impulses. These authors felt that fear of being killed was the punishment for the hostile aggressive fantasies. In the Freudian theory of depressive neurosis, the factor of guilt was superimposed on the mechanism of punishment for aggression. In obsessive-compulsive neurotics, death anxiety was understood by Freudian investigators as the expression of sado-masochistic wishes toward the love object. However, a great deal of evidence has accumulated suggesting that in neuroses, psychoses, and "normal" individuals the fear of death can be a universally held attitude. In fact, it was argued that in neurotics, the fear of death serves as a retriever and multiplier of their other fears, namely the fear of castration.[12]

More recently psychoanalysts have begun to look at disorders of the self in relation to severe character problems. Based very loosely on Horney's delineation of character defense, three neurotic styles for defending against the loss of the self have been defined in terms of avoidance aggression, and withdrawal. Kastenbaum, et al., saw the fear of death as the fear of suffering and helplessness in the adult and the fear of abandonment in the child.[13] Others have also suggested that the anticipation of death is intrinsic to neurosis and psychosis and further that depression is maintained by the expectation of the loss of the self.[14] From this vantage point, neurotics' real failures in living and their falling short of adult goals contribute to the fear of death. Their consequent depression and feelings of helplessness prolong the anxious fear of life and death. In the present view, the anticipation of the loss of the self contributes in part to the emergence of neurotic defensive patterns. The neurotic's death anxiety is often expressed in depression. He or she therefore alternately fears death and wishes for it, as an unconscious reunion and reincorporation into the good parent.

Emily Dickinson's subconscious fear of death and Ahab and Ivan Ilych's less conscious fears of death suggested the helplessness and defensiveness that underlie the neurotic's character adjustment. Her withdrawal, and their acting out and avoidance, smacked of the fear of helplessness and ambivalence about attempts at psychological growth. Like in Kafka's short story "The Dream of Joseph K.," none of the three was able to sufficiently grapple with the death anxiety that dominated the self. These three did not possess sufficient insight into themselves to discern the lack of autonomy, unrelatedness, depression, and death anxiety inherent in their particular personality style. Conflicting wishes and fears of being devoured or reincorporated paralleled their terrible fear of the loss of the self. The prospect of death was described as being unconsciously frightening to all three, either as the anticipated punishment for separation and autonomy, or as a projection of their depressed lifelessness. In other words, these speculations about the neurotic self were intended to substantiate the relationship between death anxiety and neurotic living. Ahab's aggression seemed much less a freely chosen, self-directed behavior than a driven obsession with narcisstic revenge. Ivan Ilych's fastidious avoidance of life and Emily Dickinson's withdrawal from life for a half-life of thought equally documented their alienation from self. This insufficiency of the self lies at the heart of neurotic impairment in interpersonal psychoanalytic theory.

The expression of the self in the defense against death anxiety also corresponds to the individual's attitude toward life roles. In the description of the Rorschach human movement response devise by Piotrowski, there are three prototypical life roles or action tendencies embedded in the type of percept. The human movement response encompasses the individual's original style for dealing with reality and people and organizing perceptions. Piotrowski observed that the prototypical roles vary from assertive and compliant to blocked movement. The roles also parallel the preferred style of neurotic defense against the fear of death. Whatever the specific defensive pattern, these deficiencies of the self emerge in the three neurotic character solutions that inevitably manifest as the fear of death. Avoidance, aggression, and withdrawal equally document neurotic defensiveness. The components of death anxiety comprise an integral aspect of neurotic adjustment problems and they are often manifest in depression underlying character problems. The character defenses and relevant modes of relating reflect the passivity and fearful living of neurosis. Neurotic fearful living mirrors K's willingness to jump into his own grave in his dream and Prometheus' precarious balance between the appetite of the hungry vulture and the whimsy of a parent god.

CHAPTER TEN

Psychotherapy and the Fear of Death

Summary:
Death Anxiety—The Loss of the Self

In my view, the relationship between separation anxiety, depression, and the fear of death persists in its psychodynamic interplay in personality functioning. This three-part fear of death complex can by no means be conceptualized as a purely structural problem in the development of the psyche. Rather, it persists both as a continuous aspect of defensive functioning and as an influence on neurotic character organization that is designed to limit threats to the self and self-representations. In contrast to the early emphasis on castration anxiety as fundamental to the origin of the fear of death, a broader inquiry into death anxiety—as the fear of the loss of the self—has been traced through psychological research, clinical psychiatry, and psychoanalytic personality theory. The relationship between depression and unconscious ambivalence about death stands out among individuals who have high death anxiety, and the degree of death anxiety can often be attributed to the influence of separation conflicts, i.e., wishes for separation-individuation, fears of abandonment, and corollary wishes or fears of psychic merger and fusion. In earlier chapters these latter factors have been called in to account for the vacillation in death fears throughout life at points of psychological change, and for the well-documented higher incidence of death anxiety in women. The fear of death as a central construct in personality functioning has been explored in previous chapters in its relation to philosophical or religious issues as well as the difficulties inherent in depression and neurotic living. Fromm's notion of the fear of death being synonymous with the fear of life, and hence the fear of freedom, provides a focal point and clarity to the diverse expression of death fears in clinical problems.

Sullivan's psychology of the self system can also be emphasized in high-lighting the emergence of death anxiety. His notion of the simultaneous emergence of anxiety and the self provides a groundwork for understanding the unconscious fear of the loss of the self in interpersonal relations.[1] Thus feeding, weaning, toilet training, and sleeping disturbance in children all have the potential for the unfolding of separation problems, depression, and death anxiety. The developmental tasks of each particular phase of early childhood bear object-relational aspects. They cannot be abstracted or divorced from the parents' emotional communication to the child and the child's consequent attitudes about self, mastery, and autonomy. Neurotic conflicts in children contain some of the same formal elements as those in adults and their symptoms of emotional disturbance have a greater meaning when looked at in terms of their developmental implications and as an outgrowth of the psychodynamics of the family. Rather than trauma in toilet training, castration threats, or drive disturbance, one might argue that it is the self that lies at the source of death anxiety. It is the attachment of the self in a unconscious symbiotic relationship with the internalized parents that is most threatened in ambivalent attitudes about death. As unconscious attitudes toward death arise in developmental problems and later depressive and neurotic conflicts, threats to the self may emerge in childhood the set contents often the unconscious fear of being devoured or the unconscious wish to be devoured. Part of the neurotic's conflicts and the etiology of his or her depression may be pointed out in the individual's type of death attitude and death fear.

The fear of death, with its tripartite dimensions of depression, separation anxiety, and ambivalence about death, needs to be understood in clinical work in terms of the individual's experienced threats to the self and fear of loss of the self. An experimental examination of the fear of death, religion and existential sense of purpose in life summarized in Chapter Five, demonstrated that a lack of purpose in life is congruent with a high fear of death.[2] I suggested that intense death anxiety in a healthy individual represents depression and failures in psychological separation inherent in neurotic living. Beginning with Freud's observation that religion constitutes an efficient defense against the fear of death religious experience might be considered neurotic to the extent that it is dominated by the fear of living and the fear of death. The interrelation of depression to separation anxiety and death anxiety illustrates Erikson's concept of identity confusion as well as the existential view of meaningfulness and distorted purpose in life as the central core problem of neurosis. The fear of death in its earliest manifestations in the horrible, yet unarticulated terror of abandonment originally emerges in the infant and young child's experience with the mother. At that point in development, the relationship with the mother either restrains death anxiety or allows it to grow. The oral quality of death anxiety is later manifest in the adult in neurosis, depression, and adjustment disturbances. The fear of living is equivalent to the emergence of the three aspects of death anxiety in the neurotic adjustment problems.

It is the fate of the self in relation to the internalized parents that provides the psychodynamic key for understanding much of these phenomena in children and adults. The representation of the self in the context of death imagery and in the symbolism inherent in the individual's dreams, and neurotic problems needs to be stressed against the grounds of the internalized family atmosphere. Ernest Shachtel's term "embeddedness" beautifully describes the experience of the self without mature differentiation that the neurotic, like the child, grapples with in trying to arrive at more legitimate self-definition and autonomy.[3]

The myth of Narcissus, as Rank interpreted it, the myth of Prometheus, and the Old Testament book of Jonah might be regarded as illustrations of the mythological abundance of the struggle of the embedded self for autonomy. Rather than the fear of death being synonymous with neurosis or psychosis, as many have argued[4] it can be proposed that the fear of death has two salient characteristics. First, that it has a much closer relationship to depression because of the earliest ties between all three components of death anxiety and separation problems. Second, that as a continuous aspect of growth and functioning, it retains a strong unconscious influence on the development of neurotic character organization. These hypotheses stand as theoretical correlates of the definition of intense death anxiety as the fear of the loss of the self. The diversity of defensive character movements does not obscure the underlying communality of death anxiety in neurosis. Overtones of death anxiety are commonplace in the varieties of neurotic styles and defenses for coping with purposelessness and depression. Confrontation, withdrawal, and avoidance constitute principal neurotic mechanisms for countering death anxiety organized into consistent characterological defenses. All three stylistic defensive trends may also be defined as very clear manifestations of death anxiety. The fear of death can, in addition, be understood as a defense against depression as well as an expression of it.

Psychoanalytic Psychotherapy

The implications of the three aspects of death anxiety for psychoanalytic psychotherapy assume a priority in clarifying the relevance of death anxiety to clinical work. Psychoanalysis and analytic therapy are the only treatment modalities considered here because of the intensity of the analytic therapeutic relationship and because of their in-depth investigation of anxiety, transference, resistance, countertransference, and unconscious influences on current personality organization. A thorough treatment of death anxiety from the perspective of all of the psychoanalytic psychotherapies exceeds the scope of this work. That effort would entail a much more complete study of the concepts of ego, self, and anxiety as they have evolved in the course of the history of psychoanalysis. Death anxiety as a clinical construct in psychotherapeutic work either touches the very core of the therapy or remains a peripheral consideration, depending on the particular metapsychology of the self and anxiety. For example, Alfred Adler believed that the early awareness of death contributes to the sense of inferiority to such an extent that single encounters with death in childhood influence the molding of the lifestyle.[5] Paradoxically, Adler felt that the fear of death was rather insignificant in itself. It gained its importance only as a spur for later attempts at compensation, as with the undertaker or physician who has suffered from exposure to death as a child. Rollo May attributed the origin of anxiety to the hostile threatening milieu in which Western man lives and its function to the purpose of signaling a threat to man's existence or to some valued ideal.[6] Death for May then becomes a common symbol for anxiety. Other authors have noted that the fear of death is central in neurotic disturbances in that it is a mask for neurotic symptoms, and in turn is masked by them.[7] Jung described a psychology of death attitudes in his concept of the collective unconscious, and further defined the fear of death in the aged as a clinging to the past and a withdrawal from life. For Fromm and the interpersonal psychoanalytic theoreticians, however, the latter position pinpoints the essence of the neurotic process at all stages of life. Fromm's equation of the fear of death with the fear of life acquires more specific meaning as the fear of the loss of the self in neurotic distress.

In the Freudian theory of anxiety as expanded by Fenichel, the fear of death was defined most clearly as the fear of castration and the result of the resolution of the Oedipal complex or of primal scene traumata. In Helene Deutsch's Freudian elaboration of female psychology, for example, the fear of death was closely tied to masochism.[8] For Deutsch, death anxiety became intense in the woman's fear—of intercourse, orgasm, sexual pleasure, childbirth, and rape fantasies. Deutsch claimed that death anxiety is aroused in rape fantasies at the mobilization of aggression and underlying repressed masochistic wishes.

The work of Bertram Lewin, Sandor Rado, and particularly the latter's early psychoanalytic papers on oral and narcissistic disturbance in depression, provided a theoretical framework for understanding unconscious ambivalent wishes for death as they became evident in death anxiety. Among contemporary Freudians, Stern has stressed the role of the fear of death in the patient's unconscious symbiotic wishes;[9] Rheingold attributed neurotic death fears to the unresolved residue of early maternal destructiveness.[10] In Melanie Klein's theory, the fear of death was of central importance in that it constituted an inherent aspect of the infantile depressive position. For Klein, the death instinct was primary and the fear of death formed the basis for other types of later anxiety and feelings of persecution. Jacobson, Winnicott, Farbairn and others have studied the struggle for the survival of the self in the world of normal and pathological object relations. The concepts of self are quite different across the broad range of psychoanalytic personality theories. Yet there seems to be some common ground between the neo-Freudian-interpersonal and the Freudian assessment of death fears in relation to threats to the self, particularly with Fromm and Fromm-Reichmann's dialectical theory of psychopathology.

For Fromm-Reichmann, each symptomatic manifestation of neurosis or psychosis served the function of maintaining or enhancing life—literally enabling the person to survive.[11] She accordingly accounted for neurosis as a struggle for psychic survival, that enmeshed the individual in failures of living. Fromm—Reichmann saw anxiety as the simultaneous expression of both a symptom and a defense. From this vantage point, the psychoanalytic situation, by definition, reverberates with life and death with each therapeutic movement. The loss of the patient's symptom or neurotic character organization signifies death or the loss of the neurotic self. It is not unreasonable to suggest that in analysis, each movement of growth or resistance to it may vitalize the unconscious fear of death with its concommittant depression and separation anxiety. It follows that growth at first often brings depression. Death anxiety and depression then complicate the specific psychodynamic and characterological pattern that is being addressed in treatment. It is therefore part of the nature of psychotherapeutic work that the tripartite dimensions of death anxiety influence the working through of conflicts among neurotics and borderline psychotic individuals. Death anxiety becomes manifest in specific symptoms, more generalized character trends, transference, or in all three areas. For Sullivan and Horney, the maintenance of the neurotic's character traits signified alienation from self, a quasi-death of the "true self." The movements of the self in the psychoanalytic situation can be better understood in light of the relationship of death imagery to depression and the anxiety of individuation. In a similar vein, Erwin Singer defined resistance as a reflection of the patient's erroneous belief in the necessity of his neurotic operations for maintaining his life and dignity.[12] Singer has delineated the nuances of the symbolization process in neurotic character traits and, in aggreement with Fromm, has defined the goal of psychoanalysis to be the accomplishment of psychic independence through genuine self-awareness.

What is being implied here is not a body of technique for lowering death anxiety but a framework for listening to the patient's report of his or her experience and an appreciation of the ambivalence of the patient's struggle. If the goal of the psychoanalytic work is the patient's freedom and autonomy, and the patient retains the unconscious fears that autonomy equals death or the loss of the self, then the positive outcome of the analysis may be as anxiety-provoking as the original inner conflicts. The person's fear of change is understandable, since it threatens the loss of the self as it originally developed in the context of the family atmosphere. Several preliminary clinical implications derive from these considerations. First, when the patient's fear of death, becomes evident in the therapeutic work, then the two remaining aspects of the fear of death complex may be present in the transference or in other aspects of the pa-

tient's experience. Second, the three aspects of death anxiety can complicate or block movement in the therapeutic work, particularly at those
moments of confrontation, growth, and resistance to it. Both of these
clinical implications are particularly true of the uncovering and working
through of the elements of the transference relationship. The importance
of death fears and wishes can be observed, particularly in the transference relationship with the analyst, as death anxiety becomes intertwined
with character defense. To paraphrase Horney's designation of neurotic
trends, the expansive types have to confront death to assuage their fear;
the self-effacing types wish for death; and the resigned types embody the
fear of death with each flight of withdrawal.[13] As a major source of anxiety in the formation of neurotic trends death anxiety may underlie the
surface expression of much of the neurotic's suffering and the recreation
of his or her survival fears and wishes in the analysis. The working
through of the interrelated death fears, depression, and separation conflicts cannot be limited to any particular type of patient or phase of
psychoanalytic work. To the extent of its influence on a person's character, death anxiety constitutes a principal counterpoint to the harmonies
of the psychodynamic themes and the patterns of transference and countertransference. The analytic uncovering of that anxiety in relation to
neurotic functioning and resistance contributes to part of the healing
process of the therapist-patient dialogue.

The fear of death therefore plays a role as a major source of anxiety
in the formation of neurotic character traits. It functions as a continuous
psychodynamic aspect of human growth that first emerges in the infantile symbiosis. In psychoanalytic treatment death anxiety and depression
accompany the patients growth. Death Anxiety is equally significant in
clinical work with psychotic individuals as a major source of their anx-
eety and as an influence on their character formation. The fear of death,
separation anxiety, and depression all play a dynamic role in schizophrenia equal to that of their role in neurosis. The terror of death for the
dschizophrenic might correspond to waat Sullivan called the "not me," the
amorphous disorganizing state of profound anxiety usually reserved for
nightmares. The more intense the fear of death becomes for the schizophrenic, the greater becomes the threat to the poorly integrated self and
the greater the possibility of disassociation.

Death Anxiety and Schizophrenia

The self that is protected from death anxiety by neurotic defensiveness limits the person in avenues for creative living. In the schizophrenic, the threat of the loss of the self becomes translated even more
directly into specific symptoms. Harold Searles has presented the most
compelling contribution on the significance of death anxiety in schizophrenia. On the basis of his extensive experience in treating schizophrenics, Searles has come to the twofold conclusion that the certainty of

death constitutes one of the major sources of anxiety in the schizophrenic, and that schizophrenia becomes the defense against anxiety
about death.[14] In the schizophrenic, death anxiety accounts for a meaningful aspect of the adaptation process equal to that of its pertinence to
neurotic character defense. It is Searles' position that the schizophrenic's
interpersonal losses in early childhood lead to a disintegration of self and
a clinging to the omnipotent fantasy that personal death can be avoided.
Thus, some schizophrenics give the impression that they are not really
alive, which further serves to deny their anxiety about death. In other
words, if the disintegrating self is experienced as already being half
dead, what difference does it make that one is lifeless in interpersonal relations, and what can be frightening about death? Searles has reported
the case of a delusional young woman whose bizzare fantasies about
witchcraft and science fiction served to enhance her denial of death. In
the course of her analysis, she collected dead leaves and dead animals,
which she tried to bring to life to protect herself from the acceptance of
the death of her parents and the realization that she too would die. In his
history of the interpretation of schizophrenia, Silvano Arieti reported
about a schizophrenic young woman who had regressed to the point
where her only defense against catatonic stupor was constant looking at
her body and surroundings. This patient's obsession with looking at herself controlled her fear that corpuscles had not fallen on her or off her
body. Her solution to her anxiety about disintegration became the relinquishment of willing and the fear of improvement of any kind. When
she eventually preferred not to move at all, so that no more pieces of her
body would fall off, she spent her time in bed, with her parents feeding
her, changing her, and assuring her that she had not moved or lost any
pieces of herself. When unable to satisfy the requirements of the obsessive compulsive thoughts and rituals, she lapsed into a severe catatonic
stupor.[15] In both of these examples, the patient's fear of death was intimately tied to the fear of the loss of the self. They both illustrate the
view that the schizophrenic has to face death without ever having been a
person who is well integrated, as Searle, pointed out. Having never lived
fully, the schizophrenic is terrified of death's finality and his own inepti-
tude in living. The experiencing self is therefore not a whole person but
rather a fragment of a person who exists in the twilight of infantile symbiosis and omnipotnece. The avoidance of death anxiety in the schizophrenic influences the choice of technique in analytic work with borderline and schizophrenic patients. Searles, for example, recounts that there
is a therapeutic stage of the "pre-ambivalent mother-infant symbiosis"
in which the schizophrenic patient and the therapist simultaneously experience the mother and infant roles and treat each other in relation to
them.[16,17]

Dr. Arieti's patient also illustrated the omnipotence of the catatonic's
regression and withdrawal. Because of this woman's conflicts about autonomous behavior independent of her parents it seems to me that her
schizophrenic break represented a life-saving defensive operation that

returned her to the safety of symbiotic union with them. Since they fed, covered, and changed her, monitored all stimulation, and reinforced her thoughts, there was slim chance of any movement or thought that would break the symbiotic tie to them and threaten her with death. Giving up her will was this woman's ultimate defense against the depression and fear of annihilation that came with attempted individuation. If her will was indistinct from that of her father and mother, then there could be no possible threat of separation from the safety of her catatonic womb. The fear of losing pieces of one's body signifies death or the fear of fragmentation of the self—a very common source of anxiety among schizophrenic patients. The self-mutilation of chronic schizophrenics often can be understood in this context as a defensive attempt to blot out feelings of depersonalization and to inhibit further disintegration. Their cutting themselves and bleeding or even attempting suicide may thus serve the defensive function of trying to inhibit the degree of disintegration of the self. Ironically, schizophrenic or borderline persons who attempt suicide under these circumstances could be characterized as trying to kill themselves in order to stay alive. In both of the above case illustrations, the symptoms of their illnesses denied the inevitability of death and its personal reality. Trying to revitalize dead birds and animals or having one's parents care for one's bodily needs illustrates the schizophrenic's childlike omnipotence add illusory power in prolonged psychic symbiosis.

A brief clinical vignette will further illustrate the significance of death anxiety in schizophrenia and its relevance to treatment issues. A middle-aged woman who was gradually improving from a profoundly catatonic state following a long hospitalization and a series of electroshock treatments reported to her therapist the recovery of her earliest memory. Prior to the time she was able to walk, she remembered that she had been left momentarily in her carriage on the street while her mother attended to some errand, only to look up at the sight of a huge vicious dog growling at her and baring its angry fangs. She remembered quite vividly the abject terror of that moment and the conviction that she would be killed and eaten by the hungry dog. There was no reason to doubt the truthfulness of her reportage, but what is one to make of this situation? Fact or fantasy, the memory clearly illustrated the affective component of her early experience, at least as she needed to reconstruct it—the absolute terror of death and the fear of being devoured. At a point when she was unable to flee from danger under her own power, a brief, momentary separation from her mother had had the meaning of total annihilation and utter helplessness. As an adult, the depth of her withdrawal from life had certainly insured protection from any such malevolent force, whether external and real or internal and projected. Her catatonic regression was akin to a silent, motionless state of symbiotic merger in which no foreign element could possibly intrude to threaten the self. This point illustrates the survival function of the schizophrenic's (and neurotic's) symptom constellations. They are adaptive mechanisms for sustaining life.

Does this woman's therapist represent the mother, the vicious dog or the helpless infant who needs protection from the patient's vehement hostility and destructiveness? Have the shock treatments stimulated memories of real cruelty she had been subjected to by one of her parents? Is she communicating a deep yearning for symbiotic merger with the therapist that would blot out the external world and shield her from responsibility for her behavior, or both? What was she communicating to the therapist by the recovery of the memory at that moment? If separation signified death for her, then what would be the outcome of any genuine intimacy or shared mutuality that might develop between patient and therapist? Is the exposure of her memory a sign of recovery, in that it illustrates death anxiety's emergence in the transference as a function of the patient's growth? Is this woman saying that her therapist will abandon her and kill her if she fully recovers, or devour her and rob her of her individuality, or vice versa? The answers to these questions suggest three possible overlapping avenues of therapeutic investigation that I would be inclined to follow.

The historical explanation of the memory or myth and its relevance to real family events and attitudes might clarify the nature of the patient's early experience.The memory may be a statement about the maternal relationship and its influence on the origins and exacerbations of her schizophrenic illness. A particularly important aspect of this part of the work would be exploring the parents' emotional attitudes toward the patient's ego functioning and their role in the psychology of her withdrawal. Second, a contemporary "here and now" investigation of the residue of the memory and myth would be fruitful in terms of its relevance to general character trends and the patient's difficulties in interpersonal relationships. Third, its relevance to the interaction with the therapist and the working through of one or more of the above patterns in the transference would eventually facilitate the reintegration of the self and an increased capacity for tolerating severe anxiety. By allowing for the development of the transference through a psychoanalytic approach, the therapist simultaneously allowed this woman to evolve whichever course was essential to her growth, used the transferential material as the medium for working through her death anxiety and symptomatic schizophrenic survival mechanisms, and also attempted to validate her symbolic language. By a flight into psychosis, this woman had chosen to protect herself from the external world and from the rage of a hostile, devouring mouth that dominated her inner psychic world. She seemed to have withdrawn in order to avoid the loss of the self in abandonment and to have sought survival through symbiotic fusion.

In that single report of the memory, whether accurate or imagined, she communicated a significant statement about her internal object relations in her own symbolic language and a momentarily ambiguous, but ultimately quite powerful message about death anxiety in the transference. Like both of the patients in the above case examples, this patient's behavior and verbalizations equally demonstrated the influence of death anxiety on personality structure and functioning. Her schizophrenic way of living expressed the fear of death that was characteristic of her way of relating to significant others with its need for rigid detachemnt, withdrawal, and defense against her oral-destructive rage. Consequently, a strategy of power and an innate intelligence was contained in her retreat from sanity and helplessness. Despite the differences in psychic structure and quality of ego functioning, the intelligence of that characterological stance stamps the schizophrenic psychotics with the same mutual fear of living and dying endemic to the neurotic's fearful living.

Death Anxiety and Transference

From this contemporary psychoanalytic perspective, death anxiety with its juxtaposition of life and death imagery lies close to the heart of the therapeutic inquiry. The fear of the loss of the self stood out in the above patients as an organizing concept that summarized their experience and character problems. It was not simply a Ranklan abstraction of the symbolic wish for return to the womb. The transference becomes the major arena for the workirg through of the fear of death complex and its gradual resolution. The fear of death imagery particularly escalates at points of regression, change, or growth and resistance, as the work of the analysis threatens the individual's security operations or uncovers psychotic disassociations. In the transference, the therapist then becomes murderer, ally, omnipotent parent, helpless victim, etc., via the transference projections with the neurotic, borderline, and psychotic patient. With the borderline or psychotic patient, however, the fear of death emanates from a disintegrating self. As the patient unconsciously seeks to merge with the therapist or separate and individuate in harmony with the analytic movement, depression and ambivalence about death can lie close at hand. Consider the following incident:

A schizophrenic adolescent frequently complimented his female therapist on her appearance and hairdo. He often expressed the wish to look like the therapist and became upset if he noticed any change in her hairstyle. After several months of analytic therapy, he remarked, "I like your hair—it's pretty (touching his own hair), it's cut. Are you going to see her (another patient's) hair too?" His interest in the therapist's hair did not simply imply identity confusion or wish for identification with the therapist. His obsession with her hair marked a struggle for control of oscillating self-representations and a loss of boundaries between himself and his therpaist. He did not experience himself or his therapist as a whole person or as separate, but rather as merged, as hair. The therapist's presence was needed desperately by this boy to complement his impaired ego functioning and to inhibit his fragmentation. In conjunction with the use of splitting and a loss of ego boundaries, he had vacillated between a fragmented self that was either good or bad, ugly or handsome. He did not experience himself as a person, but rather as the hair on his therapist's head. The therapist existed for him, only as hair on his head. The symbiotic maternal transference brought to light his depression and the anxiety that he would be abandoned by the therapist-mother if she saw other patients. The anticipation of any threat to the symbiotic tie with her provoked a great deal of anxiety in the patient. That anxiety accounted for his fragmentation and the confusion within which he could safely cling to his therapist. It would be more correct to say that he could cling to her hair—that part of her he was at first able to more fully experience. Just as the infant first grasps the breast or bottle and then later reaches out for parts of the mother's face and body, it is only after the symbiotic attachemnt that he or she later differentiates parts and the whole gestalt of the mother's distinct separate physical presence. The loss of the therapist's hair or even a minor change in her hairstyle signified separation and the death of the symbiotically attached fragmented self. The therapeutic task at the moment of this boy's remark consisted of, at first, simply trying to get him to think and helping him examine his experience in the session or whatever it was in the therapist-patient interactoion that had elicited his mental state. The therapist's attempt to thereby bolster his ego functioning simultaneously took the first step in the examination of the meaning of his communication.

For the therapist to have remained silent or not actively participated with the boy would have been to miss the point that at that moment something had touched his very survival. Since the boundaries between self and other had been blurred for this boy, the prospect of separation from his therapist represented death and a loss of the self in the transference. By means of his communication, this patient had been telling the therapist that his need for her and fear of losing her was a matter of life and death. The investigation of the boy's remarks signified that the therapist understood his feeling that his life was in danger and that she would neither kill him nor permit him to be killed. Her intervention suggested that her active participation would continue to protect him from death. It suggested further that it was crucial for the patient to seek the meaning of his fear of death at that moment in her presence. The resolution of the symbiotic transference permitted him to emerge individuated from the analytic work with more autonomous and adequate ego functioning. On the one hand, this remark might be considered as a regression in the transference to a symbiotic state and an expression of the patient's rage at the mother—the true symbiotic partner. It was not so much a regression as a recreation in the analytic situation of the patient's inner world, in which self is not differentiated from object. To the degree that self and other are identical, separation means death. Thus, the fear of death via separation or fusion may characterize the transference of either the borderline or schizophrenic patient.

Finally, the three aspects of death anxiety may become apparent in specific resistances or general character traits manifest in the transference. It has already been noted that the fear of death may exert the greatest influence on the backward and forward ebb of the analytic movement at the points of the patient's genuine growth, regression, and resistance. This influence has been accounted for on the basis of the threat of the loss of the self and early childhood feelings of helplessness and dependence upon parents for survival. At stake here again is the psychodynamic linkage between separation anxiety, depression, and ambivalence about death as the analytic movement confronts a resistance in the transference. Resistance needs to be understood in relation to the patient's self.

Following about a year of treatment, a middle-aged man reported the following dream to his therapist. "I was both at home in my bed and at the office. I was paralyzed, tried to move and couldn't, but my eyes were open. I thought a soul came into my room and tried to grab me and that I was falling into an abyss. I thought something terrible had happened at the office, and it did—an explosion. I was outside it, but also inside it, and it all depended on me. The other guys could escape, but I didn't. I was like a magical universe. I could make the explosion just by thinking about it. I thought myself out of there and that I have to be careful about what I think—all the things happen. I was afraid everyone would die in the explosion. When I was in bed, I thought: I'm really a warlock. I can make anything happen. I'm better than they are. I was a warlock because I could get away in my bed. I could move and I could move my fingers twice, so I knew that the explosion hadn't worked."

Even though he possessed generally adequate resources, judgment, and reality testing, the dream illustrates the extent of this patient's disassociation and psychic vulnerability. This man needed to resort to a magical world in which his powers were limitless and his identity was that of a warlock. As a warlock he could keep his fragmented self alive. On a characterological level this secret identity showed itself in hostility and grandiosity that counteracted feelings of alienation, shame, and inferiority. It also reflected a projection of his rage, difficulty in intimate relationships, and alienation from self. The deadly explosion occurred in two places in the dream, and the word *office* has two possible meanings—the therapist's office and the patient's place of employment. As the therapeutic investigation touched this man's rage, grandiosity, disguised feelings of omnipotence, and the fear of being influenced by the analyst, he began to fear equally that the therapist would "paralyze him" and that he would kill the therapist. In the dream the patient could fear for his coworkers safety, but he kills them through the use of his magical powers. The loss of this secret warlock self and its evil power signified death to this patient. The dream suggested, among other things, that the therapeutic encounter took on the quality of a continuous life and death struggle. The patient's unconscious struggle to retain his magical world and warlock self dictated a counterassault on the analyst's efforts to assist him toward self-knowledge and growth. The possible anal or sexual meanings of the "making" or "explosion" were only significant at superficial levels of meaning. The patient's feelings toward the analyst needed to be defended against since they insured, in the unconscious, that his efforts or presence would "grab" the patient (self), immobilize him, and then kill him. At stake here was the loss of an infantile self in a magical world reanacted in the transference. Whims and needs could be satisfied in this world by a mere expression or the slightest of gestures. Depression, shame and rage could be dismissed from the self, unlike the patients usual experience in the real world. Close, intimate contact signified the loss of magical control in the therapy, fusion with the therapist, and annihilation. The giving up of his warlock self meant death for this man. Its activity and retention also meant death for patient and therapist in the transference. If the analyst was perceived as a colleague, or an equal partner and guide in the mental analytic "office" work then the differentiated analyst-parent would be destroyed. Here again, resistance to change amounted to more than a failure in the development of adequate internal-psychic structures. The conflicts vividly experienced in the transference and the patients' resistance to change signified the early attempts at survival projected onto the psychoanalytic situation. The fear of death unconsciously influenced his need to resist the therapist's efforts to truly "keep his eyes open" to himself. The resistance denied the analyst's influence upon him and kept the patient alive. Unfortunately it reinforced the "paralysis" of his fear of living and dying.

As death imagery increasingly becomes the metaphor in the therapeutic work for the patient's internalized object relations, it can take the form of fusion with the good parent who would be a source of protection and comfort, or with the bad persecutory parent who will attack. The identification of the therapist as an extension of the patient as helpless victim is still another possible turn of event in the unconscious transference communications. Transference cannot be adequately defined just as the universal childhood wish for protection from death. This wish for invulnerability may be one aspect of transference in all types of patients. In addition, however, the transference becomes the arena for the expression of those defensive operations that have been identified with the self. The here and now interaction between therapist and patient recreates the life and death struggles of the self in the present moment. In other words, death anxiety is experienced in the transference, whatever particular form it may take. The very form of the transference demonstrates the denial of death anxiety in the symbioticlike transference. The wish for fusion and merger denies the reality of separation and, thus, the reality of death. In idealizing transferences, the patient's insecurity discloses the wish for parental protection from that anxiety. Winnicott suggested that the mother's role involves monitoring stimulation and protecting the maturing infant from harmful stimuli and trauma.[18] If excessive stimulation or overwhelming instinctual urges are not adequately monitored, a threat to the infant's self results. Part of the function of the analytic relationship, as a substitute for the "good enough mothering," includes the defense against death anxiety, protection from murderous rage, and the fear of helplessness.

In the therapy with the above-mentioned adolescent patient, his becoming his therapist's hair insured that they would not be separated since he experienced himself as a part of the therapist's body. His al-

ready fragmented self thereby became relatively more secure from internal or external stress that could evoke further disassociation. The fragmentation defended him against death, while trying to provoke the
presence of the "good enough mother" in the therapist. His blurring of
boundaries worked in the service of providing a genuine attachment to
the therapist upon which his life depended. It is particularly in this latter
type of symbiotic transference that there is the clearest illustration of the
child's terror of helplessness and sincere need for parents who, at one
point, are perceived as being omnipotent. If the paitent is merged with
the therapist or they have indistinguishable, interchangeable parts, then
death becomes much less of a threat. The attachment to the mother in
early childhood sustains the child's life, and the unfolding of the emotional relationship with the analyst provides the patient with safety from
feelings of helplessness in the face of threats to the self. It is the real relationship with the analyst that accomplishes this goal by providing the atmosphere for the patient's growth and the working through of the patient's death anxiety and character problems. As such, there can be no
specific stage in the work with psychotic, borderline, or neurotic people
in which the fear of death exclusively predominates. The imagery of
death anxiety weaves its transverse patterns in the transference at moments of regression, growth, and resistance, namely at those points at
which there is an unconscious perception of threats to the self. The three
aspects of the fear of death intensify at those moments that the person is
potentially most alive, yet paradoxically most afraid of living.

Death Anxiety and Symbolism

The investigation of death anxiety in dream imagery provides valuable clues to its significance in the patient's character problems as they
evolve in daily living and in the transference. The specific symbolism in
a person's dream language substantiates the unique personality problems heightened in the anxiety over the loss of the self. The association
of the fear of death imagery with separation anxiety and depression in
dream symbolism corresponds to one of the longest-standing traditions
in Western thought. The ancient Greeks battled with this problem via
mythologic transformation of their contemporaries into heroic gods. In
part, the quest of Odysseus in Homer's *Odyssey* superimposed an exposi-
tion of the fear of death upon the chronology of the Trojan War and its
poetic, historical record. Before traveling to the war to avenge the rape of
Helen, Odysseus despaired over leaving his beloved wife, Penelope, so
much that he feigned insanity to prevent their separation. Homeric students have described Odysseus' journey primarily in terms of Mycenaen
cultural history and the need to preserve, in epic form, the religion and
mythology contained in the Greek oral tradition. However, the themes of
death, separation, and reunion were frequent aspects of the legends of
Odysseus' journey. His relentless struggle to return to Ithaca paralleled the

devotion of his wife, Penelope, in maintaining the fantasy of their reunion in spite of twenty years of separation. After two decades of patient waiting for Odysseus' return, Penelope despaired over her loss and confusion about how to put off her suitors. The pain of separation and unresolved grief took a heavy toll on her spirit. Her loyalty to the fantasy of his return became a meek compensation for her depressed mental state.

At that point in the epic, Penelope reported the following dream:

From a water's edge twenty fat geese have come to feed on grain
Beside my house. And I delight to see them.
But now a mountain eagle with great wings and crooked beak storms
in to break their necks
And strew their bodies here.
Away he soars
into the bright sky;
and I cry aloud
All this in the dream
I wail and around me gather
Softly braided Akhaian women mourning
Because the eagle killed my geese.
Then down out of the sky he dropped to a cornice beam
With mortal voice telling me not to weep.
Be glad says he renowned Ikarios' daughter:
Here is no dream but something real as day
Something about to happen
All those geese
Were suitors and the bird was I
See now,
I am no eagle but your lord come back
To bring in glorious death upon them all!
As he said this my honeyed slumber left me
Appearing through half shut eyes I saw the geese
In a hall still feeding at the same trough.

Her conscious wish for relief from anguish provided one of the contextual clues for some of the significant latent content in her dream language. Based on the assumption that all of the components of a dream's imagery form a cohesive unit as a creative production of the dreamer, Penelope's delight at the appearance of the geese, the geese themselves, and the eagle all deserve decoding as divergent aspects of Penelope, the dreamer. In Penelope's dream, her symbolized depression and inability to mourn or relinquish the ties to her husband, complicated by the uncertainty of his fate, could be interpreted as a conflicting wish for death and fear of it. The eagle and the geese may be interpreted not only as the suitors and avenging husband, but as aspects of the dreamer herself. Penelope's delight at the arrival of the geese and identification with them as slain but free independent entities, then signifies the possible projection of a combined husband-parent figure onto the animals in the dream. Why had the geese been slaughtered, but not Penelope? Thoughts about separation and severing internal ties (not simply sexual fidelity) met with the anticipation of the punishment of death. The dream implied that she escaped death not only because of loyalty but also because of obedience or a fear of punishment. Penelope cried for herself as a victim of conflicting wishes for freedom from ties of obligation and fierce loyalty versus a yearning for reunion with the lost husband-parent. Her entire experience was related in *The Odyssey* as a twenty-year period of partial mourning and denial of loss, fortified by clinging to the fantasy of reunion. The passivity of the helpless geese (dreamer) in contrast to the power and vengeful fury of the eagle (parent) also recapitulated the helplessness and powerlessness of the childhood self in relation to the devouring, or agressive, parental images in dreams.

Penelope's depression and death anxiety, as indexed by the dream and the fantasy of reunion, duplicated the same psychodynamic pattern in Mark Twain's prose account of Tom Sawyer's fantasies about his death and reappearance at his own funeral. The anguished suffering in Penelope's depression provided a dramatic contrast to her devotion. One might infer that her devotion suited Odysseus' heroid determination to be reunited with his wife and kingdom at all costs. In Penelope's dream, and Tom Sawyer's fantasies, the three dimensions of death anxiety masked the resourcelessness of the self. The legendary queen and the fictional preadolescent boy turned to their own unique defensive armor in combating the depicted threats of the loss of the self. In the imagery of their dreams and fantasies, the conflicting wishes for death and fear of death betrayed their depression in the symbolic language at points of ambivalence about change or psychic growth. The inexplicable series of delays and adventures that befell Odysseus all involved a common ingredient. In each adventure from Circe to the Cyclops, Odysseus alternated between dependence on the intervention of the gods and bouts of his own autonomous cunning. His reliance on the intervention of the gods corresponded to helplessness in the face of their interference, outrage, and whimsy. In this sense, his adventure in returning from Troy reiterated part of the thematic content in Penelope's dream: ambivalence about psychic autonomy versus dependence on internalized parental images.

In psychotherapy, the degree of resourcefulness of the depicted self in the patients' dream imagery provides a symbolic statement of the extent of their freedom from depression and death anxiety. When the fear of death imagery does emerge in the symbolism of dream language or fantasy, the therapist's work in part involves the uncovering of its linkage to the patient's character problems and depression. Self-reliance grows in the recognition of the mythological hero, sleeping child, or dreaming adult as distinct from the internalized parental image. Ambivalence about the emergence of the self because of entanglement with death fears and depression stands out as a central motif in mythology, children's fantasies, and adult's symbolic language.

Historically, transference has been understood as a solution to the fear of death. The attribution to the therapist of power over life and death recalls the child's reliance on the parents for lowering anxiety about the dark and the demons of the night. Robert Lifton and Ernest Becker have gone even further in understanding transference as a kind of heroic struggle in which the person engages to assure immortality. As such, transferential phenomena by definition amount to both distortion and a process of creative self-expression. The clinical work with each patient discussed above suggested an interlocking honeycomb of fear of death imagery, and depression in a threatened self, as well as creative defensive expression in the transference. Moreover, the patterns of therapy with all kinds of patients generally involve the twofold use of the transference for a projection of the life and death conflicts that threaten the self, and as the medium for the growth of the self. The therapist's participation demands sensitivity to the patient's symbolic communication of attitudes about death in the transference. The difficulty of allowing for merger and fusion in the transference while also encouraging autonomy is no slight feat. Through the merger with the analyst, whether partial or relatively complete, transferential distortions are played out and worked through in a living recreation of the patient's unique blend of character style and internalized objects. Threats to the self can be analyzed as they occur in the context of providing the opportunity for the growth of a new self. The therapeutic process assimilates such scrutiny of the individual's death anxiety in problems of living while allowing for its unfolding in the transference.

Death Anxiety and Neurosis

The juxtaposition of death anxiety and character trends finds fullest expression in the transference and a concise lexicon in the individual's symbolization process. Both areas demand therapeutic investigation and decoding of that juxtaposition, whatever the nature of the person's psychopathology. It is my impression that the fear of death becomes manifest in its three dimensions in the interaction of transferential reactions with character trends in all types of individuals. The fear of the loss of the self correlates with the degree of resourcefulness of the person's ego functioning and style of adapting to perceived threats to the self. The difference between the neurotic symbiotic transference wishes or death anxiety and those of the schizophrenic or borderline person lies in that in the latter individual, there is a more complete loss of reality testing or intactness of ego boundaries. The neurotic's merger with the therapist never becomes so complete nor are the boundaries so blurred that he, for example, becomes the therapist's hair. Giovacchini observed that it is primarily in the borderline person or more severely disturbed personality that the symbiotic transference allows for the unfolding of the individual's developmental problems; even in neurotics, the transference "recapitulates symbiotic elements."[19] The neurotic patient may unconsciously merge with the therapist and become terrified about the loss of the self, but there is always intact psychic structure and a sphere of healthy adaptive functioning. The borderline person's nuclei of ego strengths, however, are rather like islands in a stream that surface sporadically in daily life and in the life and death imagery of the transference. Guntrip acknowledged the reality of the fear of death to psychotic, borderline, and schizoid people in their frantic activity and dreams of annihilation. He felt that such dreams reflected their intense psychic struggle to keep themselves alive.[20] Anxiety about death, anxiety about separation versus fusion with internal objects, and depression have a prominent position in the borderline patient's inner psychic world.

For the neurotic, the integration of death anxiety with defense is less debilitating but equally pertinent in the transference and stylistic modes of fearful living. The neurotic's improvement and escape from death anxiety frequently involves symbiotic like fusion with the therapist and growth through individuation. Freedom from ambivalence about death and depression grows out of the movement and reorganization of the self in the transference. Consider the harmonies between death anxiety, character defense, and the patient's self in the transference in the following incident. Shortly following the installation of new carpeting in my office, a twenty-year-old college student appeared for a session wearing for the first time a sport jacket that was the same color as the carpet. A chronically depressed underachiever, this young man reported a dream in which he went for a ride in his sister's car and then, for the first time, was able to face angry male figures who had chased him and threatened to kill him. He then reported feeling momentarily hopeful about himself and less fearful about the demands of his rigorous academic program. Since this patient seldom, if ever, wore a sport jacket and the color of the carpeting was an unusual shade of dark red, he seemed to be saying, via his behavior and dream language that this event was not coincidental. My office had become his childhood home. In the transference, he had momentarily fused with the therapist as his sister or mother in recreating an early point in his life when sporadic support and concern for him had kept him alive. The brief but marked changed in his affect and mental state corresponded with a shift in the symbolized self in the dream and the symbiotic like fusion in the transference. This man's depressive character style had involved ambivalent fears and wishes for death as they congealed in a withdrawn type of fearful living and chronic drug use. His fear of death reported in previous dreams had captured experiences of terror and helplessness in the face of the uncertainty and cruelty of his early life. Meaninglessness and painful depression highlighted his characteristic use of withdrawal, both as a counterassault and a life-sustaining mechanism that stemmed from early childhood. The self, which was fused with the good mother in the transference, was experienced as more adaptive in the dream. It felt stronger in dealing with critical, attacking, persecutory introjects and much more resourceful in daily living. The dream provided an opportunity for the investigation of the interrelationship between the transference, the patient's anxiety about death, his characteristic way of responding to subjectively perceived slights, and his severe problems in relationships. This man's anxiety and depression in part derived from a need to convert other people into hostile persecutors and a lack of awareness of these persistent identifications. My choice at one point in this particular session was to interpret the meaning of the hostile, attacking figures as projections of both his parents and himself. A comment was then made about his new resourcefulness in handling himself in the dream. Such a comment simultaneously indicated an awareness of the different transferential qualities of the dream and the wearing of the sport jacket. The interpretative comments suggested that this patient could fuse with the therapist without fear of being destroyed, punished, or subject to revenge for any less neurotic and more successful behavior. In this sense, the content interpretation amounted to a transference interpretation more than a countertransference interpretation. It helped to pinpoint the location of the work in the anlaysis at that moment. It addressed the patient's defined conflicts over autonomy versus depression, identification with the hostile introjects, and misperception of his internal world in current interpersonal relationships. Through the recognition of the shift in the self-representation and the mode of functioning in the dream, it was being suggested that the patient's growth and individuation was indeed possible. In addition, the message had been conveyed that his autonomy would not kill either of us in the process. The patient's wish to merge with a part of his sister or mother in the transference and carry her off with him by no means amounted to a severe regression or loss of ego boundares . The unfolding of these events in the transference and their investigation in sessions allowed for the simultaneous work on a number of areas. Their exploration furthered the patient's awareness of experience of himself, his parents, his therapist, and his contemporary characterological mode of fearful living.

This man's behavior also illustrated the conflicting forces of the fear of death and the unconscious wish for death as merger. The neurotic's merger and symbiotic fusion with the therapist does not disclose the same deficiences or early developmental problems as the borderline patient's transference regression. The analytic work with a neurotic's transference fusion and death imagery has as its end the analyzing of the character flaws and distortions as they relate to limitations and threats to the self. The neurotic's fusion remains more reversible and less correlated with serious deficits in ego functioning. There is less of a need for the therapist to directly augment the neurotic patient's ego functioning as death anxiety is uncovered. In those neurotic character types who predominantly use avoidance and denial of death anxiety, ambivalence about death will be likely manifested in the transference. In the acting out or confrontational types who fear death and life, there is a more ac-

tive fight against death anxiety. Acting-out behavior of this type is counterphobic but still motivated by helplessness and rage at the perception
of death threats. He or she would be more likely to perceive the therapist
as an annihilating, threatening parent with whom intimacy suggests
death. As a continuous aspect of growth and functioning, the fear of
death accounts for an integral part of the origin of the neurotic's depression and fearful living, whatever the specific type of character organization.

Summary

Throughout the course of the therapeutic relationship, the juxtaposition of life and death fears with defensive character maneuvers persists
in the patterns of the transference. At points of resistance, regression,
and growth, the self of the patient engages in a struggle for continued
survival. It may integrate with the therapist through fusion and merger,
or push for autonomy from the influence of the analyst-parent. The
greater the investment the neurotic has in his or her style of fearful living, the more automatically he or she will respond to the analyst's intervention with withdrawal, confrontation, or avoidance. I have suggested
that the therapist's presence as significant other and transferential parent
elicits the patient's characteristic mode of dealing with death anxiety.
The confrontational or acting-out type, for example, may need to provoke a life and death struggle with the therapist to resolve death anxiety.
This would recreate for the patient a situation that entails the opportunity for mastery of his or her particular threats to the self. The more in-
flexible the patient's self, the more that creative change and the therapist's influence seem to be experienced as threats. The more vulnerable
the individual is to such threats to the self, the greater is the need to cling
to neurotic types of survival mechanisms. Yet the growth of the self does
not spring forth from soil of a truly adversary relationship. The analytic
investigation of transference and countertransference in relation to death
imagery and defensive operations renders the self of the patient less sus-
ceptible to death threats. Ideally, the healthy patient would be less afraid
of death and less invested in neurotic patterns of fearful living. With the
neurotic type who relies on denial, fusion and merger might be sought
with a nurturing, symbiotic parent in the transference. The acting-out
type, on the other hand, tries to provoke the antagonistic, confrontational
parent in the therapist just as the withdrawn or avoidance-type unconsciously hopes for withdrawal in the therapist. At the very least, such a
patient seeks to integrate with some personality traits in the therapist
that can be defended against by withdrawal or avoidance. The neurotic
who uses avoidance compliance, and self-effacing behavior might fear
death as abandonment. The neurotic may protest too much against the
fear of death via hostile operations, manipulativeness, confrontations, or
the need to constantly prove himself. He may seek either to withdraw or

to provoke life and death struggles, to the extent that he fear death as the loss of the self. Throughout all of the types of neurotic character problems, depression and separation conflicts coexist in the therapeutic process in the context of the threats to the self. These elements can be addressed therapeuticaly in the face of the awareness of the individual's unique style for defending against death and avoiding life.

A most dramatic change in the self can be observed in the recovery of psychotic and borderline patients who have been able to individuate from transferential fusion states. A lack of integration of the self corresponds with marked distortions of body image in schizophrenia. Therefore, recovery and clinical improvement in the schizophrenic's mental state can often be noted by changes in the clarity and organization of the human figure drawings. No detailed analysis may even be necessary with such patients' drawings in order to see the change in their projections of a less threatening world, and a more resourceful intact self, onto their graphic protocols. Heightened adaptive ego functioning and increased solidity of the self also earmark the improvement of the borderline child or adolescent's recovery as well. The growth of the self in the neurotic, however, takes a more circuitous path in treatment. It has been proposed that one aspect of this course lies in the interaction of the entire therapeutic process with the fear of death complex. The concepts of resistance, acting out, transference, countertransference, and unconscious defensive motivation, can all be explored in treatment with the recognition that analytic work uncovers the patients' related fears of living and dying. The uncovering and working through of death anxiety, particularly in relation to the transference harmonies, provides clarity to the patient's struggle and ambivalence about recovery. It helps to clarify the mystery inherent in those neurotic areas of difficulty that persist, as W. H. Auden put it in commenting on the death of Yeats in "the deserts of the heart." The concepts of death anxiety and the fear of living presuppose the individual's unique psychology of the loss of the self. The relationship between this psychology of the loss of the self and the threats to the self unfolds throughout treatment, particularly in the transference, whether death signifies abandonment, and disintegration or a merger that might allow for individuation and growth. Its relevance to the patient's adjustment difficulties emerges in the therapeutic work on the patient's imagery and experience. From this vantage point, the psychotherapeutic process evolves in the recognition of its relationship to the person's characteristic modes of death anxiety and of fear of living. Effective psychoanalytic psychotherapy allows for the growth of the self in the context of a medium that recreates the ongoing experience of the perceived threats to survival.

References

Chapter 1—The Fear of Death

1. Zilboorg, G.: "Fear of Death," *Psychoanalytic Quarterly*, 1943, 12, 465-475.
2. Freud, S.: "The Ego and Id." *The Standard Edition of the Complete Psychological Works of Sigmund Freud*, London, Hogarth Press, 1955, Vol. IX, 48.
3. Jones, E.: *The Life and Works of Sigmund Freud*, New York, Basic Books, 1953.
4. Bromberg, W. and Schilder, P.: Death and Dying, *Psychoanalytic Review*, 1933, 20, 133-185.
5. Bromberg, W. and Schilder, P.: The Attitudes of Psychoneurotics Toward Death, *Psychoanalytic Review*, 1936, 23, 1-25.
6. Chadwick, M.: "Notes on the Fear of Death," *International Journal of Psychoanalysis*, 1929, 10, 321.
7. Hitschman, E.: "Anxiety About Death Due to the Compulsion to Kill: A Neurotic Mechanism," *Zeitscrift fur Kinderpsychiatrie*, 1937, 3, 165-169.
8. Becker, E.: *The Denial of Death*, Free Press, New York, 1973.
9. Wahl, C.: "The Fear of Death," *Bulletin of the Meninger Clinic*, 1958, 22, 214-223.
10. Diggory, J., Rothman, D.: "Values Destroyed by Death," *Journal of Abnormal and Social Psychology*, 1970, 26, 50-53.
11. Sarnoff, L., Corwin, S.: "Castration Anxiety and the Fear of Death," *Journal of Personality*, 1959, 27, 374-385.
12. Kastenbaum, R.: "The Realm of Death: An Emerging Area in Psychological Research," *Journal of Human Relations*, 1965, 13, 538-552.
13. Frankl, V.: *The Will to Meaning: Principles and Applications of Logotherapy*, New York, World Press, 1969, Angel E. and Ellenberg H. (Eds.).
14. May, R.: *Existence: A New Dimension in Psychiatry and Psychology*, New York, Simon and Schuster, 1967.
15. Fromm, E.: *Man for Himself*, New York, Rinehart, 1947.
16. Choron, J.: *Death and Western Thought*, New York, Collier Books, 1963.
17. Bluestone, H., McGahee, G.: Reaction to Extreme Stress: "Impending Death by Execution." *American Journal of Psychiatry*, 1962, 119, 393.
18. Gottlieb, C.: *Modern Art and Death in H. Fiefel: The Meaning of Death*, McGraw Hill, 1959.
19. Freud, S.: Religion—"The Future of an Illusion," *The Standard Edition of the Complete Psychological Works of Sigmund Freud*, London, Hogarth Press, 1955, Vol. XXI.
20. Winnicott, D.: in *Collected Papers*, New York, Basic Books, 1958. "The Theory of Parent-Infant Relationships, "*International Journal of Psychoanalysis*, 1960, 41, 585.
21. Jacques, E.: *Death and the Mid-Life Crisis in H. Ruitembeck's Death Interpretations*, New York, Dell, 1969.
22. Klein, M.: "A Contribution to the Psychogenesis of Manic Depressive States," *International Journal of Psychoanalysis* 1935, 16, "Mourning and Its Relation to Manic Depressive States," *International Journal of Psychoanalysis* 1940, 20,
On the Development of Mental Functioning," *International Journal of Psychoanalysis*, 1958, 39, 84.

23. Lifton, R.: *Living and Dying,* New York, Praeger, 1974; *Death in Life: Survivors of Hiroshima,* Random House, New York, 1968.
24. Freud, S.: "Inhibitions, Symptoms and Anxiety," *Standard Edition of the Complete Psychological Works of Sigmund Freud,* London, Hogarth Press, 1955, Vol. XX.
25. Wahl, C.: *OP CIT* ref. 9.
26. Jones, E.: "On Dying Together with Special Reference to Hernich von Klists' Suicide." In *Essays in Applied Psychoanalysis,* London, Hogarth Press, 1952.
27. Grotjahn, M.: "Ego Identity and the Fear of Death and Dying, "*Journal of Hillside Hospital,* 1960, 9.
28. Bettleheim, B.: *The Uses of Enchantment,* New York, 1977.
29. Chadwick, M.: *op cit* ref. 9.
30. Poe, E.: *The Mentor's Book of Major American Poets,* New American Library, New York, 1962, p. 113. D. Williams and E. Honig, (Eds.).

Chapter 2—Death Anxiety in the Living and the Dying

1. Freud, S.: "The Future of an Illusion," *The Standard Edition of the Complete Psychological Works of Sigmund Freud,* London, Hogarth Press, 1953, Vol. XXI.
2. Swenson, W.: "Attitudes Towards Death in an Aged Population." *Journal of Gerontology,* 1961, *16,* 49-52.
3. Jeffers, F., Nichols, C., Eisdorfer: "Attitude of Older Persons Towards Death," *Journal of Gerontology,* 1961, *16,* 53-56.
4. Christ, P.: "Attitudes Toward Death Among a Group of Acute Geriatric Psychiatric Patients," *Journal of Gerontology,* 1961, *16,* 56-59.
5. Shatan, C.: "Bogus Manhood, Bogus Honor: Surrender and Transfiguration in the U.S. Marine Corps.," *Psychoanalytic Perspectives on Aggression,* Charles Thomas, 1973.
6. Lifton, R.: *Death in Life, Survivors of Hiroshima,* New York, Random House, 1967.
7. Hinton, J.: "The Physical and Mental Distress of the Dying," *Quarterly Journal of Medicine,* 1963, *32,* 1-2.
8. Kalish, R.: "Some Variables in Death Attitudes," *Journal of Social Psychology,* 1963, *59,* 137-148.
9. Cappon, D.: "The Dying," *Psychiatric Quarterly,* 1959, *33,* 466-489.
10. Freud, S.: "Beyond the Pleasure Principle," *The Complete Edition of the Psychological Works of Sigmund Freud,* London, Hogarth Press, 1955, Vol. XVIII.
11. Shakespeare, W.: *Hamlet,* Appleton Century Crofts, New York, 1946.
12. Diggory, J. and Rothman, D.: "Values Destroyed by Death," *Journal of Abnormal and Social Psychology,* 1961, *63,* 205-210.
13. Swenson, W.: "Attitudes Towards Death in an Aged Population," *Journal of Gerontology,* 1961, *16,* 49-52.
14. Lester, D.: "Experimental and Correlational Studies of the Fear of Death," *Psychological Bulletin,* 1967, *67,* 27-36.
15. Lowry, R.: "Male and Female Differences in Attitudes Towards Death," Doctoral dissertation, Brandeis University, 1965.
16. Templar, D., Ruff, C. and Franks, V.: "Death Anxiety, Age, Sex and Parental Resemblance in Diverse Populations," *Developmental Psychology,* 1971, *4,* 108.
17. Feifel, H. (Ed.): *The Meaning of Death,* Mc Graw Hill New York, 1959.

18. Rheingold, J.: *The Fear of Being a Woman: A Theory of Maternal Destructiveness,* Grune and Stratton, New York, 1964; *The Mother, Anxiety and Death,* Little, Brown, Boston, 1967.
19. Chadwick, M.: "Notes Upon the Fear of Death," *International Journal of Psychoanalysis,* 1929, *10,* 321.
20. Feifel, H.: "Older Persons Look at Death," *Geriatrics,* 1956, *11,* 127-130.
21. Shrut, S.: "Attitudes Toward Old Age and Death." *Mental Hygiene,* 1958, *42,* 259-266.
22. Corey, L.: "An Analogue of Resistance to Death Awareness," *Journal of Gerontology,* 1961, *16,* 59-60.
23. Jeffers, Nichols and Eisdorfer, *op cit* ref. 3.
24. Jaehner, D. (The Attitude of the Small Child to Death), *Zeitschrift fur Anjewandte Psychologie,* 1933, *45,* 262-288.
25. Schilder, P. and Wechsler, D.: "The Attitudes of Children Towards Death," *Journal of Genetic Psychology,* 1936, *31* 348-363.
26. Nagy, M.: "The Child's Theories Concerning Death," *Journal of Genetic Psychology,* 1948, *73,* 3-27.
27. Corey, *op cit* ref. 22.
28. Martin, D. and Wrightsman, L.: "The Relationship Between Religious Behavior and Concern About Death." *Journal of Social Psychology,* 1965, *65,* 317-323.
29. Templar, D., Ruff, C. and Franks, C.: "Death Anxiety, Age, Sex and Parental Resemblance in Diverse Populations," *Developmental Psychology,* 1971, *4,* 108.
30. Jung, C.: "The Soul and Death" *The Meaning of Death,* New York, McGraw-Hill, 1959, Feifel, H. (Ed.).
31. Rhudick, P. and Dibner, A.: "Age, Personality and Health Correlates of Death Concerns in Normal Aged Individuals," *Journal of Gerontology,* 1961, *16,* 44-49.
32. Stacey, C. and Reichen, M.: "Attitudes Toward Death and Family Life Among Normal and Subnormal Adolescent Girls," *Exceptional Children,* 1954, *20,* 259-262.
33. Swenson, W.: "Attitudes Toward Death in an Aged Population," *Journal of Gerontology,* 1961, *16,* 348-363.
34. Schilder, P.: "The Attitudes of Murders Toward Death," *Journal of Abnormal and Social Psychology,* 1936, *31,* 348-363.
35. Klein, M.: "A Contribution to the Theory of Anxiety and Guilt," *International Journal of Psychoanalysis,* 1948, *29,* 114-123.
36. Fenichel, O.: *The Psychoanalytic Theory of Neurosis,* Norton, New York, 1955.
37. Rhudick, *op cit* ref. 31.
38. Jeffers, *op cit* ref. 3.
39. Feifel, H.: "The Problem of Death," *Catholic Psychological Record,* 1965, *3,* 18-22.
40. Templar, D.: "The Construction and Validation of a Death Anxiety Scale," *Journal of General Psychology,* 1970, *82,* 165-177.
41. Templar, *op cit* ref. 15.
42. Templar, D.: "Death Anxiety as Related to Depression and Health of Retired Persons," *Journal of Gerontology,* 1971, *4,* 521-523.
43. Stern, M.: "The Fear of Death and Neurosis," *Journal of the American Psychoanalytic Association,* 1968, *16,* 3-31.
44. Weisman, A. and Kastenbaum, R.: "The Psychological Autopsy," *Community Mental Health Minographs,* New York, 1968.

45. Chandler, K.: "Three Processes of Dying and Their Behavioral Affects," *Journal of Consulting Psychology,* 1965, *29,* 296-301.
46. Le Shan, L. and Worthington, R.: "Some Psychological Correlates of Neoplastic Disease: A Preliminary Report," *Journal of Clinical and Experimental Psychopathology,* 1955, *16,* 281-288.
47. Pearson, L.: *Death and Dying,* Case Western Reserve, Cleveland, 1969.
48. Eissler, K.: *The Psychiatrist and the Dying Patient,* International Universities Press, New York, 1955.

Chapter 3—Depression and the Fear of Death

1. Deutsch, H.: *Neurosis and Character Types,* International Universities Press, New York, 1955.
2. Mahler, M.: *On Human Symbiosis and the Vicissitudes of Individuation,* International Universities Press, New York, 1968.
3. Boneim, W. "The Psychodynamics of Neurotic depression," *American Handbook of Psychiatry.* 1966, *3,* 239-255.
4. Lewin, B.: *The Psychoanalysis of Elation,* Norton, New York, 1950.
5. Mahler, *op cit* ref. 2.
6. Spitz, R.: "The Primal Cavity," *The Psychoanalytic Study of the Child,* 1955, *10,* 215-240. *The First Year of Life.* International Universities Press, New York, 1965.
7. Fodor, N.: "Nightmares of Cannibalism," *Journal of Psychotherapy,* 1951, *5,* 226.
   Fenichel, O.: "The Dread of Being Eaten," *Collected Papers of Otto Fenichel,* Norton, New York, 1953.
8. Freud, S.: "From the History of an Infantile Neurosis," *Standard Edition of the Complete Psychological Works of Sigmund Freud,* London, Hogarth Press 1955, Vol. XVIII. See Also "Mourning and Melancholia," *Collected Papers of Sigmund Freud.* London, Hogarth Press, 1950.
9. Gardner, M.: *The Wolfman by the Wolfman,* Basic Books, New York, 1971.
10. Grotjahn, M.: "Ego Identity and the Fear of Death and Dying," *Journal of Hillside Hospital* 1960, *9,*
11. Stern, M.: Fear of Death and Neurosis, *Journal of the American Psychoanalytic Association,* 1968, *16,* 3-31.
12. Rheingold, J.: *The Mother, Anxiety and Death,* Boston, Little, Brown, 1967.
13. Rado, S.: "The Psychoanalysis of Pharmacothymia," *Psychoanalytic Quarterly,* 1933, 2, 1.
14. Templar, D.: "The Relationship Between Verbalized and Non-Verbalized Death Anxiety," *Journal of Genetic Psychology,* 1971, *119,* 211-214.
15. Wolfenstein, M.: "How is Mourning Possible?" *The Psychoanalytic Study of the Child,* 1966, 31.
16. Templar, D., Ruff, C. and Franks, C.: "Death Anxiety, Age, Sex and Parental Resemblance in Diverse Populations," *Developmental Psychology,* 1971, 4, 108.
17. Anthony, S.: *The Child's Discovery of Death,* Harcourt, New York, 1940.
18. Despert, L.: "Diagnostic Criteria of Schizophrenia in Children," *American Journal of Psychotherapy,* 1952, *6,* 148-163.
19. Schilder, P. and Wechsler, D.: "The Attitude of Children Towards Death," *Journal of Genetic Psychology,* 1934, *45,* 406-451.
20. Bowlby, J.: "Separation Anxiety," *International Journal of Psychoanalysis,* 1958, *39,* 350.

21. Beck, A.: *Depression*, Univ. of Pennsylvania, Philadelphia, 1967.
22. Rado, S.: "The Problem of Melancholia," *International Journal of Psychoanalysis*, 1928, *9*, 420-438.
23. Fenichel, O.: *The Psychoanalytic Theory of Neurosis*, Norton, New York, 1945.
24. Hinton, J.: *Dying*, Penquin, Baltimore, 1967.
25. Hoffman, F.: "Mortality and Modern Literature" in Feifel, H. (Ed.) *The Meaning of Death*. McGraw Hill, New York, 1959.
26. Alvarez, A.: *The Savage God. A Study of Suicide.*, Bantam Books, New York, 1972.
27. Fenichel, *op cit* ref. 23.
28. Rank, O.: *The Trauma of Birth*, Harcourt, New York, 1929, *The Double: A Psychoanalytic Study*, Univ. of North Carolina, Chapel Hill, 1971.
29. Bender, L.: *Aggression, Hostility and Anxiety in Children*, Thomas, Springfield, 1953.
    Furman, R.: "Death and the Young Child: Some Preliminary Considerations," *Psychoanalytic Study of the Child*, 1964, *19*, 321-328.
30. Rank, O.: *Beyond Psychology*, Dover, New York, 1958.
31. Brodysky, B.: "The Self Representation, Anality and the Fear of Dying," *Journal of the American Psychoanalytic Association*, 1959, *7*, 95.
32. Seidenberg, R.: "The Trauma of Eventlessness," *Psychoanalytic Review*, 1972, *59*, 95-109.

Chapter 4—Adjustment Problems and the Fear of Death

1. Marshall, T.: *The Psychic Mariner: A Reading of the Poems of D.H. Lawrence*, Viking Press, New York, 1970.
2. Freud, S.: "Totem and Taboo," *The Standard Edition of the Complete Psychological Works of Sigmund Freud*, Hogarth Press, London, Vol. XIII, 1955.
3. Freud, S.: "Some general remarks on Hysterical Attacks," Vol. IX, *ibid.*
4. Mandelbaum, D.: "The Social Uses of Funeral Rites," in Feifel, H. (Ed.) *The Meaning of Death*, McGraw Hill, New York, 1959.
5. *Ibid.*
6. Roheim, G.: "The Panic of the Gods," *Psychoanalytic Quarterly*, 1952, *21*, 92-106. Grotjahn, M.: "About the Representation of Death in the Art of Antiquity and in the Unconscious of Modern Man, *Psychoanalysis and Culture*, 1953, 410-424.
7. Lampriere, J.: *A Classical Dictionary*, Routledge & Sons, London, 1928.
8. Sperling, M.: "Sleep Disturbances in Children," in Howell, J. (Ed.) *Modern Perspectives in International Child Psychiatry*, Brunner-Mazel, New York, 1971.
9. Bornstein, B.: "The Analysis of a Phobic Child," *The Psychoanalytic Study of the Child*, 1949, *3*, 181-226.
10. Millar, T.: *Peptic Ulcers in Children*, *op cit* ref. 8.
11. Blos, P.: *The Young Adolescent*, Free Press, Glencoe, 1970.
12. Farley, G.: "An Investigation of Death Anxiety and the Sense of Competence," Doctoral dissertation, Duke University, 1970.
13. Bromberg, W. and Schilder, P.: "Death and Dying," *Psychoanalytic Review*, 1933, *20*, 133-185.
14. Sarnoff, L. and Corwin, S.: "Castration Anxiety and the Fear of Death," *Psychiatric Quarterly*, 1959, *27*, 374-385.
15. Friedman, D.: "Death Anxiety and the Primal Scene," *Psychoanalysis and the Psychoanalytic Review*, 1961, *48*, 108-119.

16. Searles, H.: "Schizophrenia and the Inevitability of Death," *Psychiatric Quarterly*, 1961, 35, 631-635.
17. Kafka, F.: *The Complete Stories of Franz Kafka*, Glatzer, N. (Ed.), Schocken, New York, 1971.
18. *Ibid.*
19. Reik, T.: *The Search Within.* Minerva Press, New York, 1956.
20. Edgar, I.: *Shakespeare, Medicine and Psychiatry*, Philosophical Library, New York, 1970.
21. Deutsch, H.: *The Psychology of Women*, Grune and Stratton, New York, 1967.
22. Freud, S.: "The Theme of the Three Caskets," *Collected Papers*, Vol. IV, Hogarth Press, London, 1925.
23. *op cit* Reference 21.
24. Sullivan, H.: *The Interpersonal Theory of Psychiatry*, Norton, New York, 1953. Mullahy, P.: *Psychoanalysis and Interpersonal Psychiatry*, Science House, New York, 1970.
25. Blake, W. in *Mentor Book of Major English Poets* New American Library, New York, 1963. O. Williams (Ed.).

Chapter 5—Religion and the Fear of Death

1. Wahl, C.: "The Fear of Death," *Bulletin of the Menninger Clinic*, 1958, 72, 214-223.
2. Soustelle, J.: *Daily Life of the Aztecs*, Weidenfeld and Nicolson, London, 1961.
3. Bychowski, G.: "The Ego and the Introjects: Origins of Religious Experience," *Psychoanalysis and the Social Sciences*, 1958, 5, 246-279.
4. Feldman, S.: Notes on some Religious Rites and Ceremonies. *Journal of Hillside Hospital*, 1971, 8, 36-41.
5A. Freud, S.: "A Neurosis of Demonic Possession in the Seventeenth Century. American Imago," 1923, IX.
5B. "A Seventeenth Century Demonological Neurosis," Vol. XVII. *The Standard Edition of the Complete Psychological Works of Sigmund Freud*, Hogarth Press, London, 1955. "Moses and Monotheism," Vol. XXIII, *ibid.* "The Future of an Illusion," Vol. XXI. *ibid.* "Totem and Taboo," Vol. XIII, *ibid.* "Notes upon a case of Obessional Neurosis," Vol. X, *ibid.*
6. James, W.: *The Varieties of Religious Experience*, Collier-Macmillan, New York, 1967.
7. Fromm, E.: *Psychoanalysis and Religion*, Yale University Press, New Haven, 1967.
8. Allport, G.: *The Individual and His Religion*, Doubleday, New York, 1954. *Personality and Social Encounter*, Beacon, Boston, 1959. "Religion and Prejudice," *Crane Review*, 1959, 2, 1-10. "The Religious Context of Prejudice," *Journal for the Scientific Study of Religion*, 1966, 5, 418-451. *The Person in Psychology*, Beacon, Boston, 1968. Allport, G. and Ross, M.: Personal Religious Orientation and Prejudice," *Journal of Personality and Social Psychology*, 1967, 5, 432, 443.
9. McCarthy, J., "Death Anxiety, purpose in Life and Intrinsicness of Religious orientation among nuns and Roman Catholic female undergraduates," Doctoral dissertation, St. Johns University New York, 1973.

Chapter 6—Children and the Fear of Death

1. Gesell, A. and Ilg, F.: *The Child from Five to Ten*, Harper, New York 1946. Gesell, A. and Ames, L.: *Youth: The Years from Ten to Sixteen*, Harper, New York, 1956.
2. Schilder, P., Wexler, D.: "The Attitudes of Children towards Death," *Journal of Genetic Psychology*, 1934, 45, 406-451.
3. Nagy, M.: "The Child's Theories concerning Death," *Journal of Genetic Psychology*, 1948, 73, 3.
4. Anthony, S.: *The Child's Discovery of Death*, Harcourt, New York, 1940.
5. Scott, H.: "Old Age and Death,"*American Journal of Psychology*, 1896, 8, 67-122.
6. Caprio, F.: "A Study of some Psychological Reactions During Prepubescence to the Idea of Death," *Psychiatric Quarterly*, 1950, 24, 495-505.
7. Klein, M.: "On the theory of Anxiety and Guilt," in *Developments in Psychoanalysis*, Hogarth Press, London, 1952.
8. Despert, L.: "Diagnostic Criteria of Schizophrenia in Children," *American Journal of Psychotherapy*, 1952, 6, 148-163.
9. Bender, L: *Aggression, Hostility, and Anxiety in Children*, Thomas, Springfield, 1953.
10. Gould, R.: *Child Studies Through Fantasy*, Quadrangle, New York, 1972.
11. Freud, A.: *The Ego and the Mechanisms of Defense*, Hogarth Press, London, 1937.
    Normality and Pathology in Childhood, International Universities Press, New York, 1965.
12. Kestenberg, J.: "From Organ Object Imagery to Self and Object Representations" in *Separation-Individuation*," International Universities Press, New York, 1971, Devitt, M. (Ed.).
13. Mahler, M.: "On the Significance of the Normal Separation Individuation," *Drives, Affects and Behavior*, International Universities Press, N.Y., 1965, Schur, M. (Ed.).
14. Spitz, R.: "The Primal Cavity," *Psychoanalytic Study of the Child*, 1955, 10, 215-240.
15. Bruch, H.: "Obesity in Childhood and Personality Development," *American Journal of Orthopsychiatry*, 1941, 11, 467-474.
16. Bruch, H.: "Transformation of Oral Impulses in Eating Disorders," *Psychiatric Quarterly*, 1961, 35, 458-481.
17A. Bruch, H.: "Perceptual and Cognitive Disturbances in Anorexia Nervosa," *Psychosomatic Medicine*, 1962, 24, 187.
17B. McCarthy, J. "Infantile Narcissism: A Study of Symbiosis and Agrression in Borderline Children," *Modern Psychoanalysis*, 1979, 4, 71-81.
18. Fenichel, O.: *The Psychoanalytic Theory of Neurosis*, Norton, New York, 1945.
19. *ibid*
20. Freud, S.: "A Phobia in a Five-Year Old Boy," *Standard Edition of the Complete Psychological Works of Sigmund Freud*, Hogarth Press, London, 1955, Vol. X., Strachey (Ed.).
21. *ibid.*
22. *Ibid.* p. 110.
23. Furman, R.: "Death and the Young Child: Some Preliminary Considerations," *Psychoanalytic Study of the Child*, 1964, 19, 321-328.
    Death of a Six-Year Old's Mother During his Analysis. Psychoanalytic Stucy of the child, 1964, 19, 377-397.

24. Wolfenstein, M. and Kleinman, G.: *Children and the Death of a President*, Doubleday, New York, 1965.
25. Morrissey, J.: "Death Anxiety in Children with a Fatal Illness," *American Journal of Psychotherapy*, 1964, 18, 606.

Chapter 7—Purpose in Life and the Fear of Death

1. Lamont, C.: *The Illusion of Immortality*, Philosophical Library, New York, 1959.
2. Frankl, V.: *Man's Search for Meaning*, Beacon, Boston, 1962.
   The Doctor and the Soul: An Introduction to Logotherapy, Knopf, New York, 1955.
   "Logotherapy and the Challenge of Suffering," *Review of Existential Psychiatry and Existentialism*, Washington Square Press, 1967.
   "The Spiritual Dimension in Existential Analysis and Logotherapy," *Journal of Individual Psychology*, 1959, 14, 157-165.
   "Beyond Self Actualization and Self Expression," *Journal of Existential Psychiatry*, 1960, c, 7.
   "Dynamics, Existence and Values" *Journal of Existential Psychiatry*, 1963, 4.
3. Crumbaugh, J. and Maholick, L.: "The Case for Frankl's will to meaning," *Journal of Existential Psychiatry*, 1963, 4, 43-48.
   "An Experimental Study in Existentialism: The Psychometric Approach to Frankl's Noogenic Neurosis," *Journal of Clinical Psychology*, 1964, 20, 200-207.
   Manual of Instructions for the Purpose in Life Text, Psychometric Affiliates, Chicago, 1969.
4. Allport, G.: *The Individual and His Religion*, Macmillan, New York 1950.
   Personality and Social Encounter, Beacon, Boston, 1960.
   The Person in Psychology, Beacon, Boston, 1968.
5. Templar, D.: "The Death Anxiety Scale," *Proceedings of the 77th Annual American Psychological Association Convention*, 1969, 4, 737-738.
   "The Construction and Validation of a Death Anxiety Scale," *Journal of General Psychology*, 1970, 82, 165-177.
   "The Relationship between verbalized and non-verbalized Death Anxiety," *Journal of Genetic Psychology*, 1971 119, 211-214.
   "Death Anxiety as Related to Depression and Health of Retired Persons," *Journal of Gerontology*, 1971, 4, 521-523.
6. Feifel, H., (Ed.): *The Meaning of Death*, McGraw-Hill, New York 1959.
   "The Problem of Death," *Catholic Psychological Record*, 1965, 3, 18-22.
   Feifel, H. and Heller, J.: "Normality, Illness and Death," *Proceedings of the Third World Congress of Psychiatry*, 1962, 2, 1252-1256.
7. Horney, K.: *Neurosis and Human Growth*, Norton, New York, 1950.

Chapter 8—Existential Psychology and the Fear of Death

1. Breisach, C.: *Introduction to Modern Existentialism*, Grove Press, New York, 1962.
2. Fromm, E.: *The Forgotten Language*, Grove Press, New York, 1951.
3. Corngold, S., (Ed.): *The Metamorphosis*, Bantam Books, New York, 1972.
4. Kierkegaard, S.: *The Sickness Unto Death*, Doubleday, New York, 1954.
5. Heidegger, M.: *Sein und Zeit* Tubingen, Neomarius, 1949.

6. Kierkegaard, S.: *The Concept of Dread*, Princeton University Press, Princeton, 1967.
7. Heidegger, M.: *An Introduction to Metaphysics*, Doubleday, Garden City, 1960.
8. Kaufman, W.: *Nietzsche—Philosopher, Psychologist, Anti-Christ*, Princeton University Press, Princeton, 1966.
9. Marias, J *Miguel de Unamuno*, Harvard University, Cambridge, 1966.
10. Mora, J. *Miguel de Unamuno A philosophy of Tragedy*, University of California, Berkeley, 1962.
11. Unamuno, M. de: *The Tragic Sense of Life*, Macmillan, New York, 1926.
12. Satre, J.: *Existential Psychoanalysis*, Philosophical Library, New York, 1953.
13. Binswanger, L.: "The Case of Ellen West" *Existence: A New Dimension in Psychiatry and Psychology*, Simon and Schuster, New York, 1967, May, Angel and Ellenberger's (Eds.).
14. May, R.: *Existential Psychology*, Random House, New York, 1960.
15. May, R.: *Man's Search for Himself*, Norton, New York, 1953.
    The Meaning of Anxiety, Ronald Press, New York, 1950.
16. *op cit* ref. 13.
17. May, R.: *op cit* ref. 15.
18. Frankl, V.: *Man's Search for Meaning*, Washington Square Press, New York 1963.
19. Frankl, V.: *The Doctor and the Soul*, Knopf, New York, 1960.
20. Maddi, S.: "The Existential Neurosis," *Journal of Abnormal Psychology*, 1967, 72, 311-324.
21. Kantor, R. and Herron, W.: *Reactive and Process Schizophrenia*, Science and Behavior Books, Palo Alto, 1966.
22. Binswanger, L.: "Existential Analysis and Psychotherapy" In *Progress in Psychotherapy*, Grune and Stratton, New York, 1965, Fromm-Reichmann and Moreno (Eds.).
23. Binswanger, L.: "Existential Analysis and Psychotherapy" *Psychoanalysis and Existential Philosophy*, Dutton, New York, 1962, Ruitenbeek's (Ed.).
24. Searles, H.: "Schizophrenia and the Inevitability of Death," *Psychiatric Quarterly*, 1961, 35, 631.
25. Kotchen, T.: "Existential Mental Health: An Empirical Approach," *Journal of Individual Psychology*, 1960, 16, 174-181.
    Crumbaugh, J. and Maholick, L. "An Experimental Study in Existentialism: The Psychometric Approach to Frankl's concept of Noogenic Neurosis," *Journal of Clinical Psychology*, 1964, 20, 200-207.
26. Laing, R.: *The Politics of Experience*, Ballantine, New York, 1967.
    Laing, R.: "Ontological Insecurity" in Reuitenbeek's *Psychoanalysis and Existential Philosophy*, Dutton, New York, 1962.
27. Laing, R.: *The Divided Self*, Tavistock, London, 1959.
28. Frankl, V.: "Paradoxical Intention: A Logotherapeutic Technique," *American Journal of Psychotherapy*, 1960, 15, 520-535.

Chapter 9—Neurosis and the Fear of Death

1. Horney, K.: *The Neurotic Personality of Our Time*, Norton, New York, 1937.
2. Horney, K.: *Neurosis and Human Growth*, Norton, New York, 1950. *Our Inner Conflicts*, Norton, New York, 1945.

3. Freud, S.: "Notes Upon a Case of Obsessional Neurosis," *Standard Edition of the Complete Psychological Works of Sigmund Freud,* Hogarth Press, London, 1966, Strachey (Ed.).
4. Tolstoy, L.: *The Death of Ivan Ilych,* New American Library, New York, 1960.
5. Melville, H.: *Moby Dick,* Abridged Edition, Washington Square Press, New York, 1949.
6. Dickinson, E.: *The Complete Poems of Emily Dickinson,* Little Brown, Boston, 1960, T. Johnson (Ed.).
7. Shands, H.: "Malinowski's Mirror: Emily Dickinson as Narcissus," *Contemporary Psychoanalysis,* 1976, *12,* 300-335.
8. T. Johnson, (Ed.): *The Letters of Emily Dickinson,* Harvard University, Cambridge, 1958.
9. T. Johnson, (Ed.): *The Complete Poems of Emily Dickinson.* Little, Brown, Boston, 1960.
10. *Ibid.*
11. Bromberg, W. and Schilder, P.: "Death and Dying," *Psychoanalytic Review,* 1933, *20,* 133-185.
    "The Attitudes of Psychoneurotics Towards Death," *Psychoanalytic Review,* 1936, *23,* 1-25.
12. Deutsch, F.: "Euthanasia: A Clinical Study," *Psychoanalytic Quarterly,* 1936, *15,* 347.
13. Kastenbaum, R. and Aisenberg, R.: *The Psychology of Death,* Springer, New York, 1972.
14. Seidenberg, R.: "*The Trauma of Eventlessness,*" *Psychoanalytic Review,* 1972, *59,* 95-109.

Chapter 10—Psychotherapy and the Fear of Death

1. Sullivan, H.: *The Interpersonal Theory of Psychiatry,* New York, Norton, 1953.
2. McCarthy, J.: "Death Anxiety, Purpose in Live and Intrinsiness of Religious Orientation Among Nuns and Roman Catholic Female Undergraduates." Doctoral dissertation, St. Johns University, New York, 1973.
3. Shachtel, E.: *Metamorphosis,* Basic Books, New York, 1959.
4. Becker, E.: *The Denial of Death,* Free Press, New York, 1959.
5. Adler, A.: *Problems of Neuroses,* Harper & Row, New York, 1964.
6. May, R.: *Man's Search for Himself,* New York, Norton, 1953.
   Contributions of Existential Psychotherapy in Existence: A New Dimension in Psychiatry and Psychology, May, R. Angel, E. and Ellenberger, H. (Eds.). Basic Books, New York, 1958.
7. Ruitenbeck, H.: *Death Interpretations,* New York, Dell Publishing, 1969.
8. Deutsch, H.: *The Psychology of Women,* Grune & Stratton, New York, 1967.
9. Stern, M.: "Fear of Death and Neurosis," *Journal of the American Psychoanalytic Association, 16,* 3-31, 1968.
10. Rheingold, J.: *The Mother, Anxiety and Death,* Little, Brown, Boston, 1967.
11. Fromm-Reichmann, F.: *Psychoanalysis and Psychotherapy,* University of Chicago, Chicago, 1959, (Ed.), D. Bullard.
12. Singer, E.: *Key Concepts in Psychotherapy,* Basic Books, New York, 1970.
13. Horney, K.: *Neurosis and Human Growth,* Norton, New York, 1950.
14. Searles, H.: "Schizophrenia and the Inevitability of Death, *Psychiatric Quarterly, 35,* 631-635, 1961.

15. Arieti, S.: *The Interpretation of Schizophrenia*. Brunner–Mazel, New York, 1955.
16. Searles, H.: *Collected Papers on Schizophrenia and Related Subjects*, International Universities Press, New York, 1965.
17. Searles, H.: "Phases of Patient-Therapist Interaction in the Psychotherapy of Chronic Schizophrenia." *Brit Jour Med. Psychol., 34,* 169–192, 1961.
18. Winnicott, D.: *The Maturational Processes and the Facilitating Environment*, International Universities Press, New York, 1965.
    Winnicott, D.: *Playing and Reality*, Basic Books, New York, 1971.
19. Giovacchini, P.: "The Symbiotic Phase" in *Tactics and Techniques in Psychoanalytic Therapy*, Science House, New York, 1972.
20. Guntrip, H.: *Schizoid Phenomena, Object Relations and the Self*, International Universities Press: New York, 1968.

Additional References

1. Alexander, I. and Adlerstein, A.: "Affective Responses to the Concept of Death in a Population of Children and Early Adolescents," *Journal of Genetic Psychology*, 1958, *93*, 167-177.
2. Colett, L. and Lester, D.: "The Fear of Death, The Fear of Dying," *Journal of Psychology*, 1972, *69*, 179-181.
3. Fulton, R.: *Death and Identity*, Wiley, New York, 1965.
4. Greenberg, I.: "An Exploratory Study of Reunion Fantasies," *Journal of Hillside Hospital*, 1964, *1*, 13.
5. Heuscher, J.: "Existential Crises, Death and Changing World Design in Myths and Fairy Tales," *Journal of Existentialism*, 1966, *1*, 45-62.
6. Hoffman, F. and Brody, M.: "The Symptom, Fear of Death," *Psychoanalytic Review*, 1957, 44, 433.
7. Howard, A. and Scott, R.: "Cultural Values and Attitudes Toward Death," *Journal of Existentialism*, 1965, *6*, 161-171.
8. Jackson, E.: "Grief and Religion in the Meaning of Death," McGraw-Hill, New York, 1960, Feifel, (Ed.).
9. Kubler-Ross, E.: *On Death and Dying*, Macmillian, New York, 1969.
10. Lester, D.:"Attitudes Toward Death and Suicide in a Non-Disturbed Population," *Psychological Reports*, 1967, *20*, 1077-1078.
11. Leveton, A.: "Time, Death and the Ego Chill," *Journal of Existentialism*, 1965, *6*, 69-80.
12. Mahler, M., Pine, F. and Bergman, A.: *The Psychological Birth of the Human Infant*, Basic Books, New York, 1975.
13. Mauer, A.: "Adolescent Attitudes Towards Death," *Journal of Genetic Psychology*, 1964, *195*, 75-90.
14. Middleton, W.: "Some Reactions Toward Death Among College Students," *Journal of Abnormal and Social Psychology*, 1963, *31*, 165-173.
15. Mitchell, M.: *The Child's Attitude to Death*, Schochen, New York, 1967.
16. Natterson, J. and Knudson, A.: "Observations Concerning Fear of Death in Fatally Ill Children and Their Mothers," *Psychosomatic Medicine*, 1960, *22*, 456.
17. Piatrowski, Z.: *Perceptanalysis: A fundamentally Reworked, Expanded and Systematized Rorschach Method*, Philadelphia, Ex Libris, 1965.
18. Portz, A.: "The Meaning of Death to Children," Doctoral dissertation, University of Michigan, 1964.

19. Rosenthal, H.: "Psychotherapy for the Dying," *American Journal of Psychotherapy,* 1957, *11,* 626.
20. Safier, G.: "A Study in Relationships Between Life and Death Concepts In Children," *Journal of Genetic Psychology,* 1964, *105,* 283-294.
21. Siligman, A.: "The Relationship Between Religion, Personality Variables and Attitudes and Feelings About Death," *Proceedings of the 1961 Annual Meeting of the Society for the Scientific Study of Religion.*
22. Sperling, M.: "Equivalents of Depression in Children," *Journal of Hillside Hospital,* 1959, *8,* 138.
23. Spitz, R.: *The Evolution of Dialogue in Drives, Affects, and Behavior.* International Universities Press, 1965, Schur, (Ed.).
24. Tate, E. and Miller, G.: "Differences in the Value Systems of Persons with Varying Religious Orientations," *Journal for the Scientific Study of Religion,* 1971, *10,* 357-365.
25. Templar, D. and Dotson, E.: "Religious Correlates of Death Anxiety," *Psychological Reports,* 1970, *26,* 895-897.
26. Weisman, A.: *On Dying and Denying a Psychiatric Study of Terminality,* Behavioral Publications, New York, 1972.
27. Williams, R. and Cole, S.: "Religiosity, Generalized Anxiety and Apprehension Concerning Death," *Journal of Social Psychology,* 1968, *75,* 111-117.

Index

Odyssey
Unification Church, 147; *See also*
   Jones, Jim
Unamuno, Miguel de, 155, 157-
   159, 161; *The Tragic Sense of
   Life*, 158
Ur graves, 49

Venus, 94
Vietnam War, 21, 31, 143

Wesley, 95
Whitman, Walt, 49, 91; "Death,
   Death, Death," 49
Wilde, Oscar; *The Portrait of Dorian
   Grey*, 50
Withdrawl, 3, 37, 39, 43, 71, 144-
   145, 167-169, 177, 181-187,
   191, 194, 198, 206, 208
Woman in the Dunes, 142
World War I, 31